Easy-to-Make

ENDANGERED SPECIES

To Stitch & Stuff

Jodie Davis

◆

Photography by Glenn Moody

Williamson Publishing • Charlotte, Vermont 05445

Library of Congress
Cataloging-in-Publication Data

Davis, Jodie 1959-
    Easy-to-make endangered species to
stitch and stuff/Jodie Davis.
        p.   cm.
    ISBN 0-913589-60-8
    1. Soft toy making.   2. Endangered species
    I. Title.
    TT174.3.D3727 1992
    745.592'4—dc20   91–38488 CIP

Cover illustration: Loretta Trezzo Braren
Cover and interior design: Trezzo-Braren Studio
Photography: Glenn Moody
Project diagrams: Jodie Davis
Printing: Capital City Press

Jodie Davis is author of the following Williamson
titles:
Easy-To-Make Teddy Bears & All The Trimmings
Easy-To-Make Cloth Dolls & All The Trimmings
Easy-To-Make Stuffed Animals & All The Trimmings

Williamson Publishing Co.
Charlotte, Vermont 05445
(800) 234-8791

Manufactured in the United States of America

10 9 8 7 6 5 4 3 2 1

CONTENTS

DEDICATION

♥

For every heart
blessed with the love
of animals

♥   ♥   ♥   ♥   ♥   ♥

*I*n this time of increasing environmental awareness, it is no less alarming to note the disturbing plight and precarious future of a steadily increasing number of wild animals. Many people agree that preservation of our earth's diversity of species may be crucial to its salvation.

As my own pawed, hooved, and winged family will confirm, I am a lover of all animals. I participate in Finchsave, a national program dedicated to naturalizing as many species of finches and softbills in aviculture as possible. Through our breeding efforts, wild birds will no longer need to be captured and imported for sale to bird fanciers.

This book is meant to bring you the fun I've had in making these stuffed animals and to celebrate some of the most fascinating creatures on earth. The making and sharing of the stuffed animals and appliqued crafts in this book offer an opportunity to understand their live counterparts' habitats, ways of life, importance to our planet, and current situations. And it is because of awareness that the first human efforts to save these creatures will be taken.

Jodie Davis

♥

♥

CHAPTER 1

The Basics

Here are the essentials for constructing the animals in this book, a review of the necessary basic sewing skills and tools needed, and a few time- and aggravation-saving methods. There is a bibliography at the end of the book listing excellent general sewing books available at your local bookstore or library.

To make the delightful creatures detailed in this book, you need only basic sewing skills and materials available at most crafts stores or by mail.

Before you begin, assemble all of the tools and materials needed for your project. Then follow the instructions one step at a time.

DEGREE OF DIFFICULTY

The following rating charts specify the degree of skill necessary in making the animals in this book. Both levels list the animals in relative order of increasing difficulty. Although I feel anyone with basic sewing skills can construct any of these animals, those in level #2 require a bit more fine detail in their construction. Whichever you choose, enjoy creating your very own huggable, endangered creature!

Level #1:	Level #2:
Chinese river dolphin	Wolf
Endangered species appliques	Bald eagle
Spotted owl	Scarlet macaw
Giant panda	Loggerhead turtle
African elephant	
Orangutan	
American alligator	
Kangaroo and joey	

GENERAL SUPPLIES

Essential

Sewing machine: Be sure to use a needle appropriate for fur. Depending upon the brand of machine you use, choose a size 90 or a 14. Use a normal stitch length for most sewing. Shortening the stitches for smaller, curved pieces such as feet and beaks will make sewing easier and smoother.

Bent-handle dressmaker's shears: Good quality shears, 7" or 8" in length, are recommended for general sewing purposes. Reserve these shears for cutting fabric only, as paper will dull them quickly.

Scissors: For cutting paper, cardboard, and other materials, a pair of inexpensive scissors will save your shears from a lot of wear and tear.

Dressmaker's tracing paper: For transferring markings from patterns to fabric.

Dressmaker's tracing wheel: A device used with the tracing paper.

Straight pins: To hold paper pattern pieces in place as you cut out the fabric.

Hand-sewing needles: For general hand sewing, choose a medium, size 8-6, sharp for heavy fabrics such as fur, corduroy, flannel, and denim. Try a crewel embroidery needle for closing seams. These are easier for grabbing in the fur, and won't be too big because the stitches aren't as small as those in regular fabric.

Embroidery needle: For embroidering the animals' noses and mouths.

Dollmaker's needle: Five inches or longer. Needed for installing the eagle's glass eyes. Also helpful to embroider mouths. Available from CR's Crafts (see Sources).

Awl: For making holes in the fur for eyes, plastic noses, and joints. Though a seam ripper can be used in its place, an awl makes a clean, round hole without breaking threads. You can buy an awl at a hardware or fabric store. A small version costs less than half the price and will do the job nicely.

Wooden Spoon: The handle end is indispensable in stuffing those hard to reach noses and paws and in packing the stuffing. For stuffing small, tight spaces, such as the orangutan's fingers, a Stuff-It™ tool proves indispensable (see Patterncrafts in Sources).

Fray Check®: A drop of this nifty product secures thread that might otherwise unravel.

Glue: A general purpose white glue for fabric, felt, wood, and paper is available at any dime, crafts, or fabric store under a variety of brand names.

General purpose thread: The all-purpose size 50 will fill most of your general hand- and machine-sewing needs. Always choose the highest quality.

Carpet thread, quilting thread, or waxed dental floss: Has the strength to withstand the tugging needed to install eyes, gather the necks of animal heads, and close openings in fur. The dental floss will slide through the fur easily. The thread or the floss will not be seen on the finished animal.

Tag board (oak tag) or cardboard: For durable animal patterns. These can be laid on the backing of the fur and traced around. This is easier and produces a more accurate transfer of pattern to fabric.

Hammer and socket or nut and washer: For panda, macaw, orangutan, kangaroo, and spotted owl to secure metal lockwashers to plastic joints for long-wearing, healthy joints. Turn to jointing section for more information.

Nice to Have

Seam ripper: A sharp, pointed tool used to tear out temporary basting stitches and goofed seams. I list this as non-essential because you can substitute the thread clippers listed below.

Thread clippers: A variation on a small pair of scissors, thread clippers are handy for trimming threads at the sewing machine, for clipping into seam allowances, and for making buttonholes. If you do much sewing, I highly recommend a pair.

Thimble: This is listed as non-essential though many, including myself, will argue that this little piece of equipment is in fact essential in guiding the needle and guarding against pinpricks.

Stuff-It™ tool: A plastic stick with a blunt metal end, used to stuff small, intricate areas where the wooden spoon handle is too clumsy (see Sources).

HOW TO MAKE PATTERNS
• CUT & MARK FUR •

All of the patterns in this book are shown in their actual size. Trace or photocopy them directly from the book. Glue the patterns to heavy cardboard, such as oak tag (tag board) or cardboard cereal boxes. By tracing around the cardboard pieces onto the fur backing you will transfer the patterns very accurately. When a pattern instructs you to "cut 2, reverse 1," trace the pattern onto the fabric, flip the pattern over so it is face down, and trace the second piece, a mirror image of the first.

MATERIALS

Tracing paper (or photocopy machine)
Cardboard for patterns
Craft glue or glue stick

INSTRUCTIONS

1. Photocopy the patterns directly from the book or carefully trace them onto the tracing paper, including all pattern markings. If tracing, be sure to transfer all markings and write in all instructions and other written markings.

Note: Those patterns that are too large to fit on one page are cut in two or more pieces and labeled (for example: body side part #1 of 2, body side part #2 of 2). When you come across such a pattern, simply photocopy or trace the pieces from the book as in step 1 above, cut them out, and butt and tape the edges together as instructed on the pattern pieces. Then continue on to step 2 below to make a permanent pattern that will be easy to use.

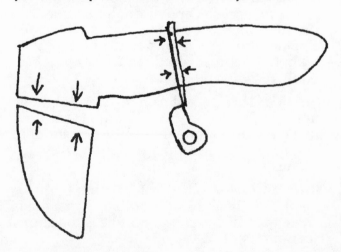

2. Lay the cardboard on your work surface. Place the copied pattern *right side* down. Apply an even coat of glue to the back. Place the copied pattern, glue side down on the cardboard. Press and smooth toward the edges to stick pattern to the cardboard.

3. Cut out the cardboard pattern. For easy transfer of dots and eye and joint markings to fur backing later, bore holes through the pattern at the markings. When you position the pattern over the fur, simply push the tip of your marking pencil or pen into the hole to mark the fur.

4. Lay the fur, backing side up, on your cutting surface. Point the nap of the fur toward you. If you stroke the fur as you would a dog, the fur should lie smoothly toward you, as if you were standing behind the dog.

5. Place the pattern pieces on the fabric, arranging them in the best way to economize on the fur. Make sure all arrows point toward you, in the direction of the nap. Remember: all seam allowances ($1/4$") are included in the patterns.

6. With a white or dark fabric marking pencil, depending upon the fur color, trace the pattern pieces. Cut out the fur pieces. For accuracy, cut just inside the drawn lines.

Slide the lower blade of the scissors along the backing of the fur, being careful not to cut the fur itself.

7. Transfer all eye, joint, and other placement markings to the wrong side of the fur backing. Instructions in the chapters themselves will instruct you when you need to transfer markings to the right (fur) side of the fabric. To do this, simply fill your sewing machine bobbin or thread your hand needle with colored sewing thread and, from the backing (wrong) side of the fur, baste over the markings. For markings for glass eyes, all you need is one stitch, leaving the thread tails hanging from the fur side of the fabric.

8. In some cases you will be instructed to trim the animal's fur. Hold your scissors parallel to the furbacking and cut the nap of the fur to within $1/4$" of the backing. Picture yourself giving the fur a crew cut.

> TIP: *Manilla envelopes (great opportunity for recycling) and resealable sandwich bags are great places to store patterns. Label and store them for future use.*

Note: The illustrations in this book follow the customary practice of depicting the wrong side of fabric dotted. The right side is left plain.

SEWING TECHNIQUES

Trimming Seams
Trimming across corners insures a smooth, finished seam and square, crisp corners.

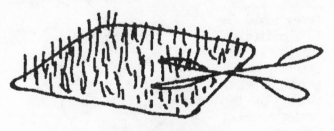

STITCH DICTIONARY

Basting Stitch
Use this long ($1/4$" by hand or longest possible by machine), temporary stitch to mark and stitch together two pieces of fabric to make sure they fit properly before the final stitching.

Ladder Stitch
Use this stitch to close the openings in the animals' bodies and limbs that had been left open for turning and stuffing. This stitch is worked from the right side. Knot your thread (I use waxed dental floss). From inside the animal, push the needle out through the machine-stitched seam to one side of the opening. From the right side of the opening, take a stitch along the seam line on one side. Take a second stitch on the other side. Work side to side, working your way up the opening with each stitch. Watch how the seam allowances are turned to the inside cleanly and effortlessly. This easy stitch results in professional-looking seam closures. After brushing the seam you'll hardly be able to see it!

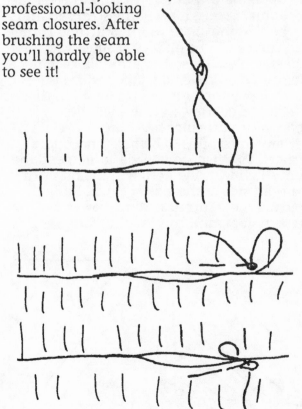

Running Stitch

This stitch is similar to the basting stitch, though it is a shorter, even stitch, for fine, permanent seams.

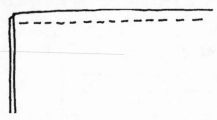

Satin Stitch

This stitch is used to attach the animal shapes to the windsock, banner, pillow, and quilt. It is a closely spaced zigzag stitch sewn over the raw edges of the animal cutouts.

Always use a tear-away stabilizer when appliqueing by machine. Cut the stabilizer larger than the animal you are about to applique. Pin the stabilizer to the wrong side of the fabric background.

If your sewing machine has a satin stitch foot, attach it. Otherwise use a zigzag foot. Adjust the top tension of the machine to a low number between two and three. A stitch length of ½ usually covers the raw edges of the applique without appearing too clumped. Experiment with a few fabric scraps to find the best zigzag stitch width. Stitching corners and curves will be difficult if stitch width is too wide. You'll also have trouble keeping the raw edges covered if stitch width is too narrow. A happy medium is found in the middle range. However, this will depend upon your particular machine.

Here's a few tips to help you negotiate corners. To stitch an outside corner, end the final stitch with the needle in the fabric at the right side of the zigzag stitch. Raise the pressure foot. Turn the fabric, lower the pressure foot, and continue stitching.

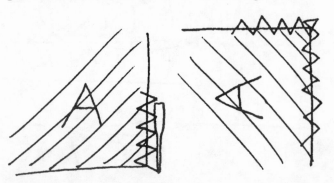

Handle inside corners by stitching three or four stitches past the corner. Stop with the needle in the fabric at the left position. Raise the pressure foot. Turn the fabric, lower the pressure foot, and continue stitching.

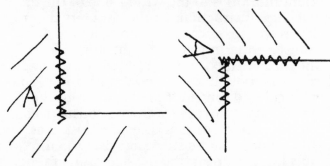

When you finish stitching, clip the threads and tear away the stabilizer from both inside and outside the appliqued shape.

Overhand Or Whipstitch

Use this to join two finished edges, as when closing the turned under edges of the ear.

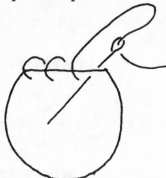

SEWING THE ANIMALS

Use a regular machine stitch and a high quality thread for sewing your stuffed animals. Always choose the appropriate size needle and a brand recommended by the manufacturer. For most furs, choose a size 90/14. A properly tuned and equipped machine will produce seams with the strength needed to withstand stuffing the animals initially and loving them for years to come.

JOINTING THE ANIMALS

The simple plastic joint pictured here will allow your animal's head, arms, and legs to move. The joint consists of a stationary disk with a threaded post, topped by a large plastic washer, a plastic lockwasher to hold the joint together, and, for long term strength, a topmost metal lockwasher.

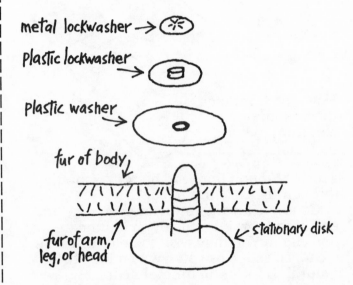

metal lockwasher →
plastic lockwasher →
plastic washer →
fur of body
fur of arm, leg, or head
stationary disk

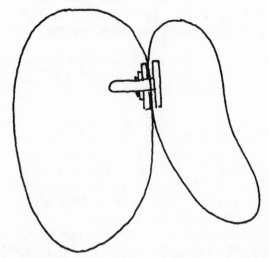

The metal lockwashers are not packaged as part of the plastic joint set. CR's Crafts (see Sources) offers them in bags of 200. Request size 7, or buy extra sets of safety eyes that have the correct size metal lockwashers and discard the eyes. This is worth the effort. Without them the animals will contract the "sleepy teddy bear syndrome," especially noticeable in the legs; over time the all-plastic joints will loosen and the animal will nod forward.

To assemble the joint, make holes in the fur at dots you transferred from the pattern to the fur backing. Look for them on arms, legs, and body. Insert the stationary disk into the head, arm, or leg so the post pokes out of the hole in the fur.

Next, poke the post through the corresponding hole you just made in the body. Make sure the arm or leg points to the front of the animal.

Working from inside the body, slip the large plastic washer over the stationary disk post. Then snap the plastic lockwasher onto the threaded post.

To snap it snugly, put the entire assembly, animal and all, on a hard surface, with the post pointing up. Place your thumbs on the lockwasher and, using the weight of your body to help you, push the washer down onto the post until it snaps — maybe more than once.

Next, snap the metal lockwasher onto the threaded post. Tighten the metal lockwasher by placing either a socket from a socket wrench set, or a large nut over the post, on top of the metal washer. Hammer the socket or nut. Check the joint by trying to move the head, arm, or leg. Moving it should be very difficult.

STUFFING

The art of stuffing is a learned skill. First, start with a quality stuffing — one of even, fluffy consistency. Always begin at the extremities — the panda's nose, alligator's tail, or the wolf's paws. Use small bits of stuffing for small parts, packing them in tightly with the aid of your stuffing tool. Graduate to larger chunks of stuffing as you progress to the larger parts of the animal. To avoid lumps, use handfuls of stuffing. Pack the stuffing as you add it, continually checking for lumps and evenness. Hold whatever part you're working on at arm's length to check for symmetry. You may have to unstuff your first attempts to get it right. Ladder stitch the openings closed when you are satisfied with your work.

Just take your time. With a bit of experience you will develop a feel for stuffing and will progress more quickly.

INSTALLING EYES

All of the animals, except the bald eagle, use plastic safety eyes. (Directions for the glass eyes are included in the instructions for the eagle.)

To install plastic safety eyes, first use an awl or seam ripper to make holes at the eye markings on the backing or wrong side of the fabric. Turn the animal or head right side out. From the right side, push the eye post into the head. Place the head on a hard surface, eye down, with a towel or a few thicknesses of fabric under the eye to protect it from possible scratches. Push the lockwasher onto the eye post. You may need a large spool of thread or a large nut centered over the post to help you push harder. I can usually snap the washer in place by positioning my thumbs on each side of the washer and standing to use my body weight to press the washer down. When making animals for children under five years of age, I suggest that you embroider eyes, nose, and mouth to avoid even a remote possibility that they will be pulled off and ingested by a youngster.

INSTALLING PLASTIC NOSES

Use an awl or seam ripper to make a hole at the nose marking (if there is not already an opening left in the stitching). From the right side of the head, push the nose post into the head. From inside the head, push the metal lockwasher onto the post and snap it in place.

EARS

Some animals' ears are stitched into the seams of the heads. Other ears are added after the animal is stuffed. With the latter, first turn the bottom edges of the ears ¼" to the inside at the bottom open edges and whipstitch with heavy thread. When you finish do not cut off the thread (see Stitch Dictionary for whipstitching).

Next, stitch the ears to the head. Place the ear on the head. With the thread coming out of the ear at one end, stitch into the head, back to front.

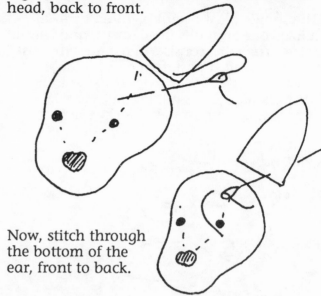

Now, stitch through the bottom of the ear, front to back.

Repeat through the head back to front, and through the ear front to back.

Continue sewing until you reach the other end of the ear. Knot the thread in the fur and clip it. You may wish to hold the ear in a cupped shape as you sew to mimic the natural shape of an animal's ear.

FINISHING

A few simple final touches will give your animal impeccable posture and jaunty character. Mold the stuffed animal with your hands. This is usually the cure for a slightly lopsided head, squashed in the jointing process. Much character can be added to an animal by molding the arms, for instance, to bend a panda's arm inward, or the elephant's tusks to point inward and upward.

Brushing the animal with a special brush, similar to a miniature metal dog brush (see Sources), will hide seams and smooth fur in the proper direction. Scrub the fur back and forth, up and down along the hand-stitched seams to pull the caught fur from the seam. Pull the fur caught in the curved ends of the ears, paws, and feet. Brush fur away from the eyes, clipping any fur that blocks the animal's vision.

Now, you're ready to make the animals!

♥ ♥

Fun &
Easy
Animals

♥ ♥

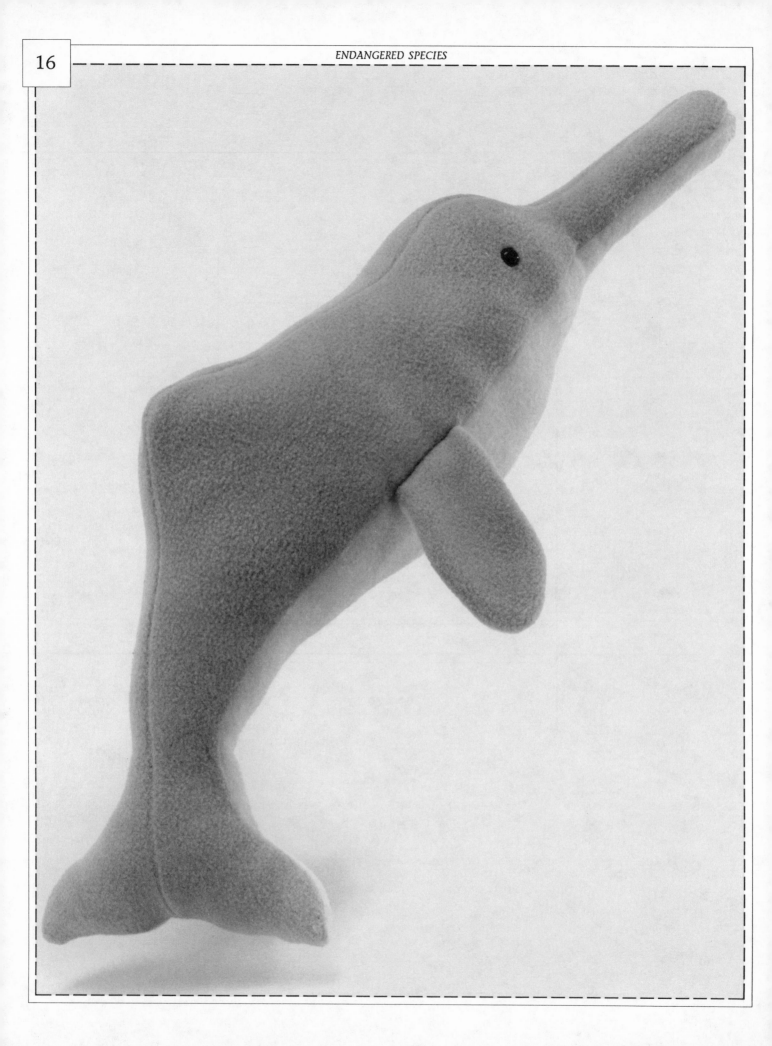

CHINESE RIVER DOLPHIN

Surprising to many people, dolphins are a type of whale. And some, like the Chinese river dolphin, live in freshwater, in this case the Yangtze River. One of the twelve most endangered species of animals in the world, the *baiji* (meaning white dolphin) is receiving critical help from a sanctuary and a research station in Tongling, the city that has adopted the baiji as its mascot.

This sewing project is perfect for a beginner: the two main pattern pieces and flipper are easily stitched, and the Polar Fleece™ fabric sews well and is easy to stuff. The finished dolphin measures 24" long.

INSTRUCTIONS

Note: All seam allowances are ¹/₄".

As instructed in chapter 1, prepare the patterns. Arrange the pattern pieces with the lengthwise grain (stretch) of the fabric along the length of the dolphin's body — following the arrows. (This is why ³/₄ yard is required.) Cut and mark the fabric.

1. Right sides facing, pin and stitch the two gray body top pieces together along the top seam.

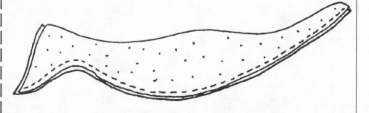

2. Right sides facing, pin and stitch the two white body bottom pieces together along the bottom seam.

MATERIALS

³/₄ yard gray Polar Fleece™

Matching thread

³/₄ yard white Polar Fleece™

Two 11 mm black plastic safety eyes

Polyester fiberfill stuffing

3. Right sides together, pin a gray flipper piece to a white flipper piece. Stitch, leaving the straight edges open.

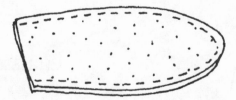

Repeat for the remaining two flipper pieces.

Turn the flippers right side out. Press flat with your fingers.

4. Pin the flippers to the right side of the gray body top between the dots as marked. Make sure the curve of the flippers is as pictured and that the gray side of the flipper is against the gray body top.

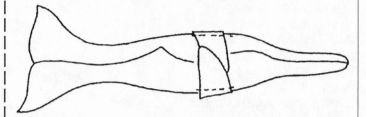

Right sides facing, pin the gray body top to the white body bottom. Match seams at tail fins and seams at tip of beak. Stitch, leaving an opening between the dots at one side as marked, and including the flippers in the seam.

5. As instructed in chapter 1, install the eyes at the markings.

6. Turn the dolphin right side out.

Stuff the dolphin, starting at the tip of the nose and working to the center. Then move to the tail fins. Stuff them; then work toward the center of the dolphin again. Finish stuffing the middle of the dolphin. Ladder stitch the opening at the dolphin's side closed.

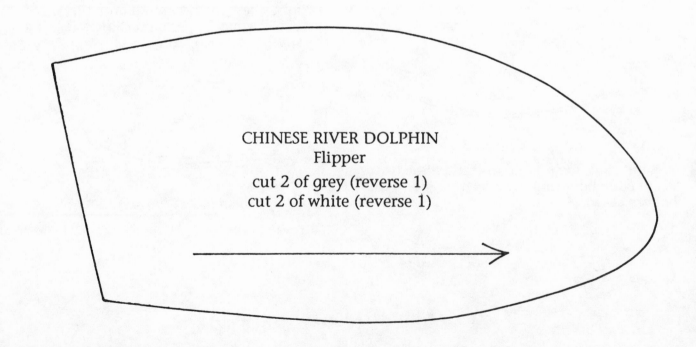

CHINESE RIVER DOLPHIN
Flipper
cut 2 of grey (reverse 1)
cut 2 of white (reverse 1)

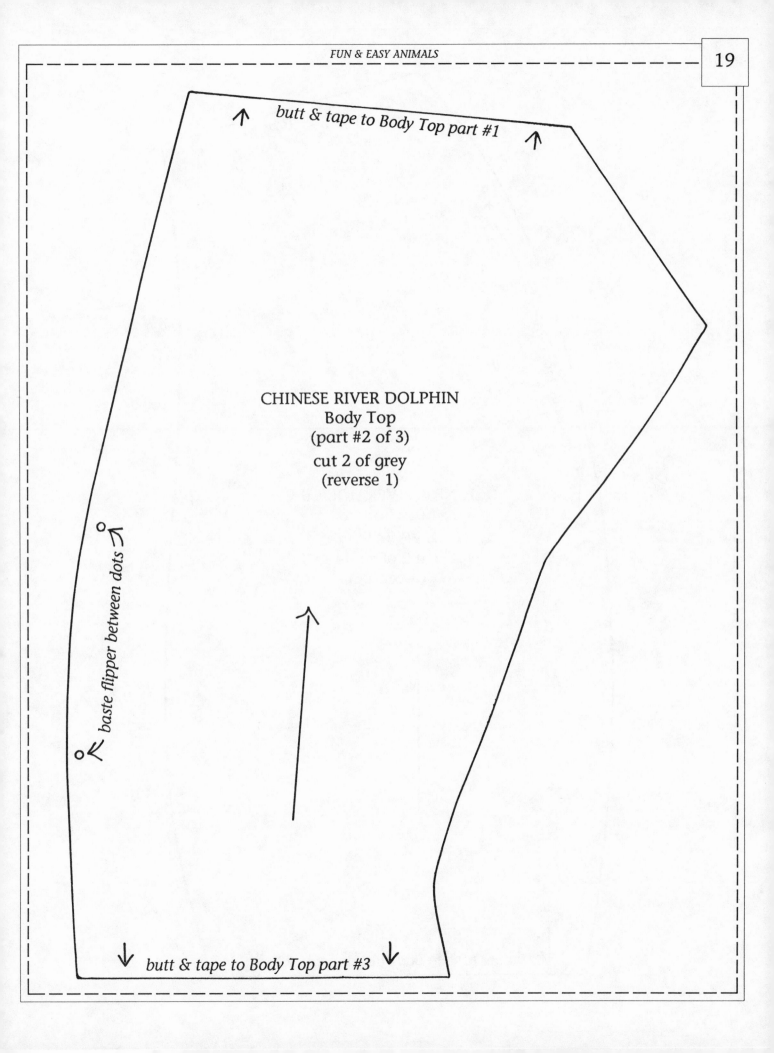

↑ *butt & tape to Body Top part #1* ↑

CHINESE RIVER DOLPHIN
Body Top
(part #2 of 3)

cut 2 of grey
(reverse 1)

baste flipper between dots

↓ *butt & tape to Body Top part #3* ↓

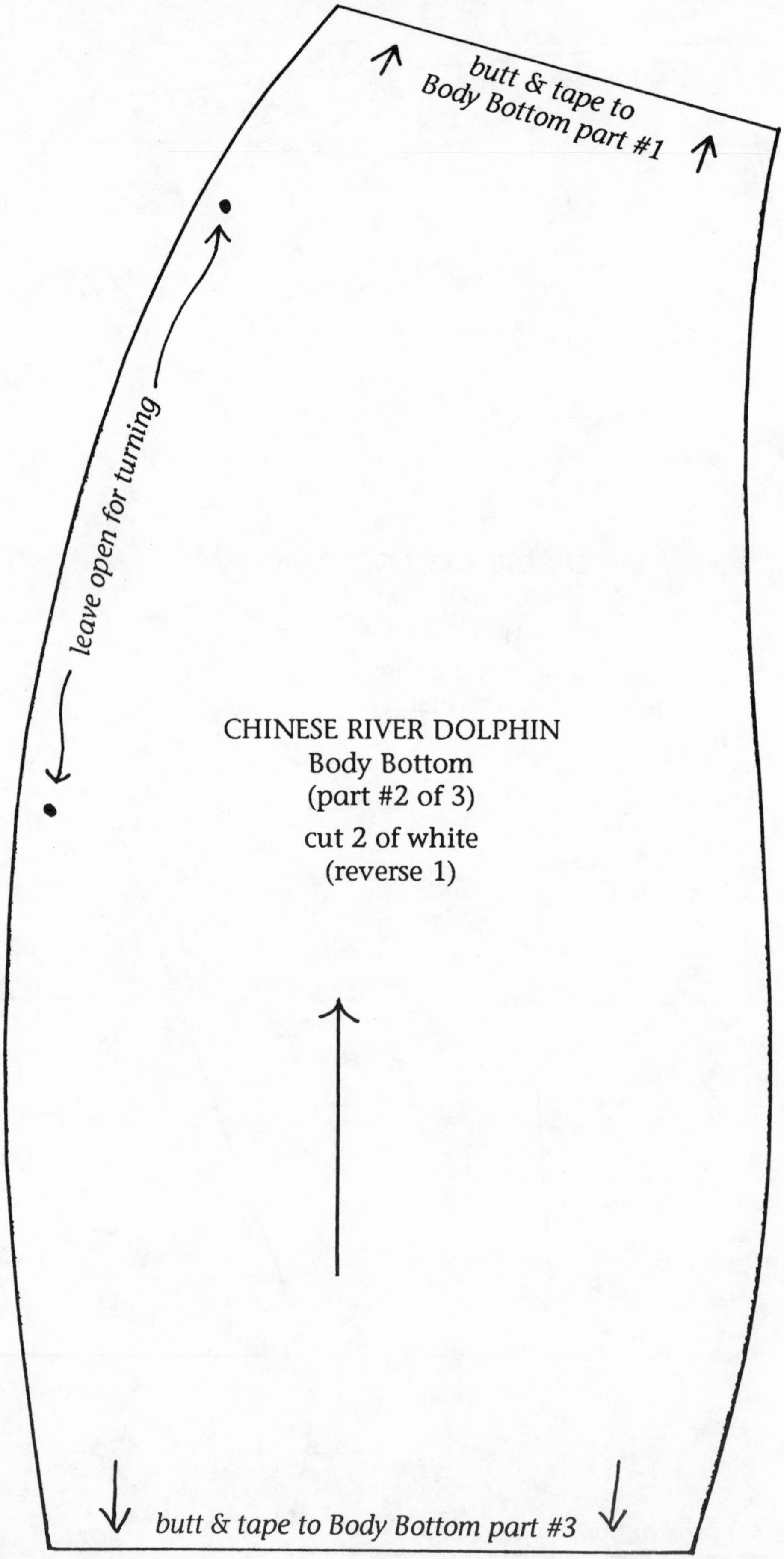

butt & tape to
Body Bottom part #1

leave open for turning

CHINESE RIVER DOLPHIN
Body Bottom
(part #2 of 3)

cut 2 of white
(reverse 1)

butt & tape to Body Bottom part #3

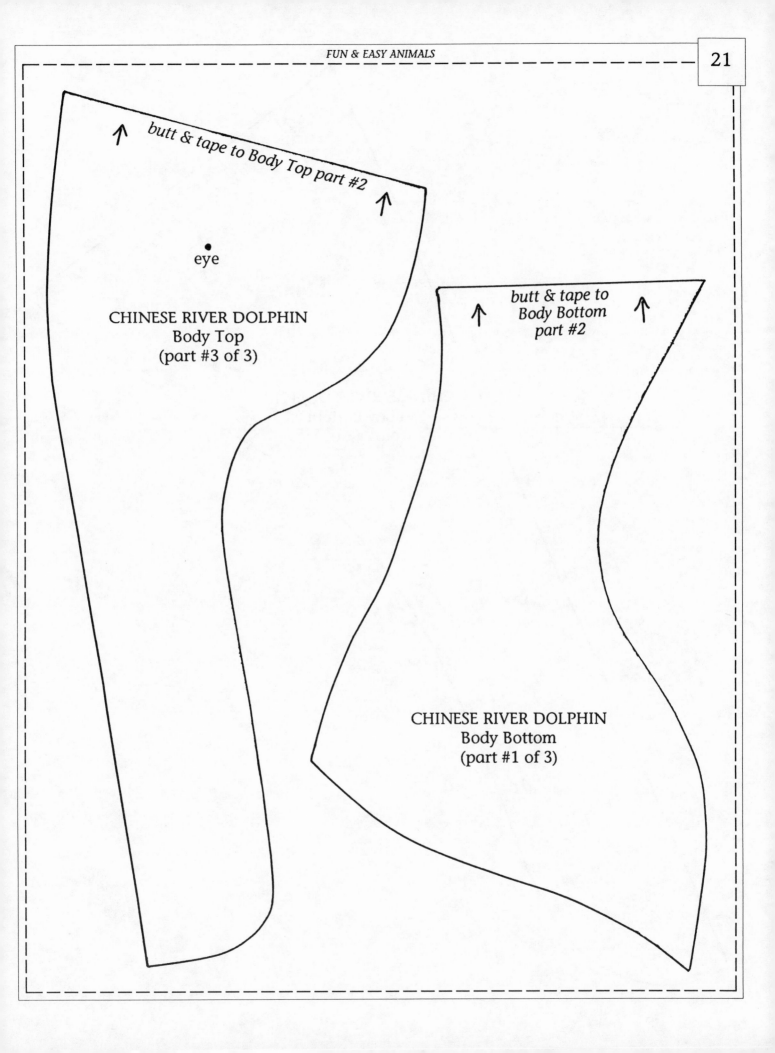

butt & tape to Body Top part #2

eye

CHINESE RIVER DOLPHIN
Body Top
(part #3 of 3)

*butt & tape to
Body Bottom
part #2*

CHINESE RIVER DOLPHIN
Body Bottom
(part #1 of 3)

butt & tape to
Body Bottom part #2

CHINESE RIVER DOLPHIN
Body Bottom
(part #3 of 3)

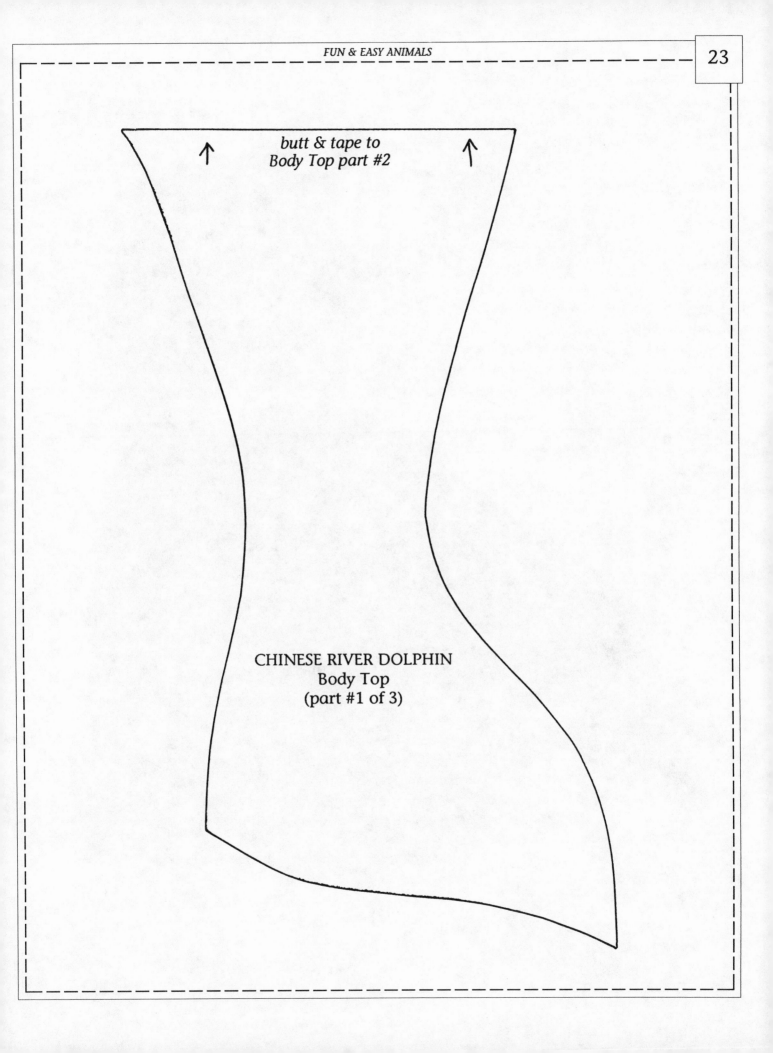

*butt & tape to
Body Top part #2*

↑ ↑

CHINESE RIVER DOLPHIN
Body Top
(part #1 of 3)

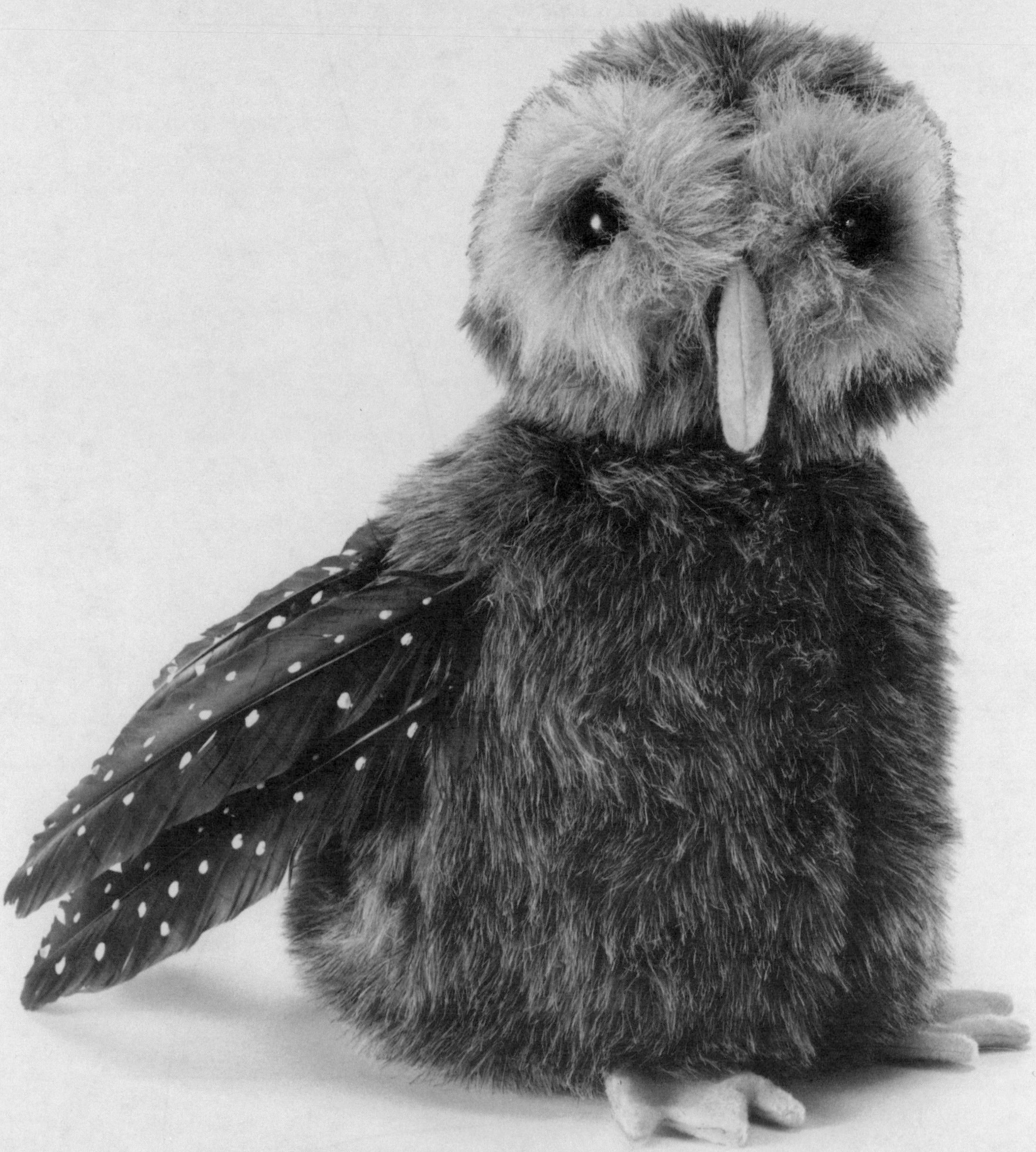

SPOTTED OWL

A symbol of old growth forests, the northern spotted owl has found its future caught precariously in the center of a raging feud between loggers and preservationists.

Our cunning crafted hooter is made of variegated fur and stands one foot tall. His wings are spotted with white paint. Eye rings and black eye patches endow him with that wide-eyed look. He is one of the easiest animals to make in this collection. And he is sure to become a favorite perched atop a bookcase or armoire.

MATERIALS

¹/₃ yard fur (904V Nutmeg from CR's Crafts, see Sources)

Matching thread

¹/₈ yard eye contrast (905G Fawn from CR's Crafts, see Sources)

Scrap of black fur for eye backings

Tan felt

Matching thread

One pair 18 mm black safety eyes

One 65 mm plastic joint set

Polyester fiberfill stuffing

5 left and 5 right brown "wing" feathers

Craft glue

White paint (in an applicator tube for T-shirt decorating)

INSTRUCTIONS

Note: All seam allowances are ¹/₄" unless noted otherwise.

Following the instructions in chapter 1, prepare the patterns, cut and mark the fur. Mark front and back edges of body and head pieces with a permanent marker, white pencil, or pen.

1. Right sides facing, pin two head front pieces together along front edge. Stitch.

2. Right sides facing, pin two back head pieces together along back edge. Stitch.

3. Right sides facing, pin and stitch head fronts to head backs.

4. Make holes at the eye markings on the head front pieces. Turn the head right side out.

Right sides facing, pin and stitch two eye ring pieces together along one straight edge. Repeat for two more pieces.

Right sides facing, pin the two halves of the eye ring together, leaving a ¹/₄" wide gap in the stitching at the center of the eye ring as shown. Repeat for the second eye ring.

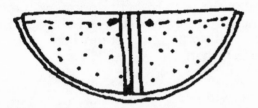

5. Make a hole at the marking on the black fur eye backing. From the right side of the fur push the post of an eye through the hole.

From the right side of the eye ring insert the post of the eye through the gap left in the stitching. Now, push the eye post through the hole in one head front. From inside the head snap a lockwasher onto the eye post as instructed in chapter 1.

Repeat for the remaining eye.

6. Double thread a needle with heavy thread and knot the end. With long stitches, gather the bottom raw edge of the head.

Stuff the head to within ¹/₂" or so of the raw edge. Insert the flat end of a stationary disk into the opening. Pull up on the gathering stitches. Stitch around another time or two, pulling on the stitches as you go. When the fabric is closed around the post, knot the thread.

7. Right sides facing, pin the two body front pieces together along the front edges. Stitch.

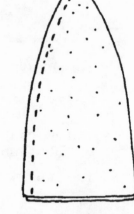

8. Right sides together, pin the two body back pieces together along the back edges. Stitch.

9. Pin the body fronts to the body backs. Stitch, leaving an opening between the dots at the top.

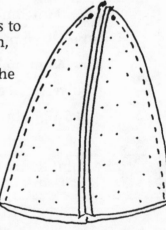

10. Pin body base to bottom edge of body, with the nap of the fur laying toward the back of the body. Stitch, leaving an opening between the dots marked on the body bottom.

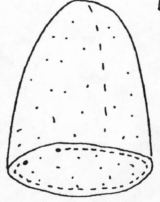

Turn body right side out.

11. Poke the post of the stationary disk protruding from the bottom of the head through the hole at the top of the body formed by the gap in the stitching in step 9 into the body. Complete the joint as instructed in chapter 1, first sliding on a large plastic washer and then the plastic lockwasher.

12. Stuff the body of the owl. Hand stitch the opening closed at the base.

13. Stitch the raw edges of the large eye patches to the head, turning the raw edges under ¼" as you stitch around.

Trim the black fur eye backing close to the eye.

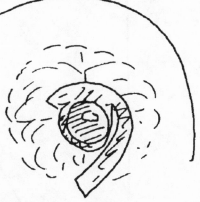

14. Using a ⅛" *seam allowance,* stitch the two felt beak pieces together, right sides facing, leaving an opening between the dots as marked. Trim the seam allowances at the tips. Turn right side out.

Stuff the beak. Whipstitch opening closed. Stitch to head as pictured.

15. Using a ⅛" *seam allowance,* stitch two felt feet pieces together, right sides facing, leaving the straight edges open, as shown. Trim the seam allowances at the tips of the toes. Turn right side out. Repeat for two remaining feet pieces.

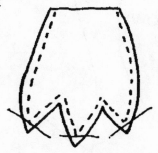

Turn the raw edges of the opening to the inside. Whipstitch. Stitch the feet to the front of the body along the body front/body base seam, each foot about ¾" to one side of the center body front seam.

16. Apply dots of white paint to the feathers. Set aside to dry before proceeding.

With a seam ripper or awl, poke holes in the fur as illustrated. Start them about 1½" from the bottom of the head and place them about ¾" to each side of the side seam. Push feathers into the holes. Trim them so they won't be too long for the owl to stand when he rests on a table. Remove each feather in turn, apply glue, and poke it back in. Allow to dry.

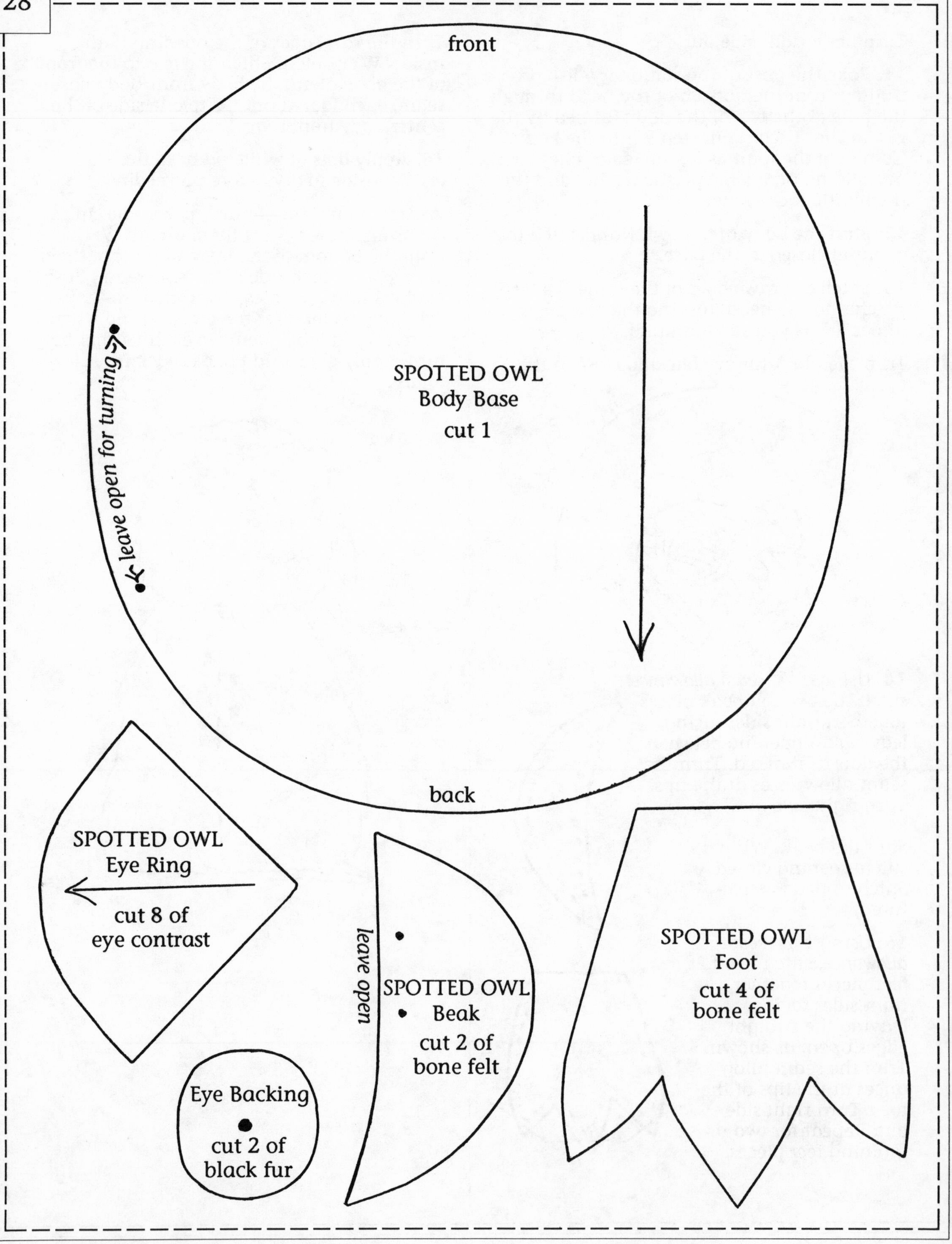

front

SPOTTED OWL
Body Base
cut 1

leave open for turning

back

SPOTTED OWL
Eye Ring

cut 8 of
eye contrast

leave open

SPOTTED OWL
Beak
cut 2 of
bone felt

SPOTTED OWL
Foot
cut 4 of
bone felt

Eye Backing
cut 2 of
black fur

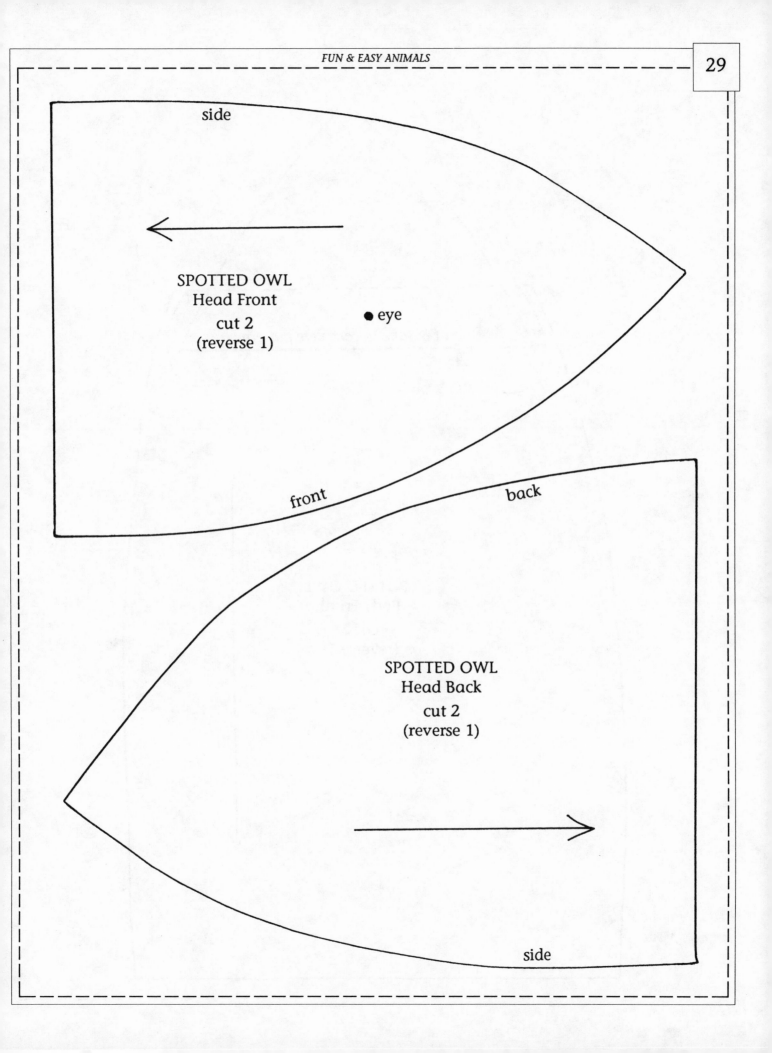

side

SPOTTED OWL
Head Front
cut 2
(reverse 1)

● eye

front

back

SPOTTED OWL
Head Back
cut 2
(reverse 1)

side

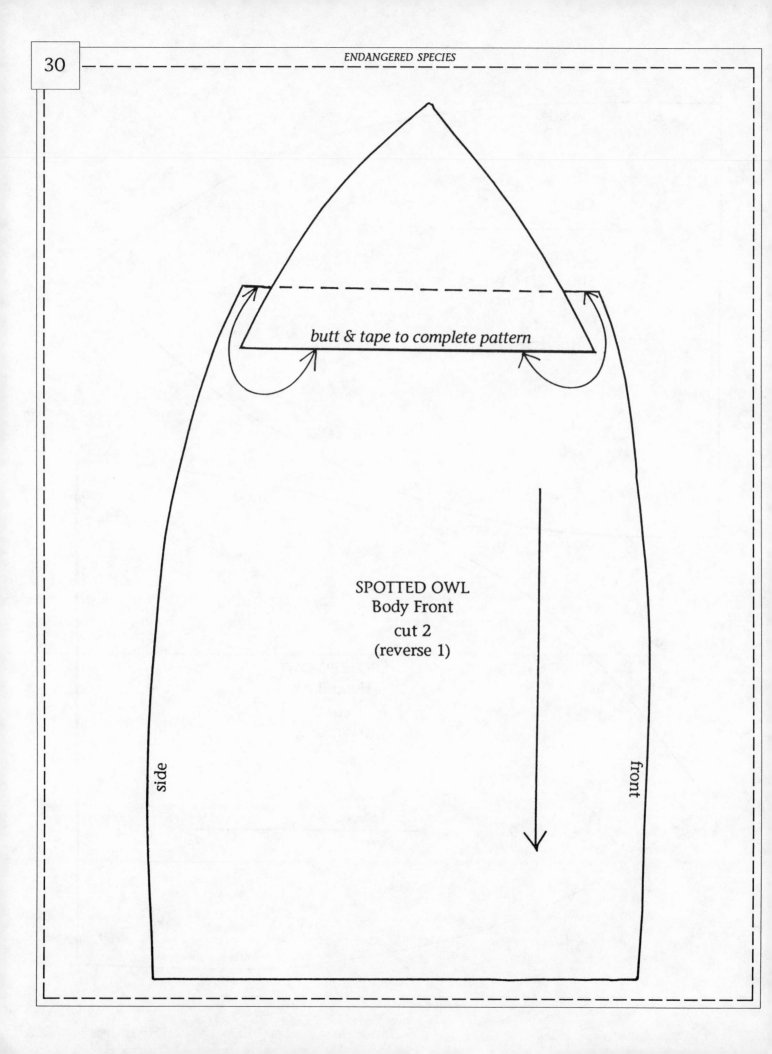

butt & tape to complete pattern

SPOTTED OWL
Body Front
cut 2
(reverse 1)

side

front

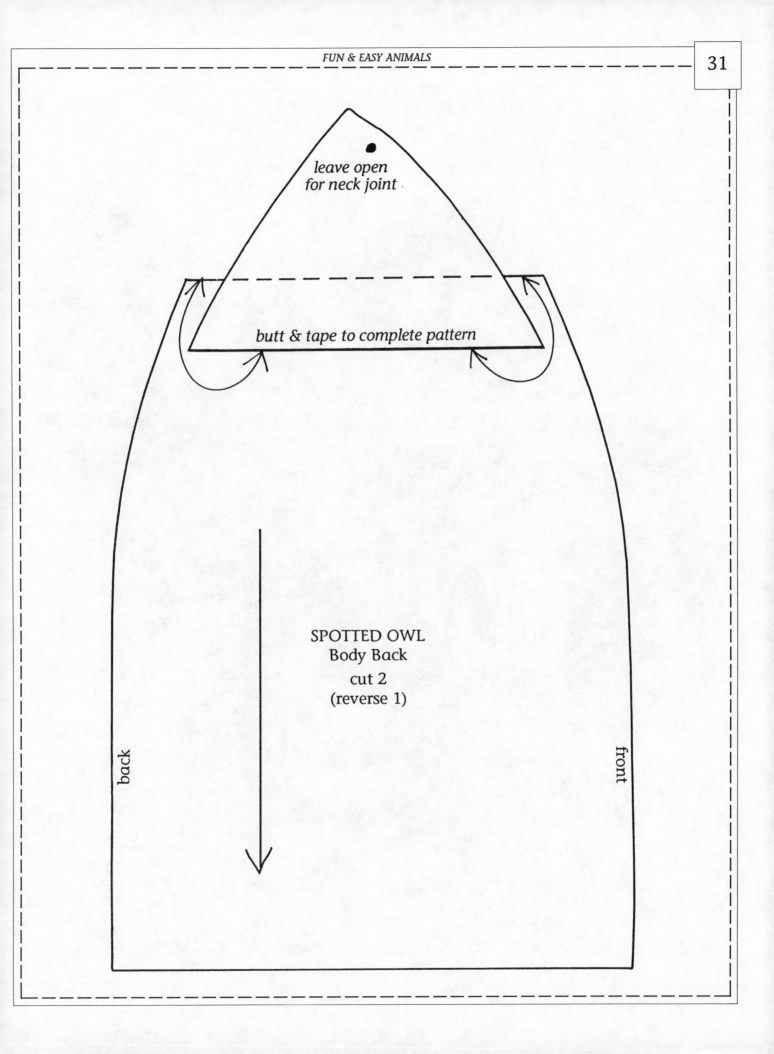

leave open
for neck joint

butt & tape to complete pattern

SPOTTED OWL
Body Back

cut 2
(reverse 1)

back

front

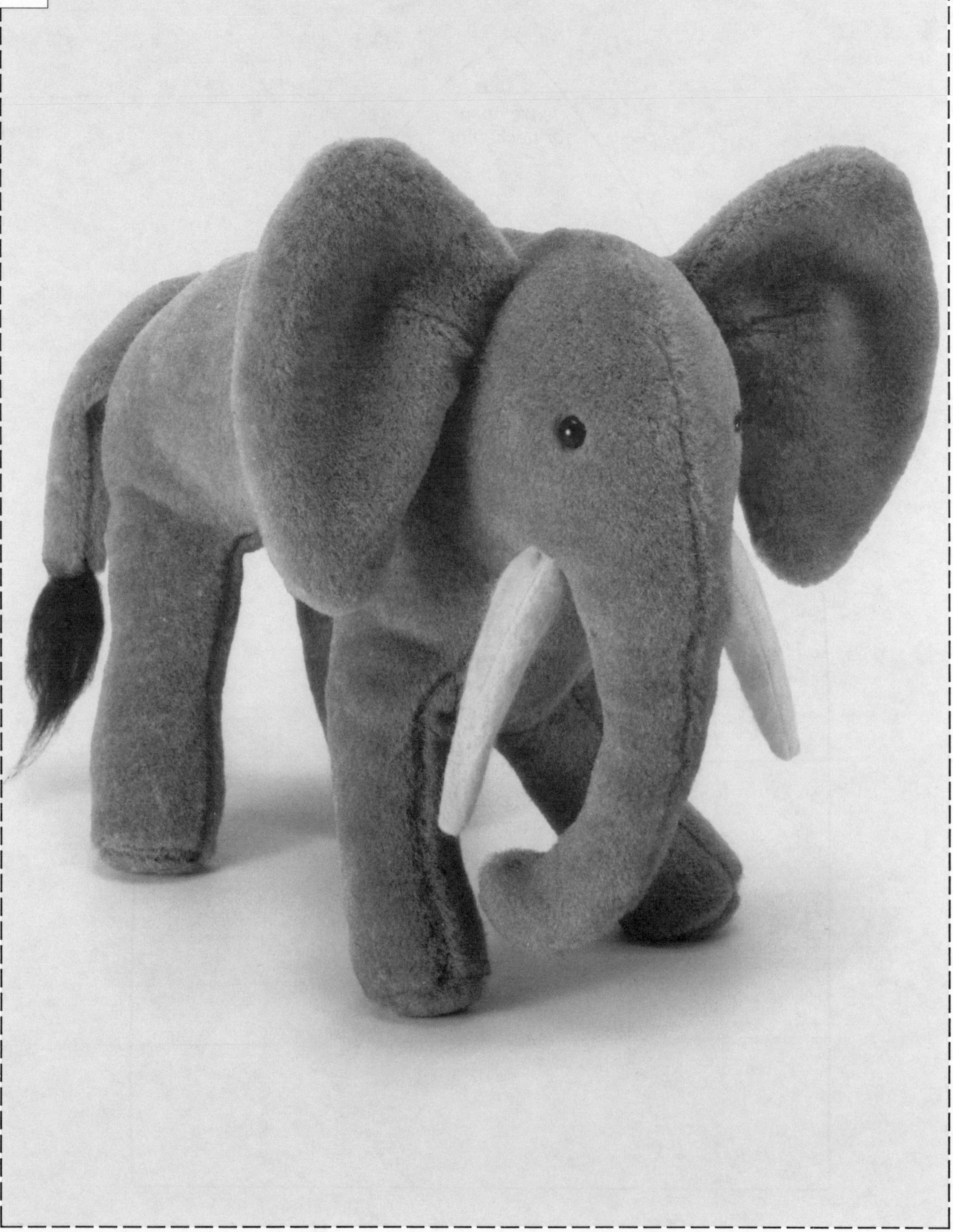

AFRICAN ELEPHANT

Here's another endangered species whose only enemies are human. Elephants live peacefully in herds, traveling mostly at night to find grass, roots, leaves, and fruit. If one elephant becomes ill or is unable to keep up with the herd, a few elephants remain behind to care for him. Elephants have about the same life expectancy as humans.

Though his real-life counterparts are the largest of all land animals, this stuffed elephant stands a more manageable 14" tall and measures 15" long. He is made of a short, coarse gray fur.

INSTRUCTIONS

Note: All seam allowances are 1/4" unless noted otherwise.

Prepare the patterns, cut and mark the fabric as instructed in chapter 1. To transfer ear and tusk markings from the backing to the right side of the fur, baste by hand or machine over the markings with red or another contrasting colored thread.

1. Cut 30 pieces of yarn 3" long or one length of Pretty Hair™ 3" long. Lay on right side of tail as shown.

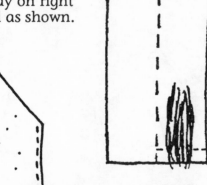

Fold tail in half lengthwise. Stitch as shown, leaving the short, angled edge (not the end where you laid the tail "hairs") open for turning.

Turn right side out.

MATERIALS

1/2 yard extra short pile fur fabric (#907K Antelope from CR's Crafts, see Sources)
Matching thread
One piece of bone-colored felt
Matching thread
Two 12 mm black plastic safety eyes
Carpet thread or waxed dental floss
Polyester fiberfill
Scrap of brown or black Pretty Hair™ (see Sources) or yarn

Pin tail to right side of one body side at dot marked tail as shown. Baste in place.

2. Matching dots A and B, pin and stitch the two inner back legs together as shown.

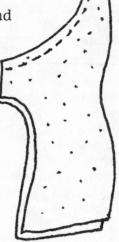

3. Pin and stitch inner back legs to underbody gusset as shown, matching dot A on gusset to dot A at seam in inner back legs.

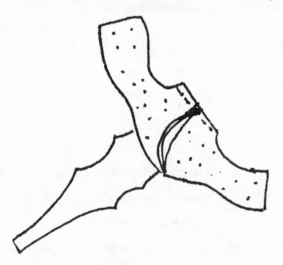

4. Pin inner front legs to underbody gusset, matching dots C and D. Stitch.

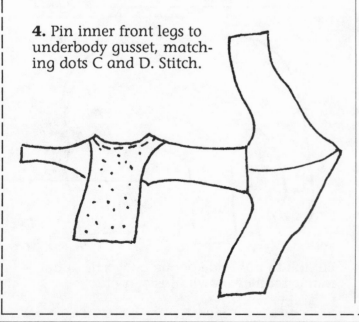

5. Starting at dot E at the underside of the elephant's trunk, pin one side of the underbody gusset/inner front and back legs to one body side, matching dots and raw edges. Match and pin all the way to dot B, just below the elephant's tail. Stitch between dots E and B as illustrated, leaving the bottom of the legs open.

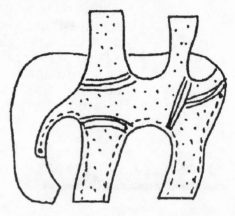

Repeat for other side of gusset and body side. This time leave an opening between the dots as marked at the tummy for turning and stuffing.

6. Pin the two body sides together from dot E under the chin, around trunk, up the head, over the back and down to dot B, under the tail. Stitch, including the tail in the seam.

7. Pin a foot sole to the bottom of a leg, matching dots to seams. Make sure nap of foot sole fur points toward the back of the elephant. Stitch. Repeat for the remaining three legs.

8. Make a hole at the markings for the eyes.

Install the eyes as instructed in chapter 1.

9. Stuff the body, paying special attention to the trunk and legs. The trunk should be stuffed uniformly, with no lumps. Fluffing the fiberfill before stuffing helps. For an elephant sure on his feet, the legs must be stuffed firmly, right up to the top. When finished stuffing, ladder stitch the opening at the tummy closed.

10. Lay the ear pieces out, wrong side up, as shown. Make darts in two ear pieces as marked. These will be the inside (facing elephant's body) of ears.

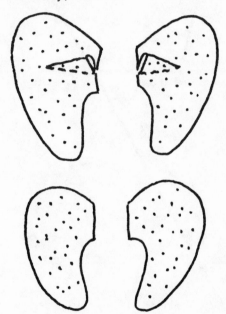

Stitch a darted to an undarted ear. Repeat. Turn right side out.

Turn seam allowances to inside. Whipstitch closed. Pin to head at markings, darts facing the back of the elephant. Ladder stitch to head.

11. Pin two tusk pieces together. Stitch, leaving short, straight edges open. Trim seam allowances to 1/8" from stitching. Repeat for other two tusk pieces.

Turn tusks right side out. Stuff. Turn 1/4" at bottom edge of tusks to center. Hand stitch across turned under edge to secure as shown.

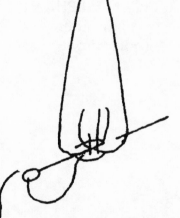

Pin tusks to head at markings. Stitch to head. Bend them gently to turn slightly up and in, toward the trunk.

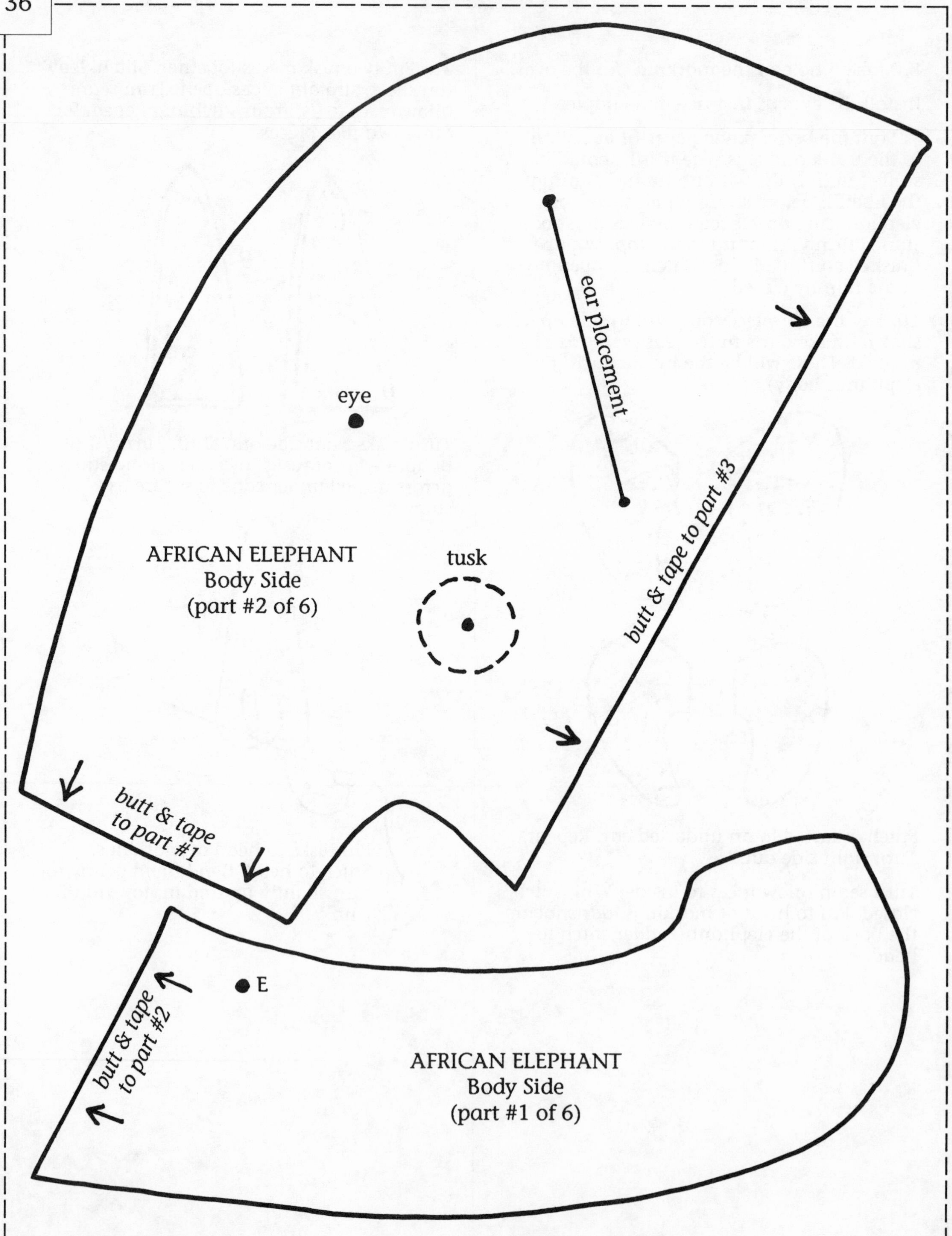

eye

ear placement

tusk

AFRICAN ELEPHANT
Body Side
(part #2 of 6)

butt & tape to part #3

butt & tape
to part #1

butt & tape
to part #2

• E

AFRICAN ELEPHANT
Body Side
(part #1 of 6)

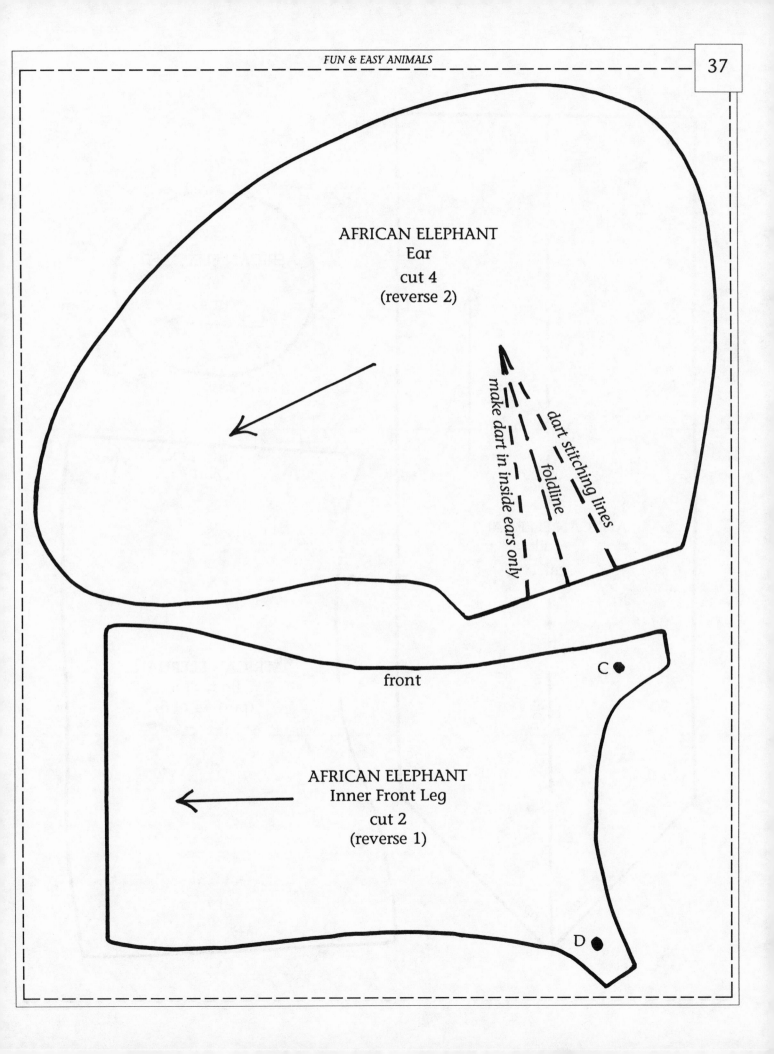

AFRICAN ELEPHANT
Ear
cut 4
(reverse 2)

dart stitching lines

foldline

make dart in inside ears only

front

C •

AFRICAN ELEPHANT
Inner Front Leg
cut 2
(reverse 1)

D •

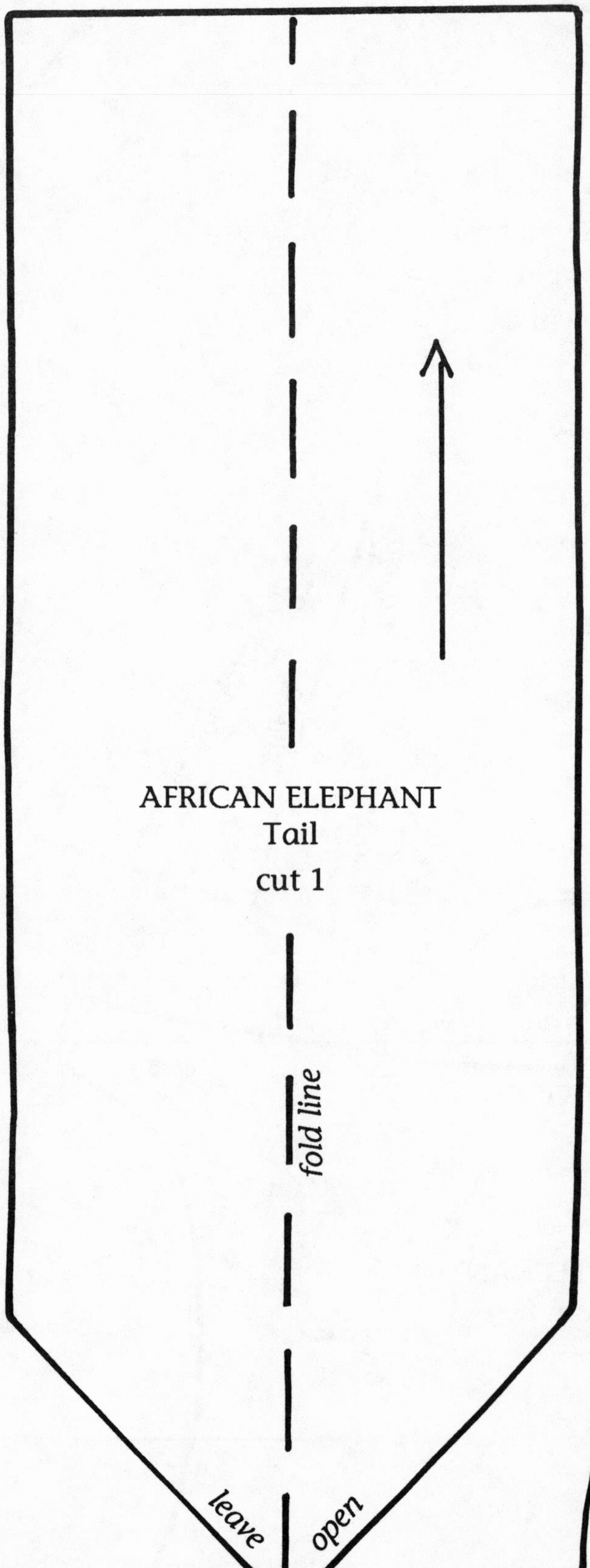

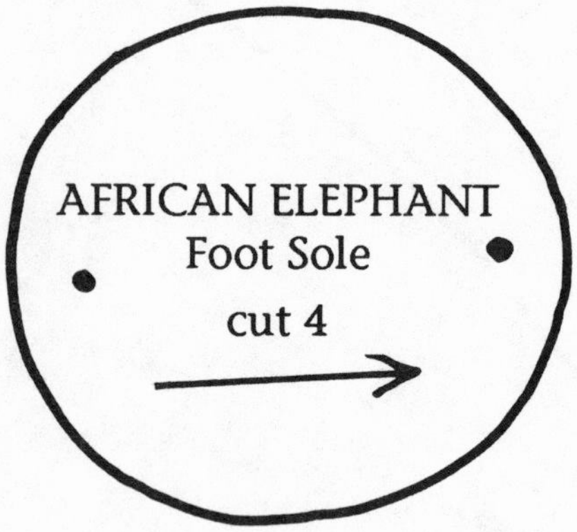

AFRICAN ELEPHANT
Foot Sole
cut 4

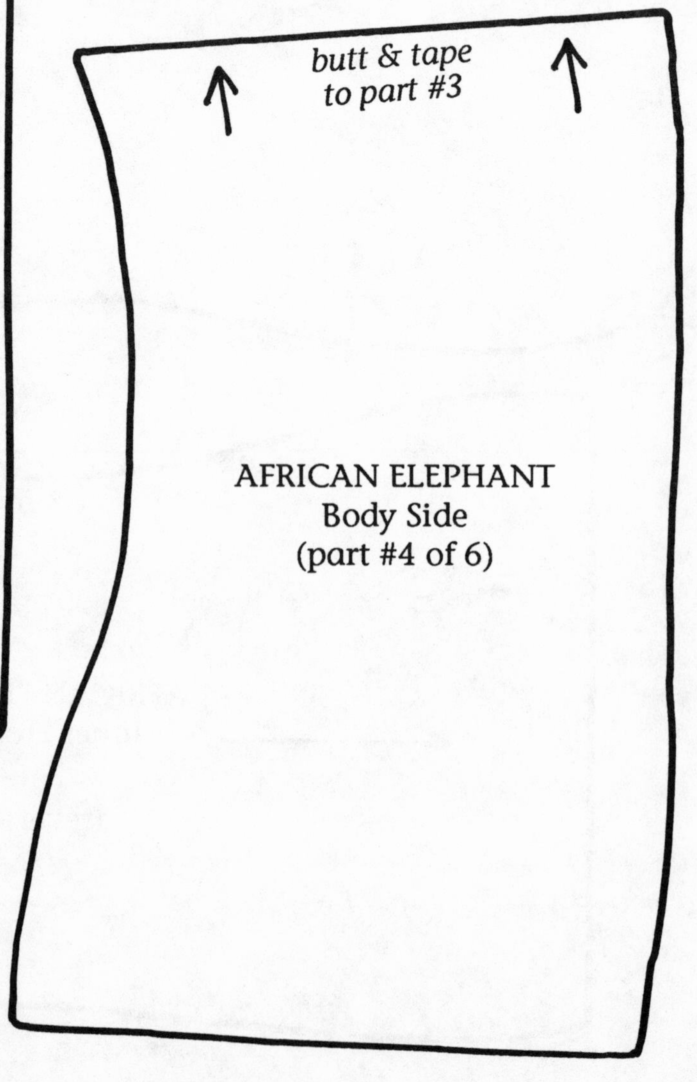

AFRICAN ELEPHANT
Tail
cut 1

fold line

leave open

butt & tape
to part #3

AFRICAN ELEPHANT
Body Side
(part #4 of 6)

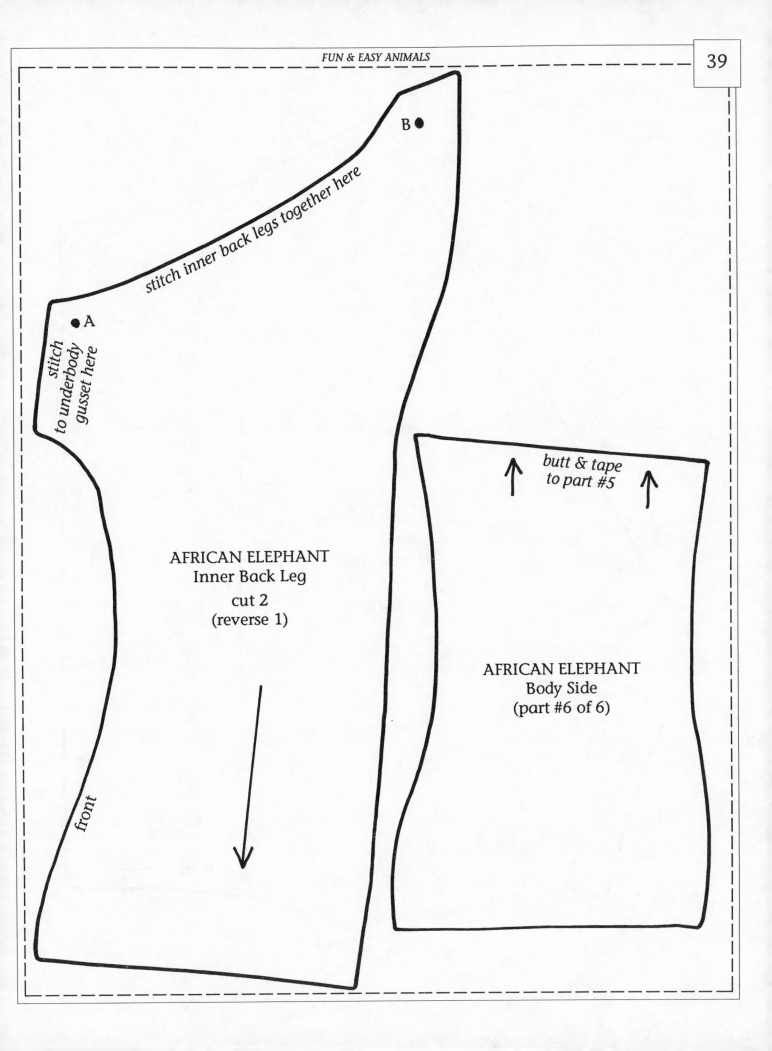

stitch inner back legs together here

B •

• A

stitch to underbody gusset here

AFRICAN ELEPHANT
Inner Back Leg

cut 2
(reverse 1)

front

butt & tape
to part #5

AFRICAN ELEPHANT
Body Side

(part #6 of 6)

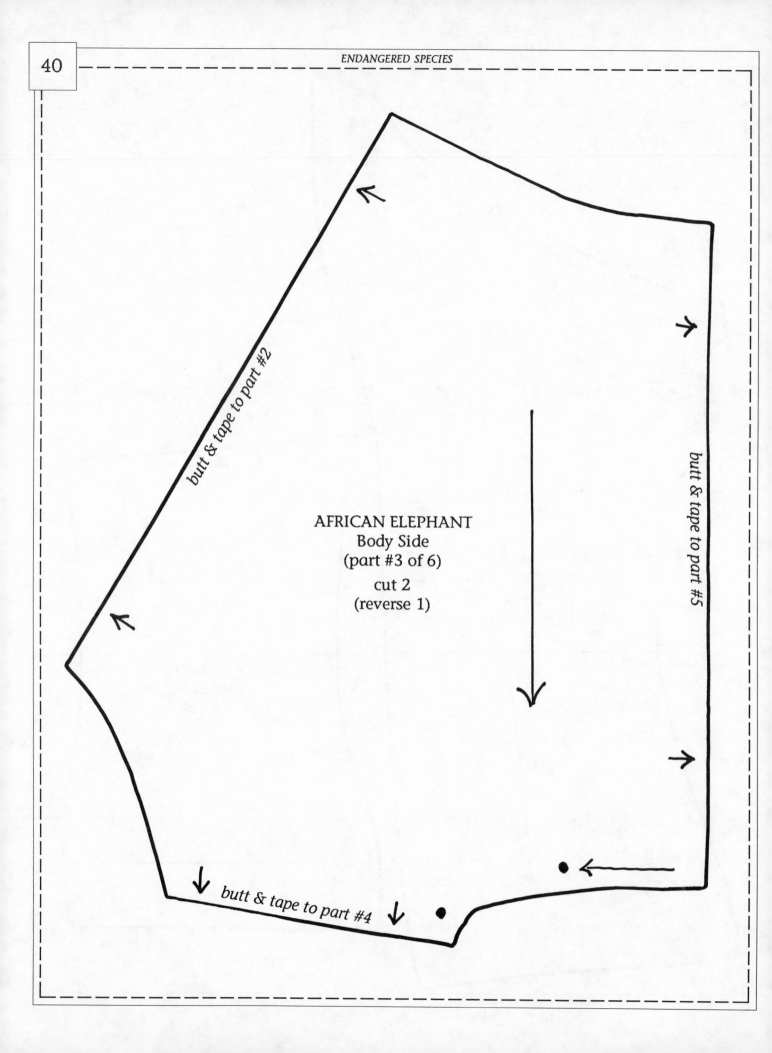

butt & tape to part #2

butt & tape to part #5

AFRICAN ELEPHANT
Body Side
(part #3 of 6)

cut 2
(reverse 1)

butt & tape to part #4

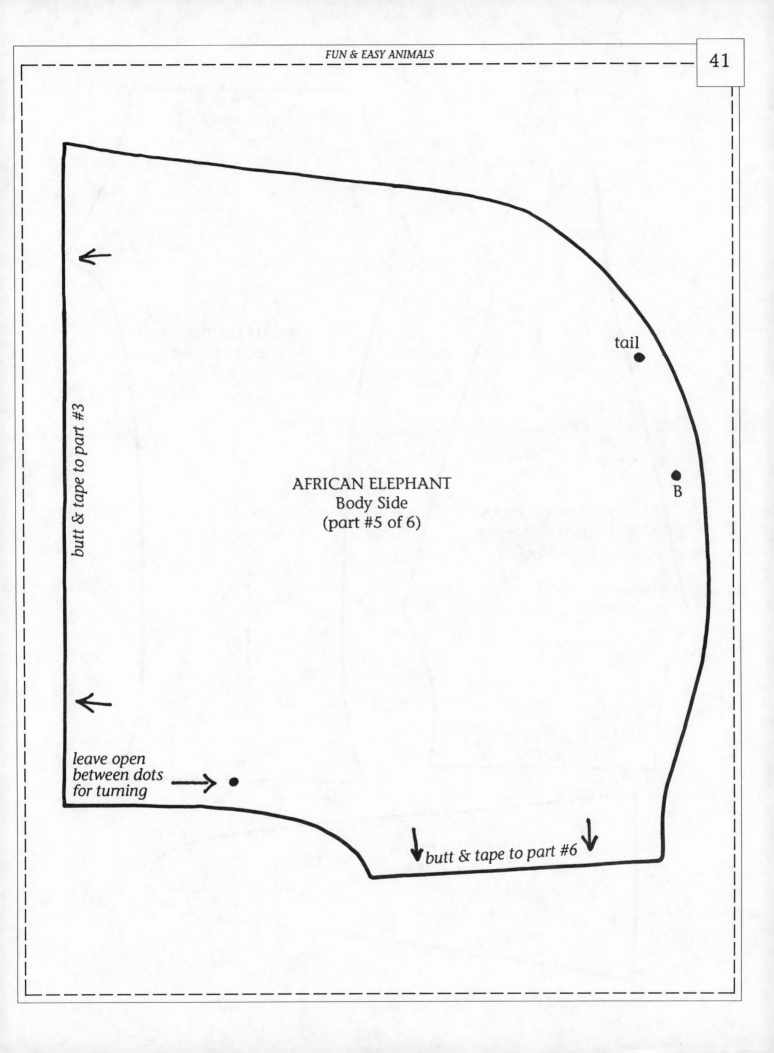

butt & tape to part #3

tail

B

AFRICAN ELEPHANT
Body Side
(part #5 of 6)

leave open
between dots
for turning

butt & tape to part #6

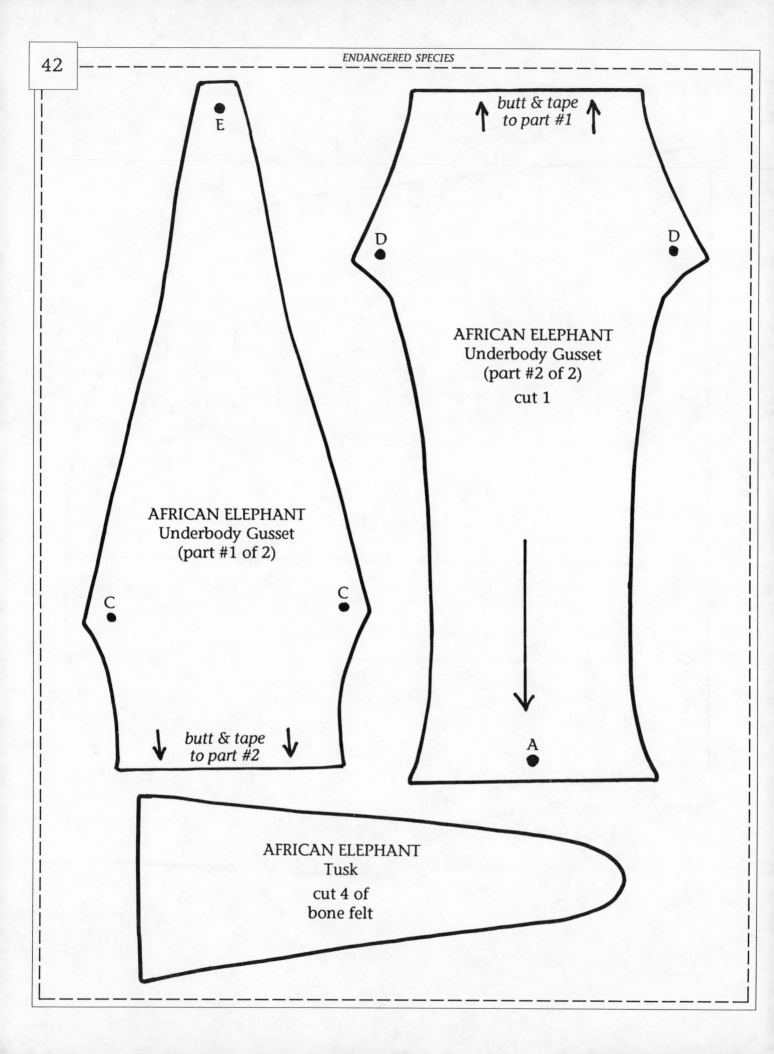

E

AFRICAN ELEPHANT
Underbody Gusset
(part #1 of 2)

C   C

↓ *butt & tape* ↓
to part #2

butt & tape ↑
↑ *to part #1* ↑

D   D

AFRICAN ELEPHANT
Underbody Gusset
(part #2 of 2)

cut 1

↓

A

AFRICAN ELEPHANT
Tusk

cut 4 of
bone felt

♥ ♥ ♥

Spectacular Species

♥ ♥ ♥

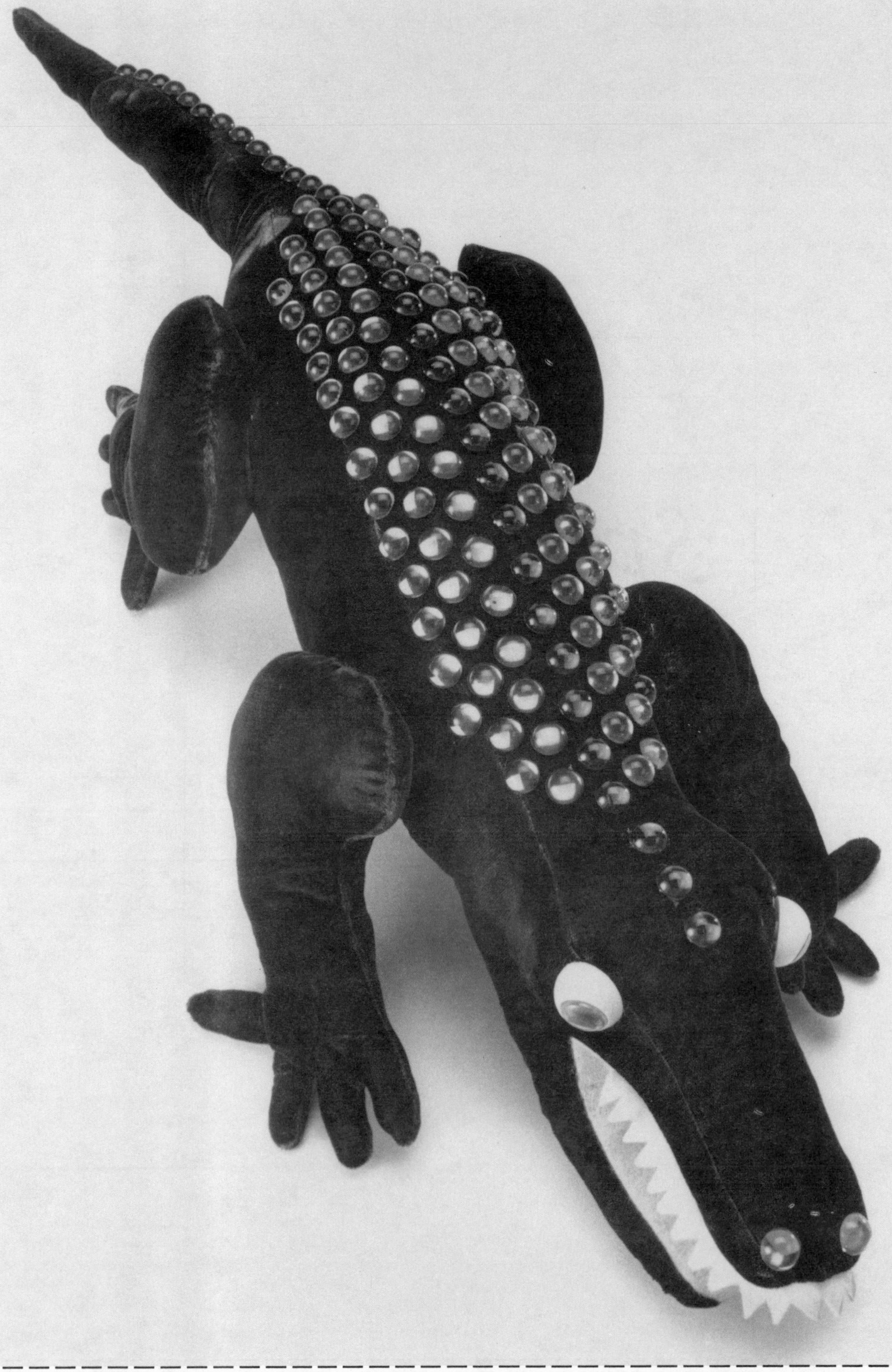

AMERICAN ALLIGATOR

A rare success in the world of vanishing species, the American alligator has responded to captive breeding and habitat protection and is thriving.

Complete with ferocious teeth and bulging eyes, our alligator is no menace. He is made of emerald felt and his back is lined with jewels, not warty bumps. He measures three feet in length.

Note: If this stuffed animal is intended for a young child, please omit the cabochons. Though they are glued on securely, small fingers could easily pull them loose. A cabochon is similar to a rhinestone except it is round and dome-shaped.

MATERIALS

⅝ yard emerald velvet

Matching thread

One pair 24 mm frog eyes (#424 from Carver's Eye Co., see Sources)

White felt

Bone-colored felt

Polyester fiberfill stuffing

Fray Check™

Cabochons in the following amounts and colors (from the Bead Gallery, see Sources):

34 ruby

36 emerald

36 topaz

26 dark sapphire

INSTRUCTIONS

Note: All seam allowances are ¼".

Prepare the patterns, cut and mark the fabric by following the instructions in chapter 1.

Note: It is crucial to prevent the raw edges of the velvet from fraying. Finish the raw edges of the cut pieces. Lay them out on a cardboard cutting board or brown paper. Apply Fray Check™ to all the raw edges and allow to dry.

1. Pin and stitch the body side pieces together from dot A at nose down to top of mouth opening.

Pin and stitch the body side pieces together from dot B at chin up to bottom of mouth opening.

2. Match and pin dot B on body bottom to dot B under chin at the body sides' seam. Match dot C on body bottom to dot C on one body side, right sides facing. Pin and stitch between these dots. Repeat for the other side of the body bottom/body side.

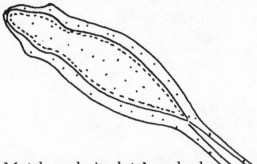

3. Match and pin dot A on body top to dot A at nose at body sides' seam. Match and pin dot D on body top to dot D on one body side. Pin and stitch between these dots. Repeat for the other side of the body top/body side.

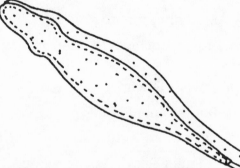

4. Pin and stitch around the tail from dot C to dot D, leaving an opening in the stitching between the dots under the tail as instructed on the pattern.

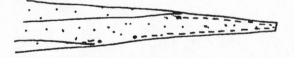

5. To find the center of the teeth, fold teeth in half. Pin the center point of the teeth to one dot on the felt mouth. Baste in place as shown. This will be the top of the mouth.

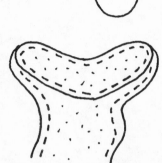

Matching dots on felt mouth to seams in body sides at center front of mouth and with teeth facing the right side of the velvet, pin mouth to mouth opening, remembering that the teeth should be stitched to the top jaw (eye side — these are top teeth) of the mouth. Stitch.

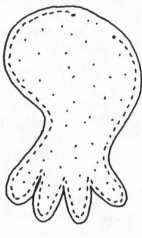

6. Turn alligator right side out. Install the eyes as instructed in chapter 1.

7. Starting at the far ends of the mouth, carefully stuff the alligator's head. Continue to stuff the body almost until you reach the stuffing opening. Now start at the tip of the tail and work your way back. Ladder stitch the opening closed.

8. Right sides facing, pin and stitch two leg pieces together, leaving an opening between the dots as marked. Repeat for the other pieces.

Turn right side out. Stuff. Ladder stitch the openings closed. Hand stitch to body sides as shown. Note that the front legs bend in the opposite direction from the back legs.

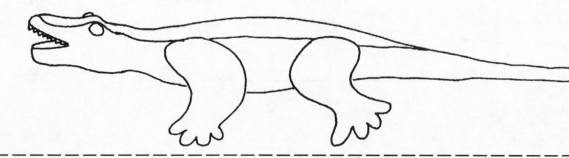

9. One at a time, apply glue to the backs of the cabochons and place them on the back of the alligator according to the overhead photograph. A single row of rubies runs down the center, a row of 18 emeralds on each side of the rubies, a row of 17 topaz to the outside of the emeralds on each side, followed by a row of 13 dark sapphires to each side of the topaz. Each is spaced about $\frac{1}{4}$" from the preceding cabochon. For nostrils, glue two topaz cabochons to the nose.

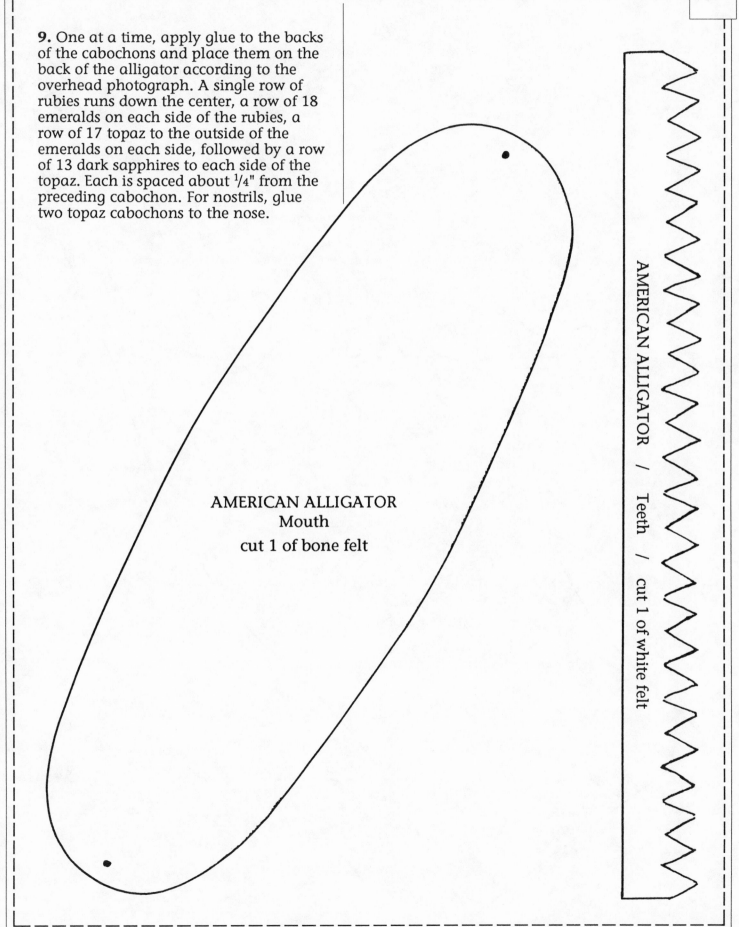

AMERICAN ALLIGATOR
Mouth
cut 1 of bone felt

AMERICAN ALLIGATOR / Teeth / cut 1 of white felt

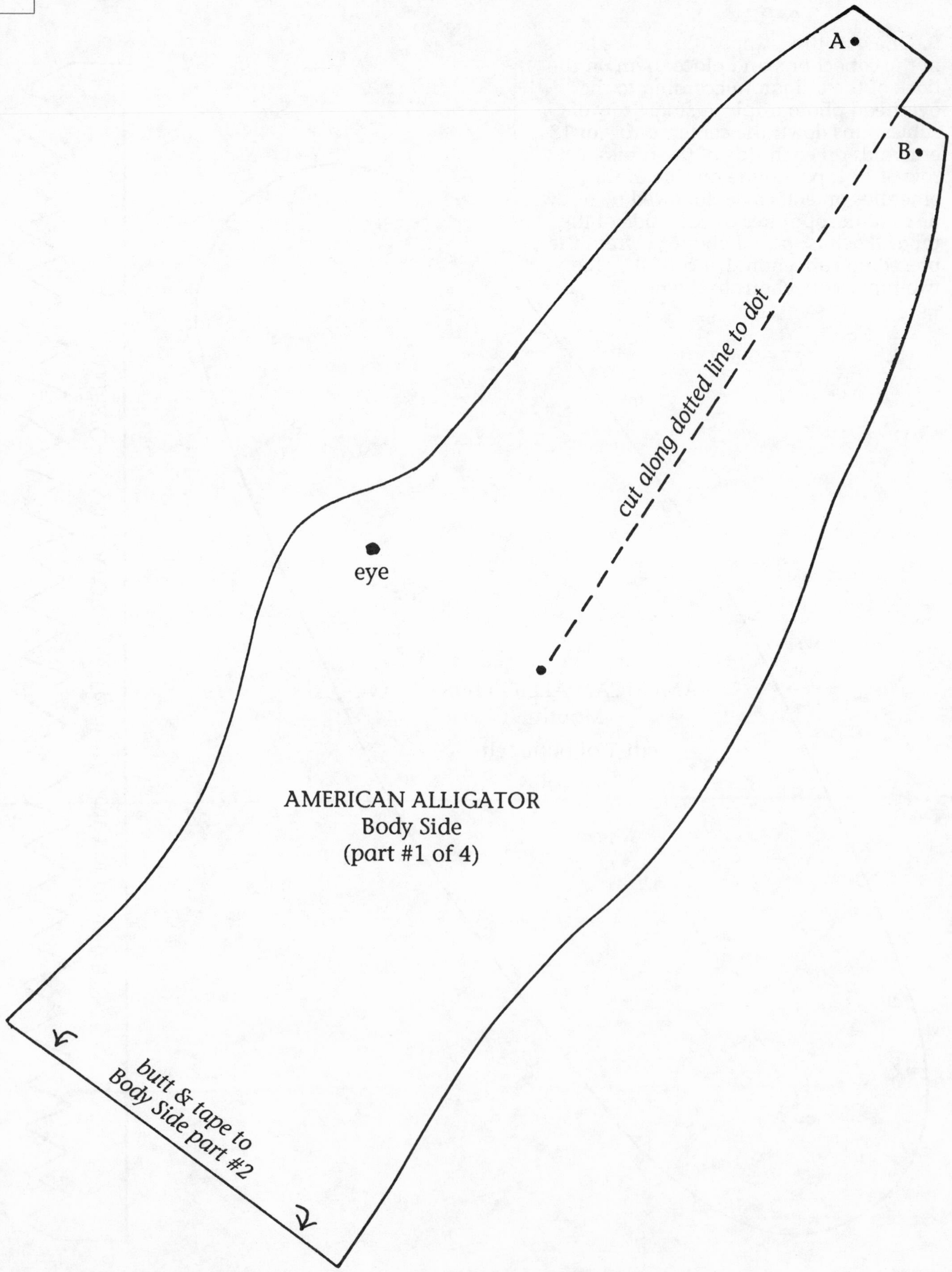

48

A•

B•

cut along dotted line to dot

•

• eye

AMERICAN ALLIGATOR
Body Side
(part #1 of 4)

butt & tape to
Body Side part #2

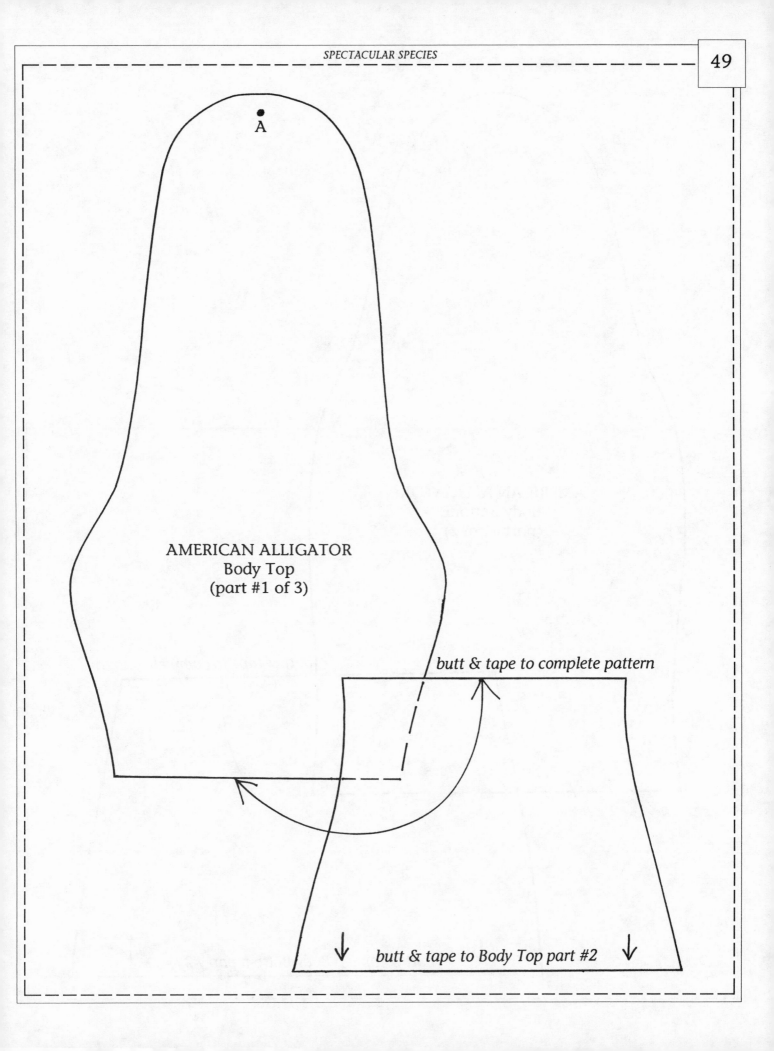

A

AMERICAN ALLIGATOR
Body Top
(part #1 of 3)

butt & tape to complete pattern

↓ *butt & tape to Body Top part #2* ↓

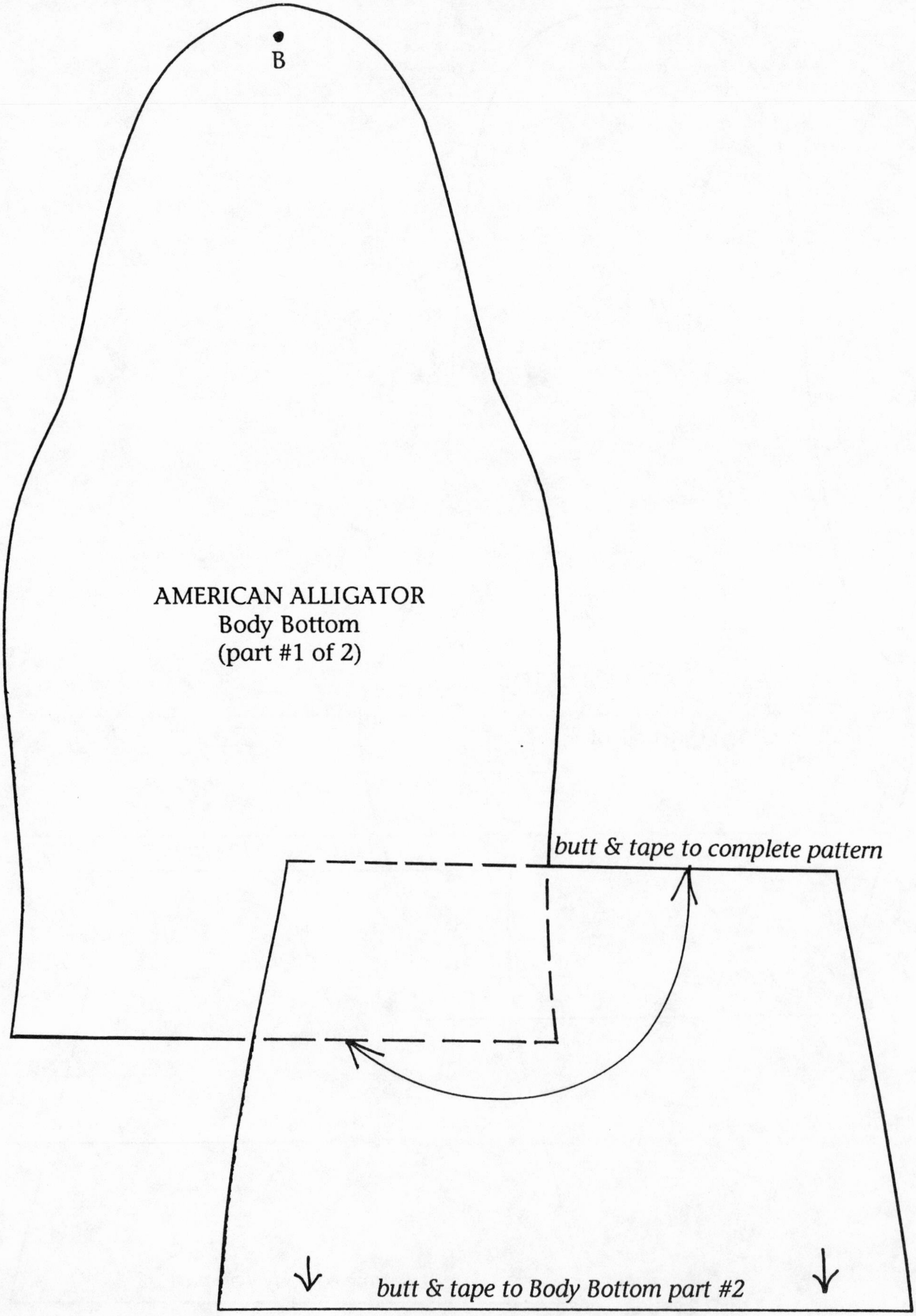

B

AMERICAN ALLIGATOR
Body Bottom
(part #1 of 2)

butt & tape to complete pattern

↓　　*butt & tape to Body Bottom part #2*　　↓

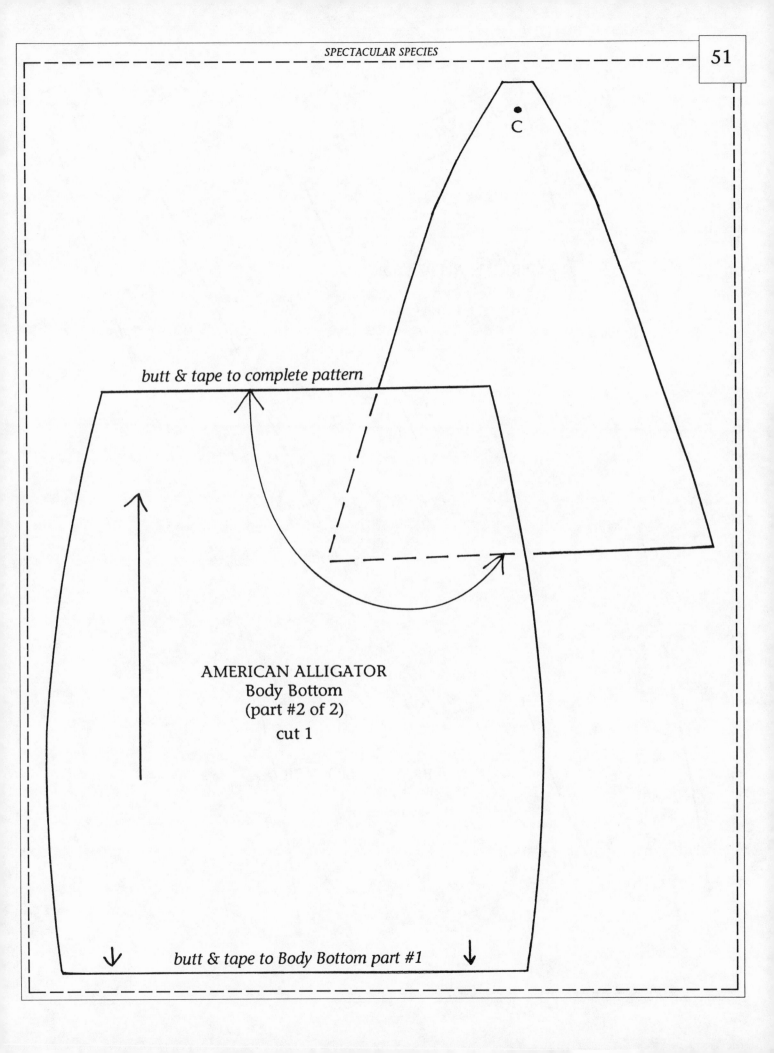

C

butt & tape to complete pattern

AMERICAN ALLIGATOR
Body Bottom
(part #2 of 2)

cut 1

butt & tape to Body Bottom part #1

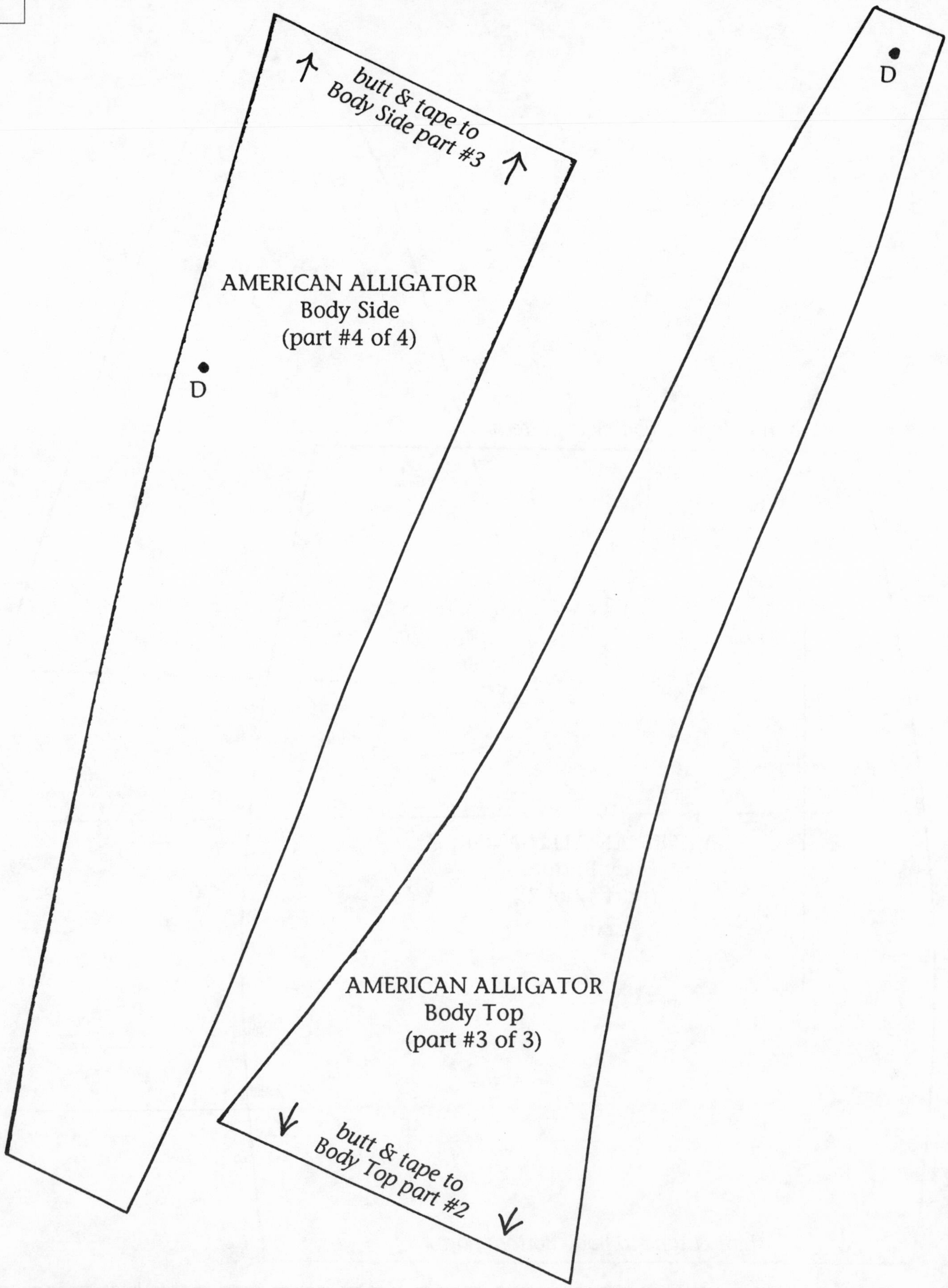

↑   butt & tape to
Body Side part #3   ↑

AMERICAN ALLIGATOR
Body Side
(part #4 of 4)

● D

D ●

AMERICAN ALLIGATOR
Body Top
(part #3 of 3)

↓   butt & tape to
Body Top part #2   ↓

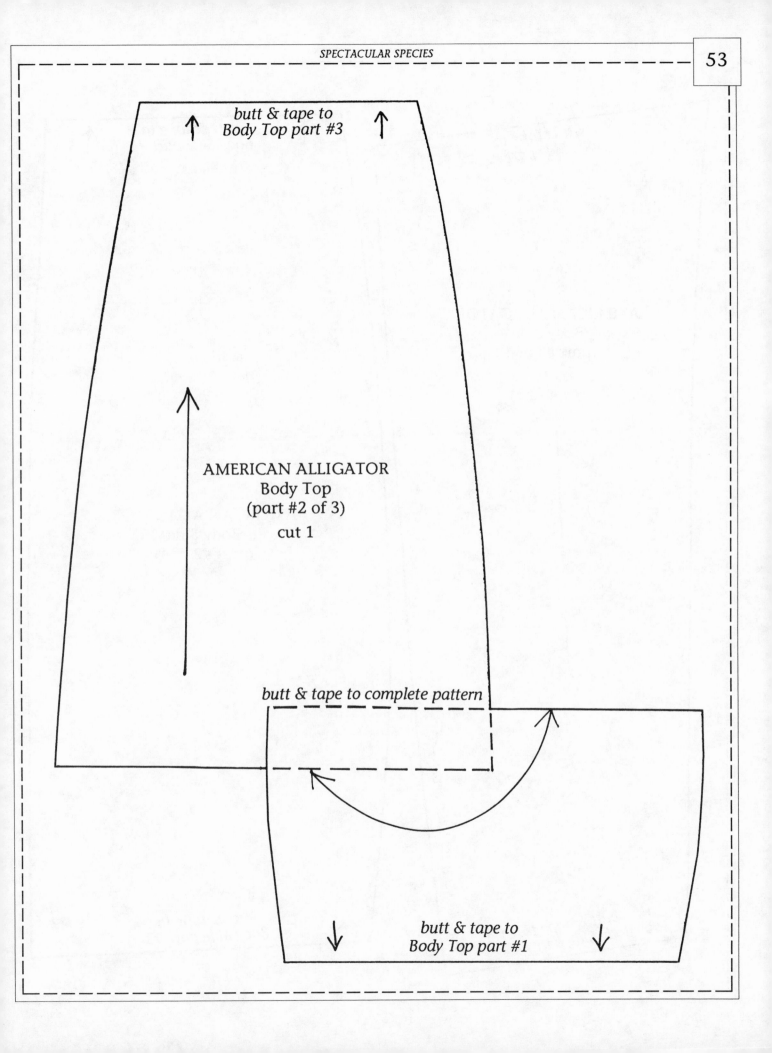

butt & tape to
Body Top part #3

AMERICAN ALLIGATOR
Body Top
(part #2 of 3)

cut 1

butt & tape to complete pattern

butt & tape to
Body Top part #1

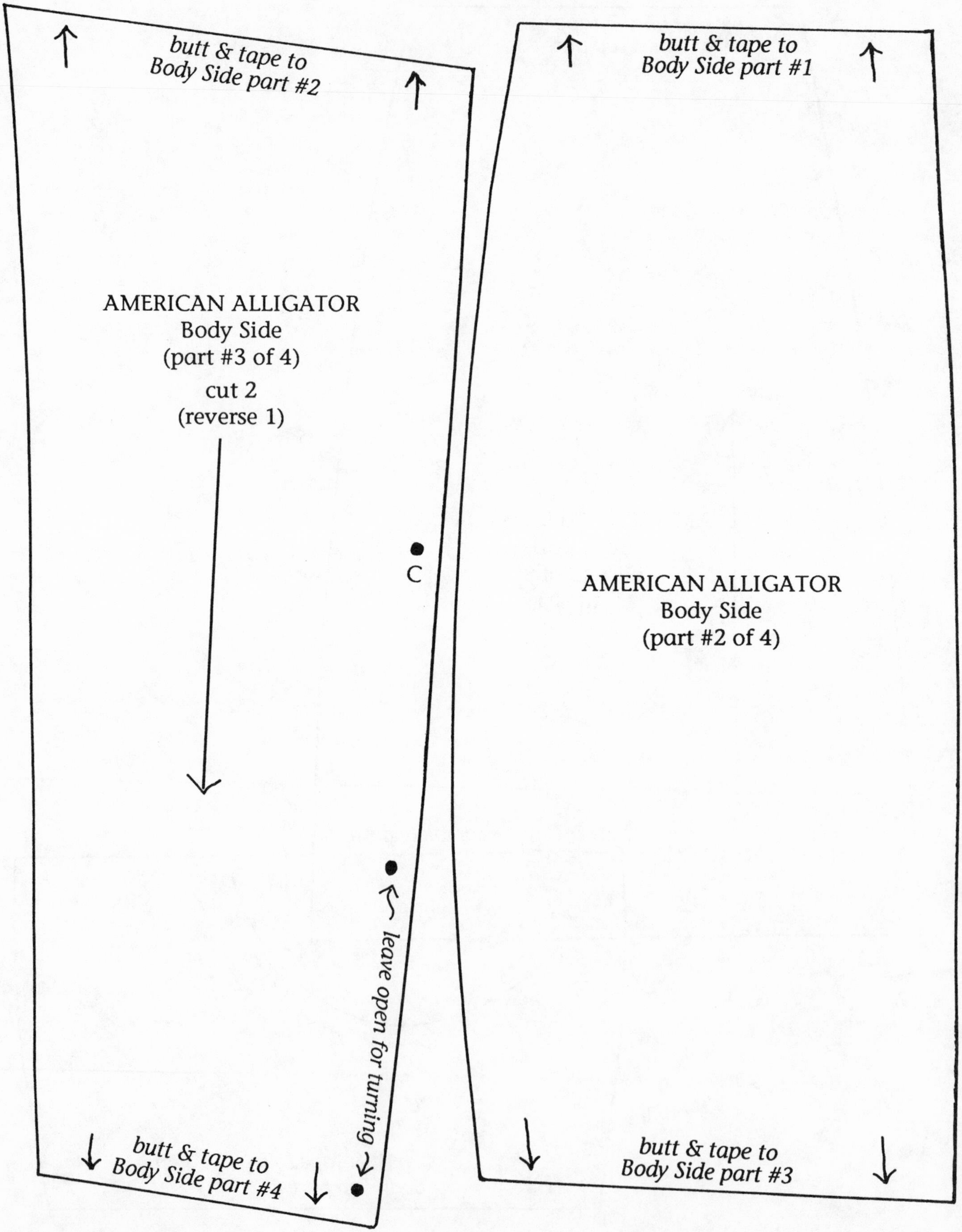

butt & tape to
Body Side part #2

butt & tape to
Body Side part #1

AMERICAN ALLIGATOR
Body Side
(part #3 of 4)

cut 2
(reverse 1)

C

AMERICAN ALLIGATOR
Body Side
(part #2 of 4)

leave open for turning

butt & tape to
Body Side part #4

butt & tape to
Body Side part #3

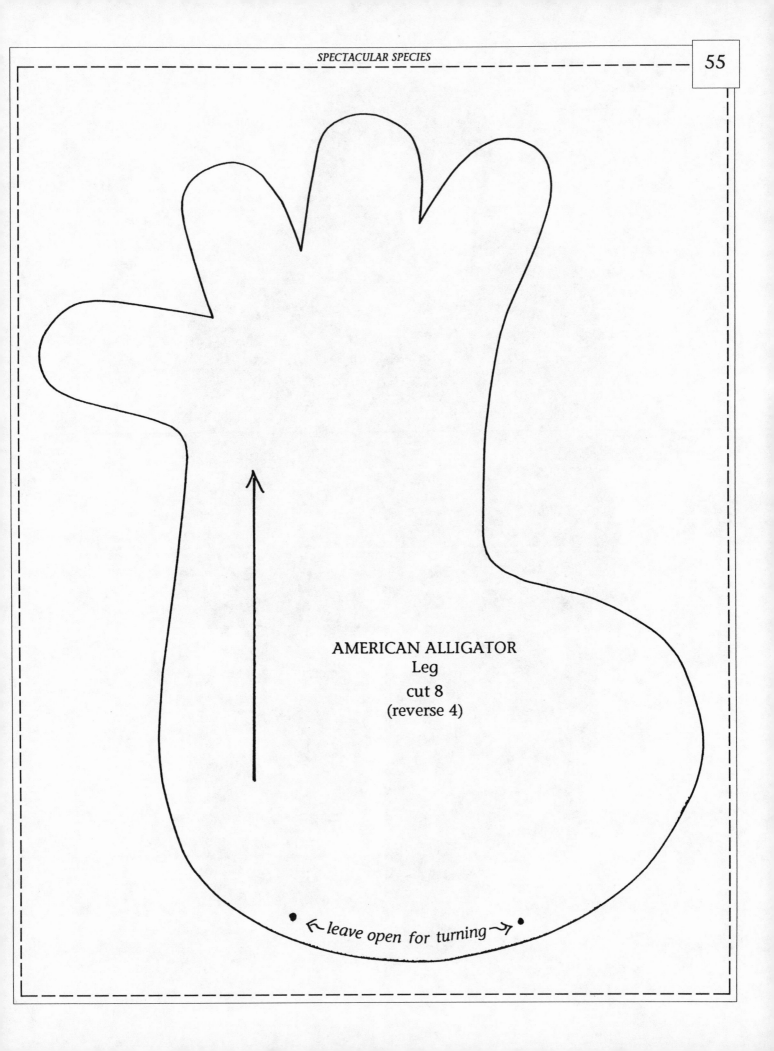

AMERICAN ALLIGATOR
Leg
cut 8
(reverse 4)

← leave open for turning →

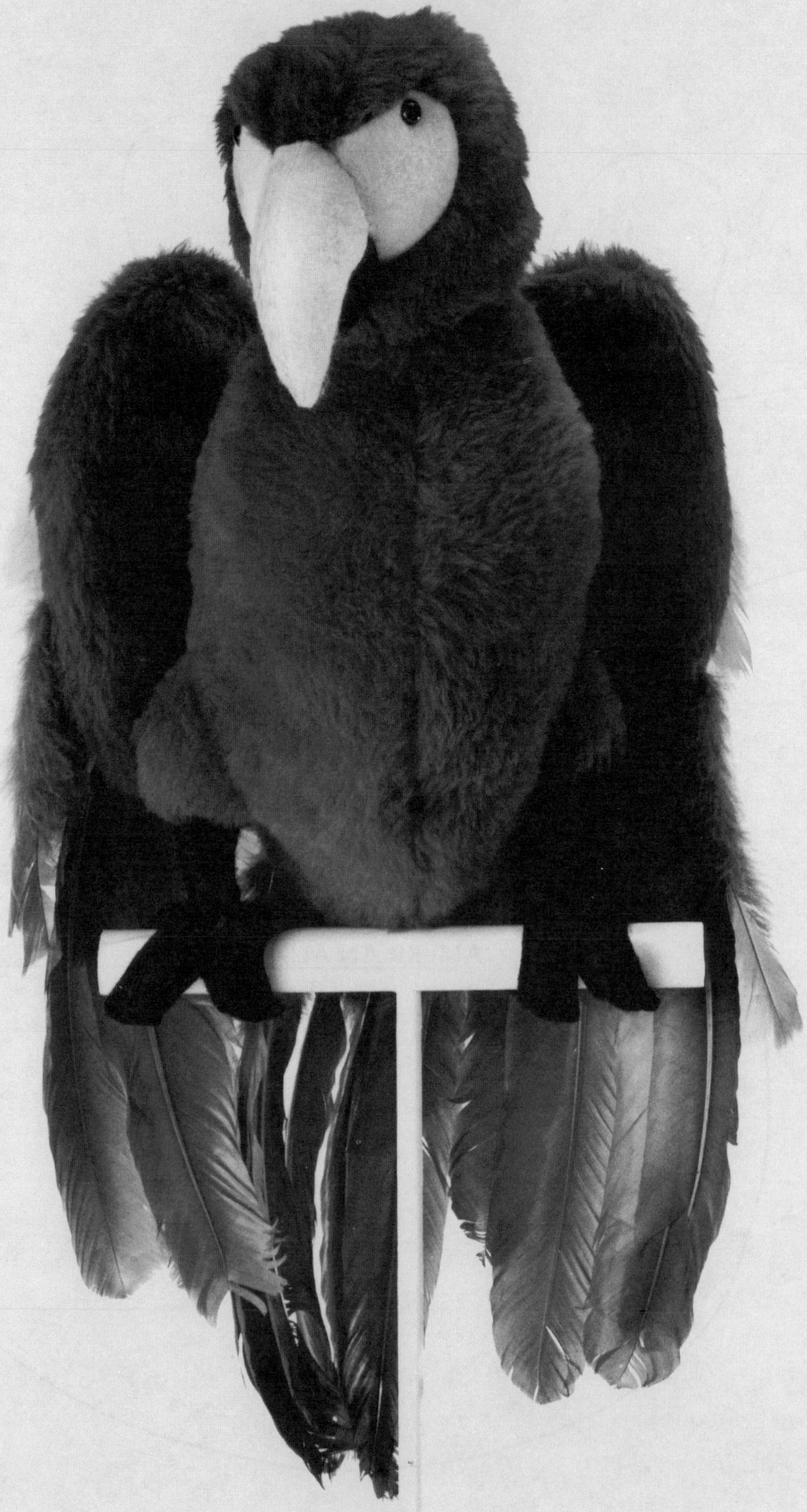

SCARLET MACAW

A living jewel, the scarlet macaw is almost too beautiful to be real. Thanks to their beauty and top pet qualities, macaws have been well-established in captivity by devoted breeders. At the same time, habitat destruction has decreased the wild populations, making the future of the scarlet macaw in its natural home dubious indeed.

This homemade red fur macaw measures 15" from top to bottom. Including tail feathers, the macaw measures 25".

MATERIALS

⅓ yard scarlet fur
(from CR's Crafts, see Sources)

Matching thread

One piece of bone-colored felt

Matching thread

Three pieces of black felt

Black thread

Two 9 mm plastic safety eyes,
brown with black pupils

20 10"-12" red "wing" feathers for wings
and tail

8 5" red feathers

16 5" yellow feathers

18 5" long blue feathers

One 55 mm plastic teddy bear joint and
metal lockwasher

Carpet thread or waxed dental floss

Masking or regular tape

Polyester fiberfill stuffing

Craft glue

20-gauge wire

INSTRUCTIONS

Note: All seam allowances are ¼" unless noted otherwise.

Prepare patterns, cut and mark the fabric as instructed in chapter 1. Transfer feather placement markings to right side of wings and bottom of body backs following the instructions in chapter 1.

1. Pin and stitch two wing pieces together, right sides facing, leaving straight edges open. Turn the wing right side out. Match and baste the raw edges of the wing together. Repeat for second wing.

2. Pin the body back pieces together at center back, right sides facing. Stitch along curve from top to bottom.

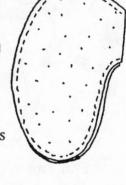

3. Pin and stitch the body fronts together, right sides facing, leaving an opening in the stitching between the dots.

4. Slash body back pieces as indicated at wing placement markings. Right sides facing, fold one body back piece along slashed line. From inside (right side) the folded body back, insert one wing into the slash, having the tip of the wing pointing downward, in the direction of the nap of the fur of the body back. Pin the two layers of the dart opening to the basted raw edges of the wing. Stitch along dart stitching line, through all thicknesses. Repeat for second body back and wing.

5. Pin and stitch body front to body back, right sides facing, leaving openings between the dots at the bottom for both legs and leaving an opening between the dots at the top of the body to insert the neck joint.

6. Pin one eye patch to one head side, right sides facing. Stitch. Repeat for second head side and eye patch.

7. Stitch one head side to the head gusset, matching dots A and B. Stitch remaining head side to other side of head gusset, again matching dots.

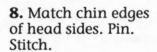

8. Match chin edges of head sides. Pin. Stitch.

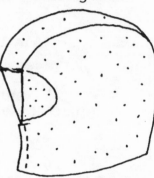

9. Stitch the top beak pieces together along the long, curved edge.

Stitch one side of top beak gusset to one remaining long edge of beak. Stitch remaining side of gusset to the other long edge of beak.

Repeat for the bottom beak.

Turn beaks right side out. Stitch the short edges of the beak gussets together at the side that places them curving toward each other.

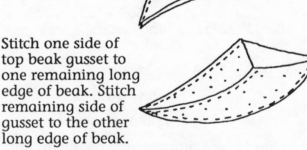

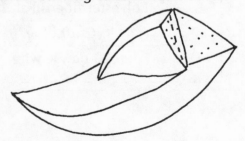

10. Install the eyes at eye markings on felt eye patches as instructed in chapter 1.

11. Stuff the head loosely: the head will be restuffed later, this is just to help you sew the beak onto the head. Pin and hand stitch the beak to the head, 1/4" in from the raw edge of the beak opening in the head. Turn the raw edges of the beak 1/4" to the inside as you sew. Take your time, and be sure to pull your stitches tight. You may want to stitch around the beak twice to achieve a good, tight fit.

12. Unstuff the head. Stuff the beak gently, but make sure the pointed tips of the beak are full. Stuff the head to within about 1/2" of the raw neck edge. Lay the flat end of the stationary disk on the fiberfill in the opening, the post sticking out. Using heavy thread and long (1/2") stitches, gather the raw edge of the opening around the post. Pull on the thread as you stitch, closing the opening tightly around the post. Knot the thread.

Attach the head to the body, following the instructions in the "Jointing the Animals" section in chapter 1.

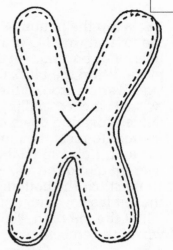

13. Stitch two foot pieces together, 1/8" from edges.

Repeat for second foot.

14. Cut four pieces of wire, each 20" long. Twist them together, leaving about 2" at each end untwisted.

Cut an "X" on top of one foot as marked. Divide the wires at the ends into two sets of toes. Fold the foot as shown and insert two toe wires into the front and two into the back toes of the foot. Spread the wires into the foot as shown and flatten them so they are perpendicular to the leg. Follow the "X-ray illustrations."

Using a Stuff-It™ tool, knitting needle or other small, pointed object, push small bits of stuffing into the foot, all around the wire.

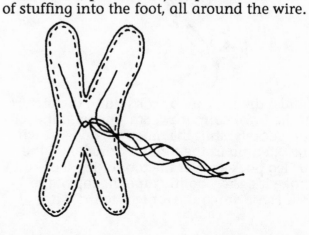

15. Wrap the bottom 4" of the twisted wire leg with fiberfill or batting. Tape in place. Wrap the black felt leg covering around the twisted wire leg, pulling the felt leg covering down over the foot to meet the top of the foot. Hand stitch the overlap along the leg. Hand stitch the bottom of the felt leg covering to the felt of the top of the foot where they meet.

16. Insert the remaining uncovered end of the wire legs into one leg opening in the body. From inside the body, poke the other leg (still just wires) out of the other leg opening, bending the middle of the wire as needed. Apply the foot and wrap the leg as above. Pull the fur down to cover the top of the felt.

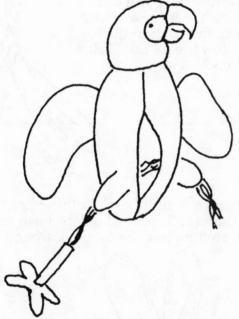

Adjust the leg wire by consulting the picture of the finished macaw. Starting with the leg top pockets, stuff the macaw. Ladder stitch the opening in the tummy closed. Pull the fur leg pockets over the tops of the felt. To make it easier, tightly tape the top of the felt. Hand stitch the fur legs to the felt.

17. With a seam ripper, make feather holes as marked across bottom of the body. Dip the tips of the long red feathers in glue and insert into holes. Consult the illustration below as a guide in placing the feathers according to their curves.

Install short red feathers above long red feathers. Adjust the feathers so they face in the desired direction before the glue dries.

Following the instructions marked on the wings, install the feathers in the wings.

18. Bend the legs and feet so that the bird will stand on the edge of a table, with the bird's tail hanging over the edge.

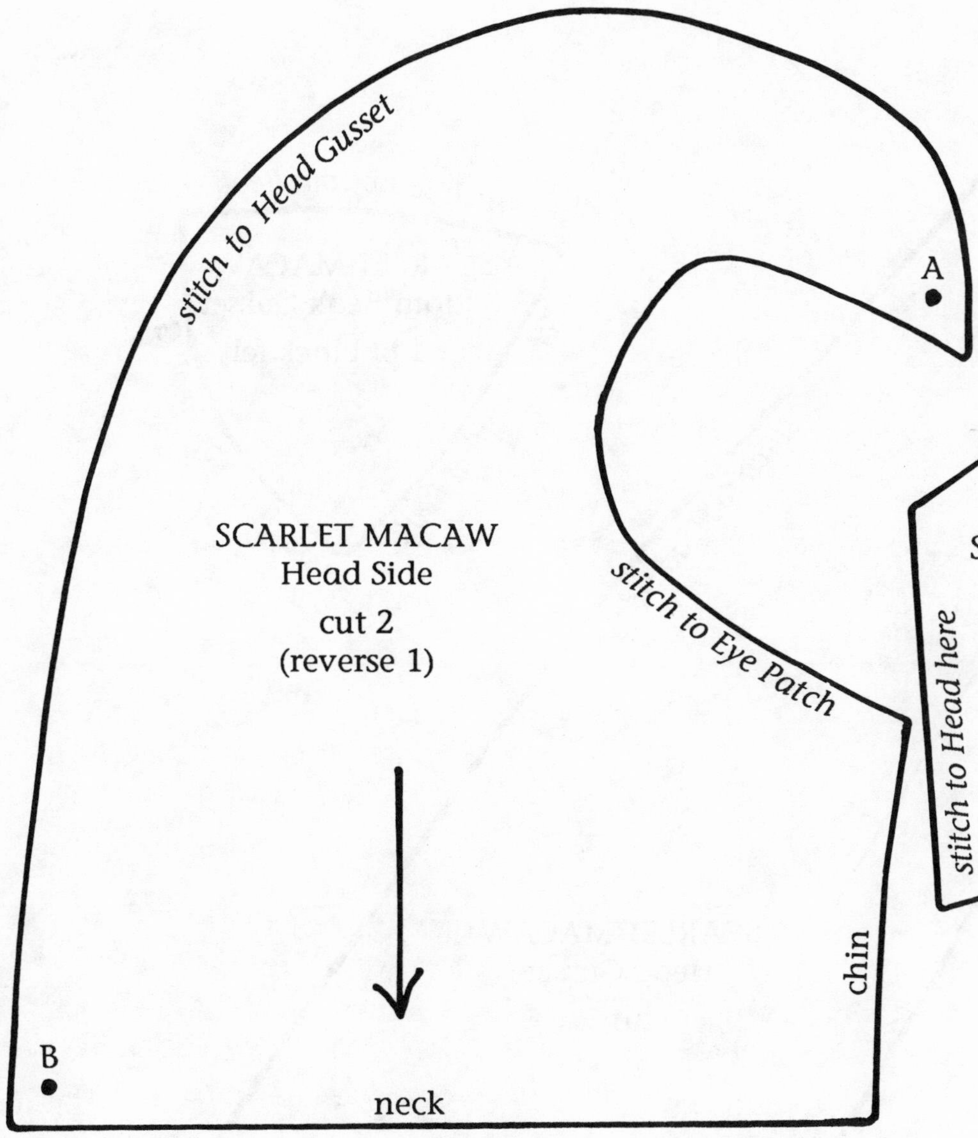

stitch to Head Gusset

A

SCARLET MACAW
Head Side
cut 2
(reverse 1)

stitch to Eye Patch

chin

B

neck

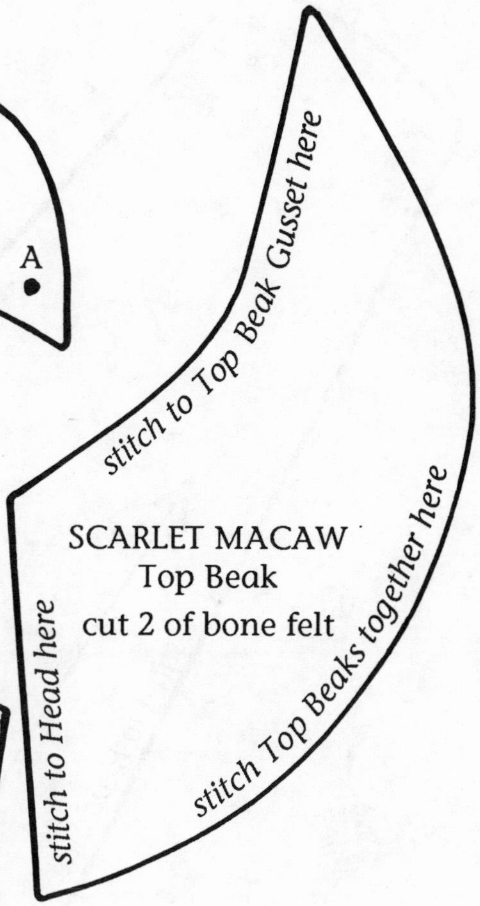

stitch to Top Beak Gusset here

stitch to Top Beaks together here

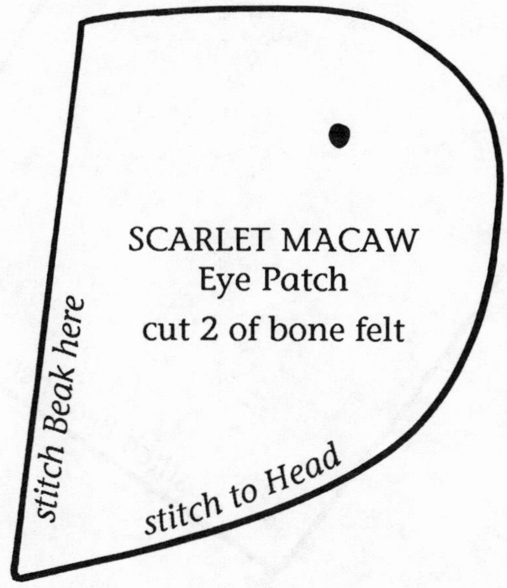

stitch to Head here

SCARLET MACAW
Top Beak
cut 2 of bone felt

SCARLET MACAW
Eye Patch
cut 2 of bone felt

stitch Beak here

stitch to Head

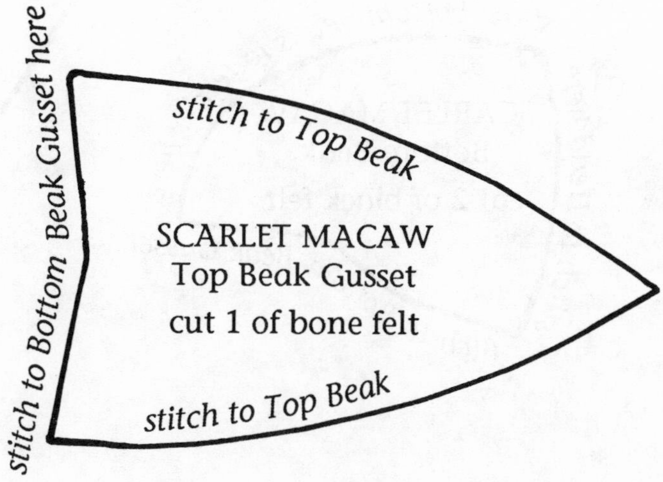

stitch to Bottom Beak Gusset here

stitch to Top Beak

SCARLET MACAW
Top Beak Gusset
cut 1 of bone felt

stitch to Top Beak

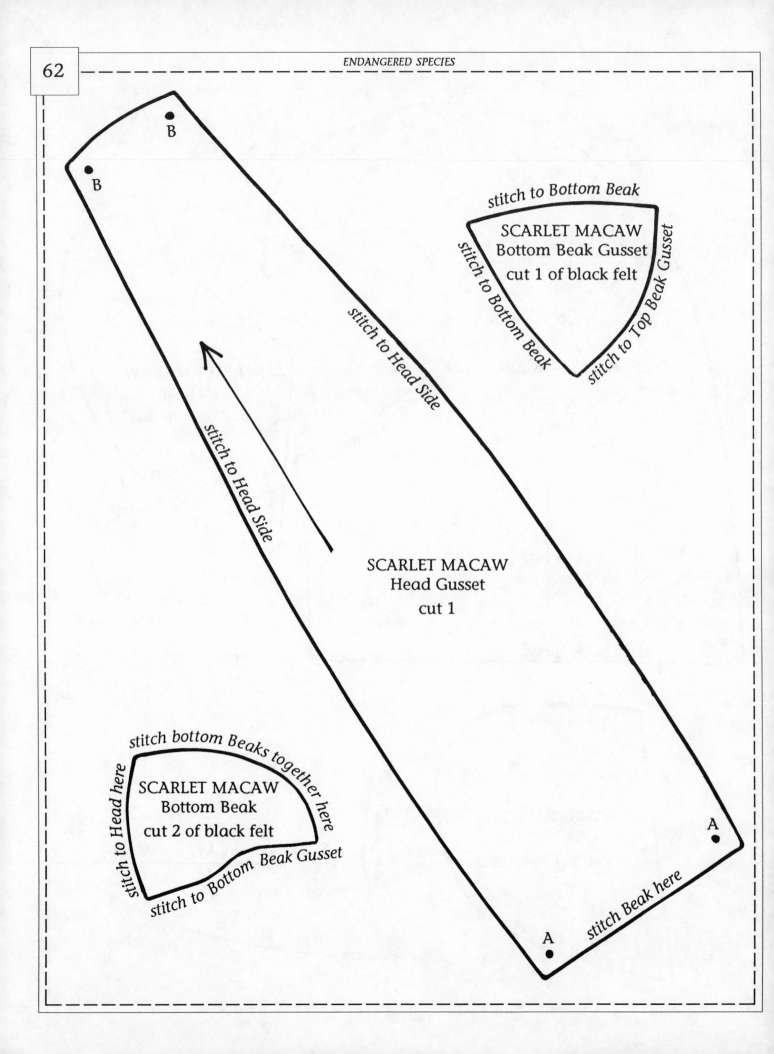

B

B

stitch to Head Side

stitch to Head Side

SCARLET MACAW
Head Gusset
cut 1

stitch to Bottom Beak

SCARLET MACAW
Bottom Beak Gusset
cut 1 of black felt

stitch to Bottom Beak

stitch to Top Beak Gusset

stitch bottom Beaks together here

stitch to Head here

SCARLET MACAW
Bottom Beak
cut 2 of black felt

stitch to Bottom Beak Gusset

A

A

stitch Beak here

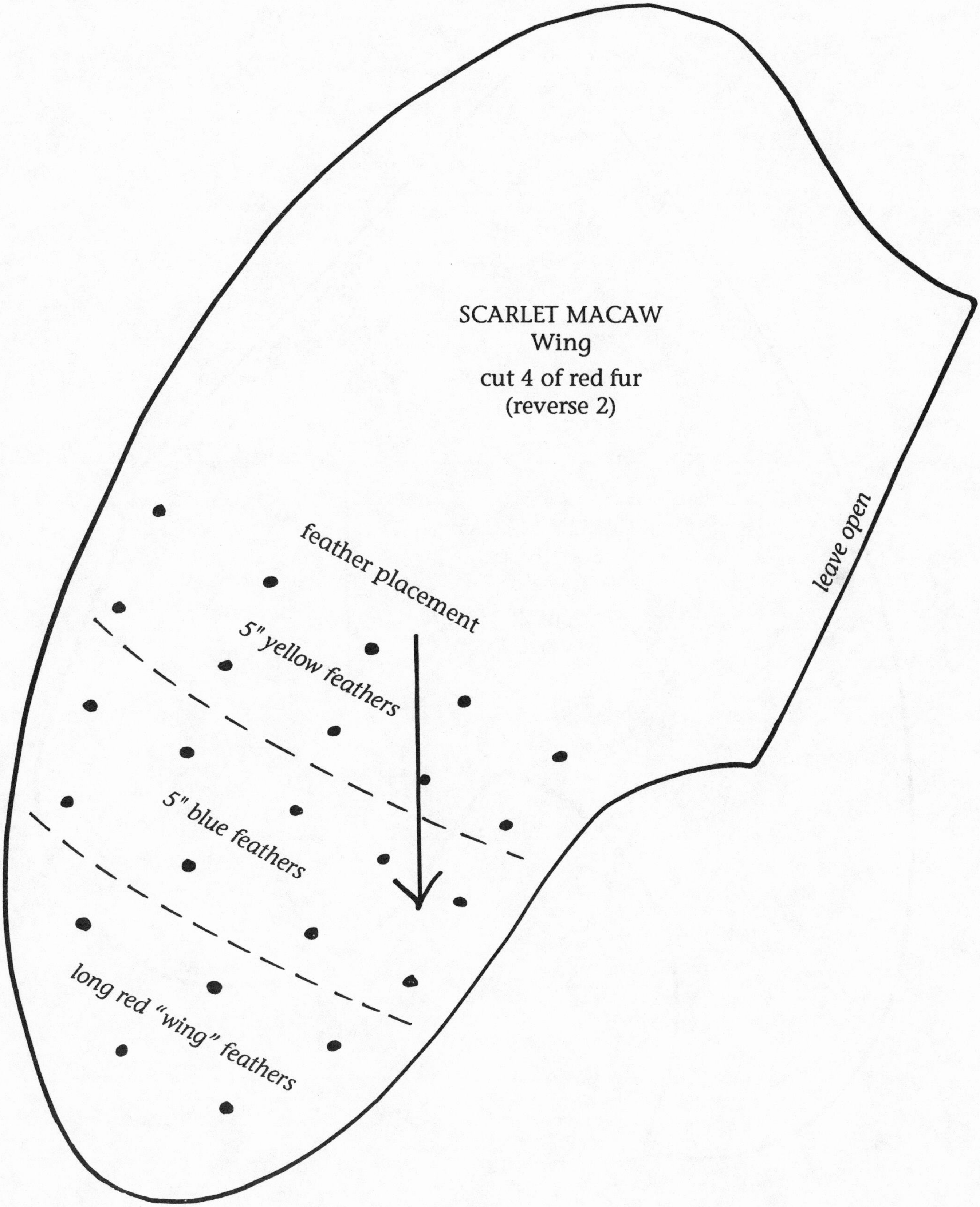

SCARLET MACAW
Wing

cut 4 of red fur
(reverse 2)

leave open

feather placement

5" yellow feathers

5" blue feathers

long red "wing" feathers

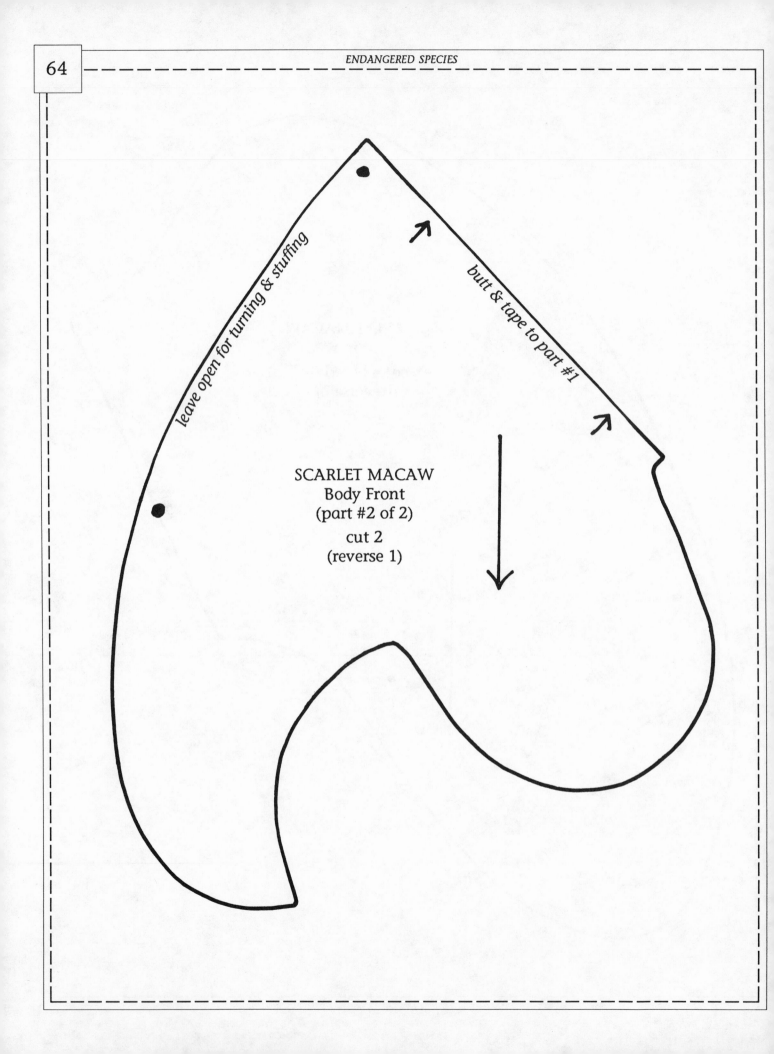

leave open for turning & stuffing

butt & tape to part #1

SCARLET MACAW
Body Front
(part #2 of 2)

cut 2
(reverse 1)

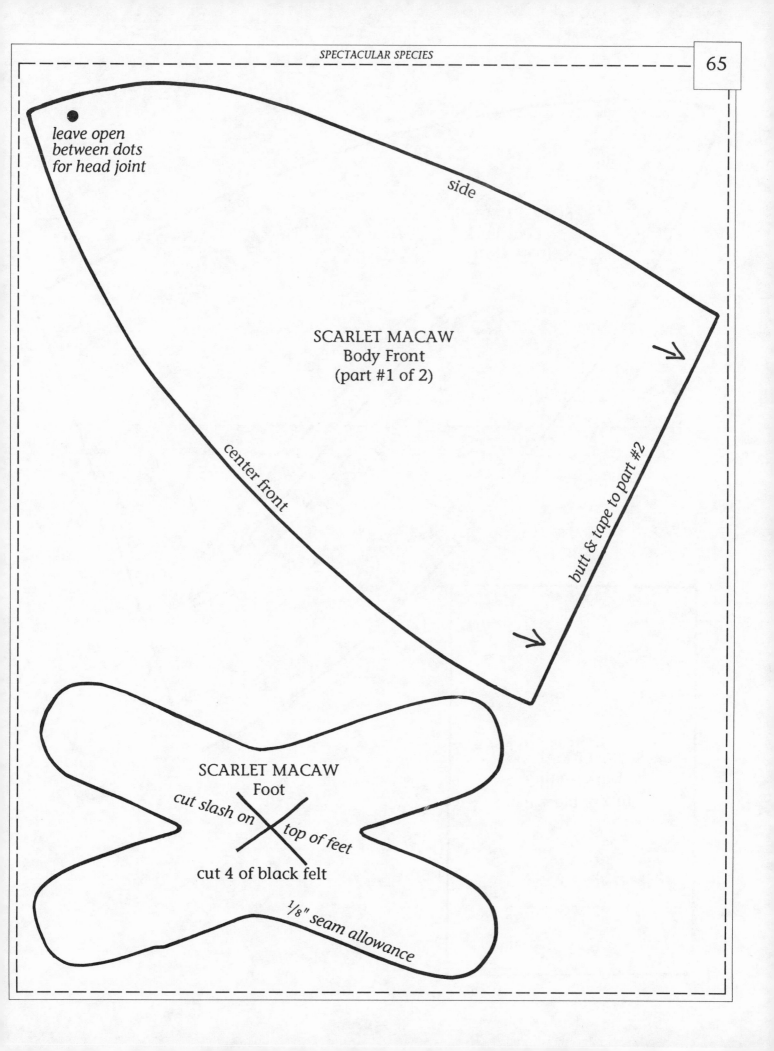

*leave open
between dots
for head joint*

side

SCARLET MACAW
Body Front
(part #1 of 2)

center front

butt & tape to part #2

SCARLET MACAW
Foot

cut slash on   top of feet

cut 4 of black felt

1/8" seam allowance

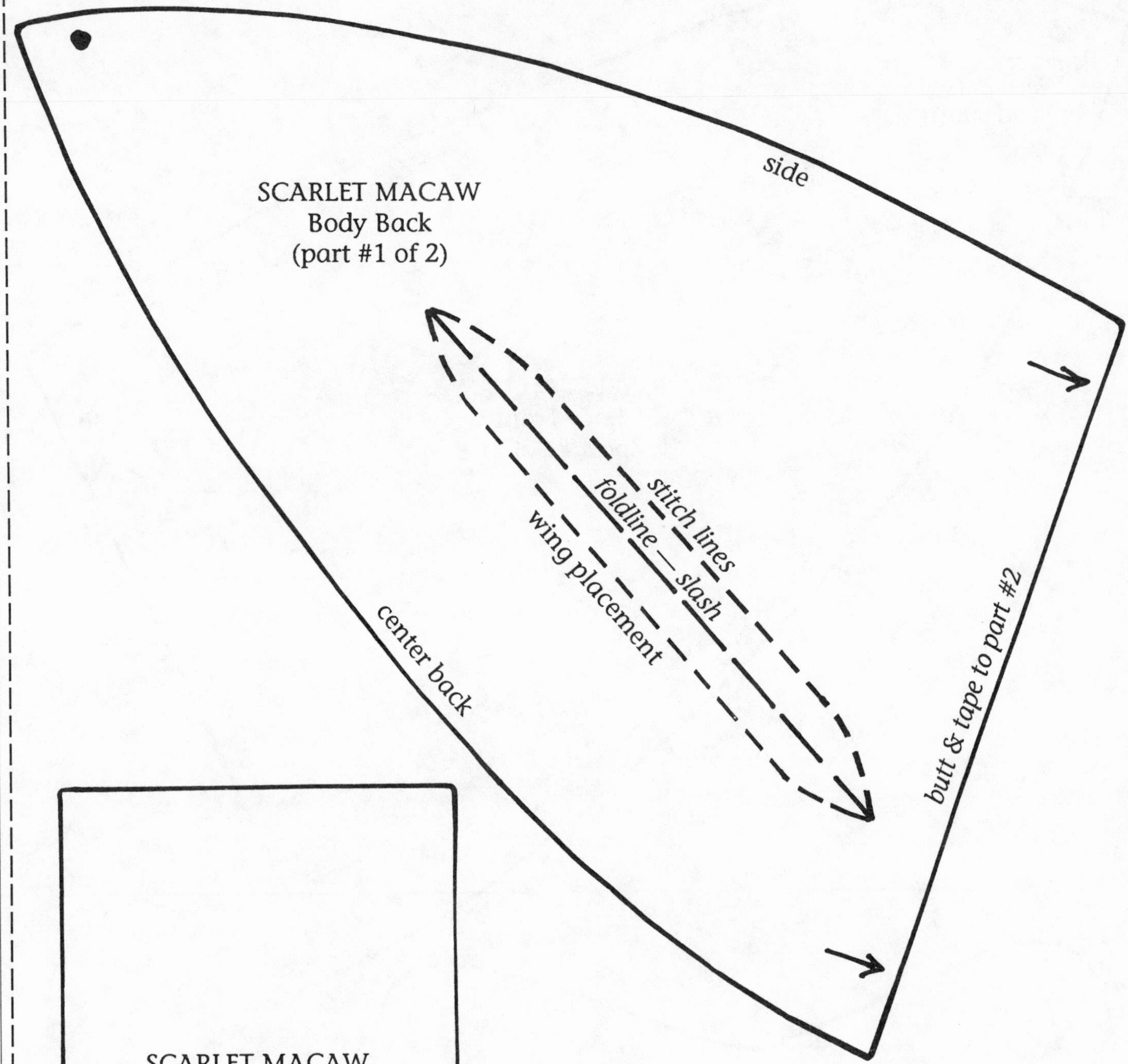

side

SCARLET MACAW
Body Back
(part #1 of 2)

stitch lines

foldline — slash

wing placement

center back

butt & tape to part #2

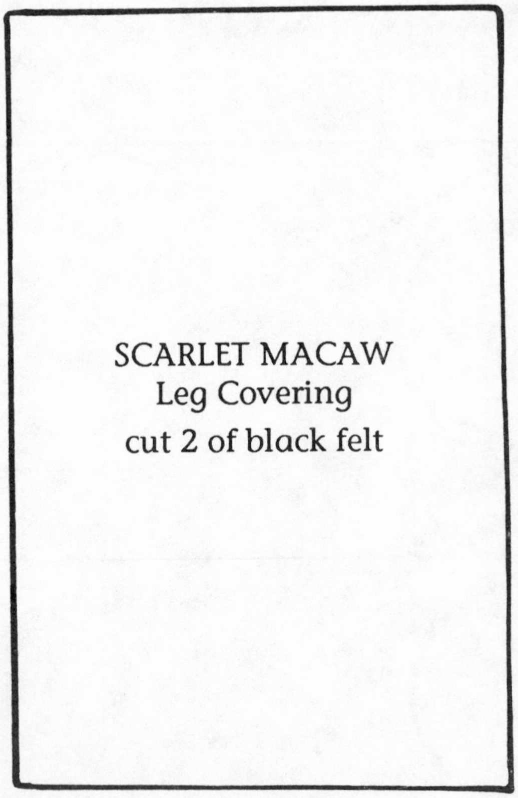

SCARLET MACAW
Leg Covering
cut 2 of black felt

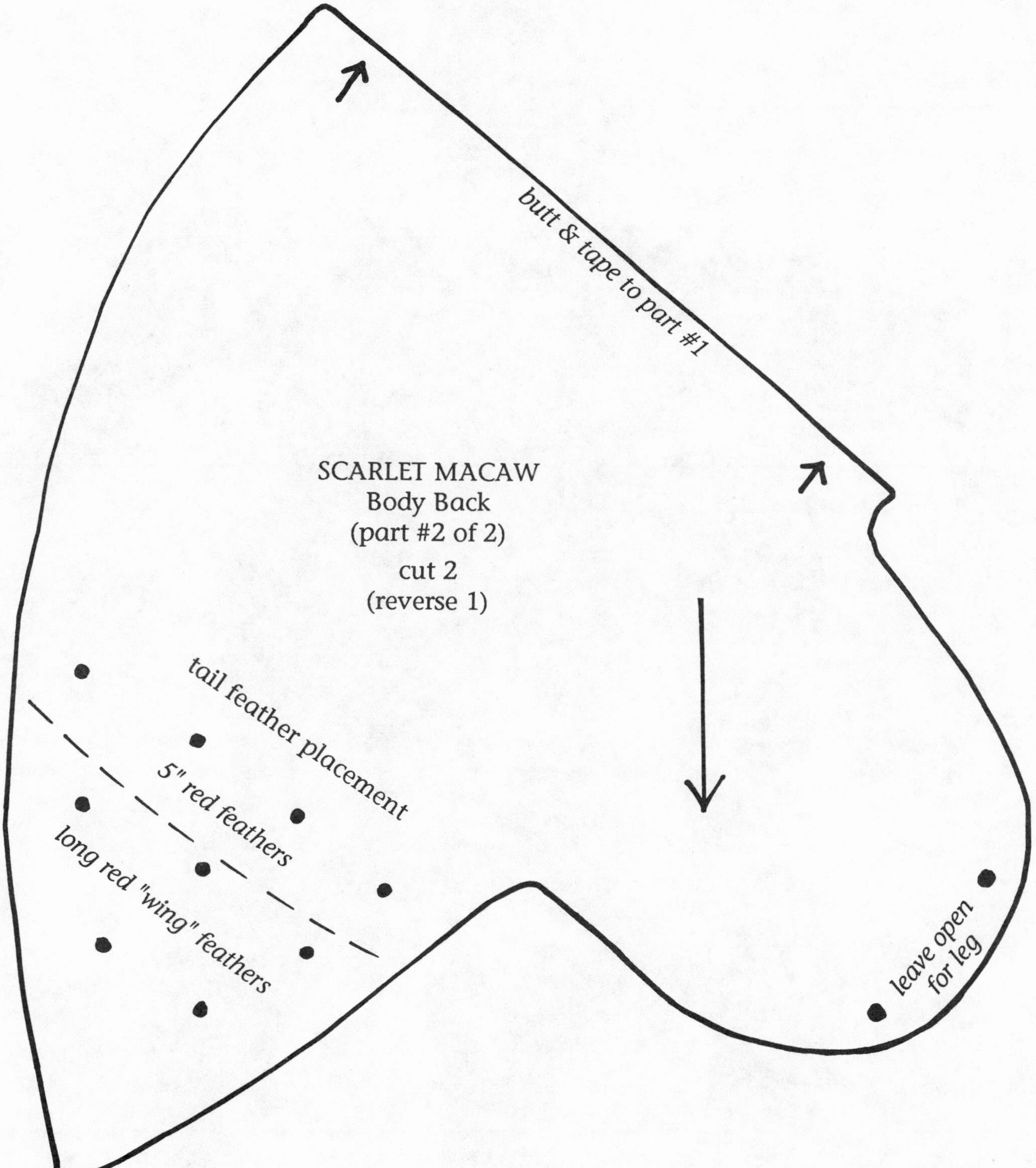

butt & tape to part #1

SCARLET MACAW
Body Back
(part #2 of 2)

cut 2
(reverse 1)

tail feather placement

5" red feathers

long red "wing" feathers

leave open for leg

LOGGERHEAD TURTLE

Often referred to as "underwater tanks," sea turtles survived the dinosaur age thanks to their ingenious protective shells. Though unchanged by evolution for more than 150 million years, this armor is no match for the turtle's greatest foe today: humans.

Here is a friendlier version of the fearsome loggerhead turtle. His shell is the old-fashioned quilt pattern called Grandmother's Flower Garden in six fabrics: two wools, two print corduroys, and two wide-wale corduroys — all in shades of green and brown. His underbody, flippers, head, and tail are handsome in green doe suede, although you can use wool. The turtle measures 24" in length.

INSTRUCTIONS

Note: All seam allowances are ¼" unless noted otherwise.

Prepare patterns, cut and mark the fabric according to the instructions in chapter 1. Transfer eye markings to wrong side of head sides and dart markings to wrong sides of flippers. For the underbody, cut one piece of doe suede, one of muslin, and one of batting, each 12" by 16". Cut the shell hexagon and shell edging patterns from heavy cardboard. Using the hexagonal shell pattern, cut 5 hexagons each from 5 of the shell fabrics and 4 hexagons each from the remaining fabric for a total of 29 hexagons. Make holes in the pattern where the six dots are and transfer the dots to the pattern pieces by poking a marking pen through the holes. Cut three shell edging rectangles from each of the shell fabrics for a total of 18 rectangles.

MATERIALS

½ yard each of six different fabrics for shell
⅝ yard green doe suede
Matching thread
Polyester batting
12" x 16" piece of muslin
Polyester fiberfill stuffing
Two 14 mm black safety eyes
One 55 mm plastic joint
Heavy quilting or carpet thread

1. Piece together the shell hexagons by following the illustration. Arrange the fabrics in a random order. Always stitch between the dots, never all the way to a raw edge.

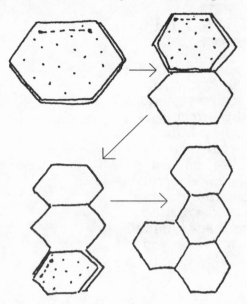

Continue piecing around the center until your shell looks like the one in the illustration.

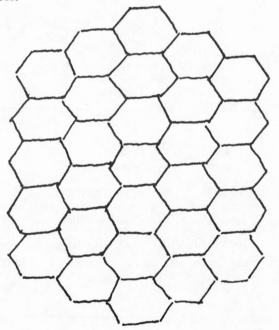

Press the pieced shell and place right side up on a flat surface. Lay the underbody pattern over the pieced shell. Center it. Pin. Trim the pieced shell to the size of the underbody pattern. Remove pattern.

2. Choosing different fabrics randomly, stitch shell edge pieces together along their longer, straight edges. When they are all pieced, press and then stitch the two end pieces together to form a ring.

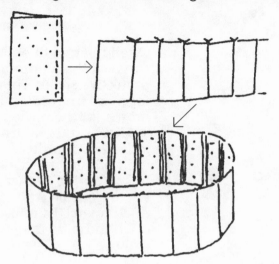

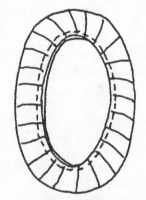

Wrong sides together, fold the ring to form a tube and match the raw edges. Pin the cylinder, lightly stuffing it as you pin. Baste.

Matching the basted, raw edges of the shell edge to the raw edge of the pieced shell, pin shell edge to right side of pieced shell as shown, easing the pieced shell to fit. Baste.

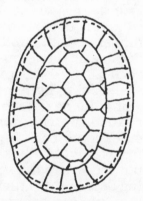

3. Center the underbody pattern over the muslin. Transfer the underbody quilting lines to the muslin. Also trace around the underbody pattern onto the muslin to mark the edge of the underbody. Remove pattern. Place the doe suede rectangle on your work surface, wrong side up. Place batting rectangle on top and marked muslin, marking side up, on top of batting. Pin layers together. Using a

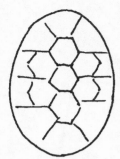

slightly long stitch and thread that matches the doe suede, machine stitch along the marked lines creating a quilting pattern, through all layers. Remove pins as you sew. Cut along the traced edge of the shell as marked through all layers. This is the turtle's bottom.

Turn the turtle bottom over, doe suede up. Lay the underbody pattern on top, matching raw edges. Mark head joint, flipper, and tail markings on right side of doe suede.

4. Right sides facing, pin quilted doe suede turtle bottom to the shell edge of the pieced shell, sandwiching the shell edge in between.

The bottom shell will be larger than the top shell, so ease the bottom shell as you pin. Stitch, leaving a 4" opening along one side for turning and stuffing.

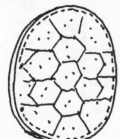

Turn right side out.

5. Pin and stitch two head sides from dot A down to mouth.

Match dot A on head gusset to dot A on head sides. Pin one head side to respective side of head gusset, right sides facing. Stitch from dot A to neck edge. Repeat for other side.

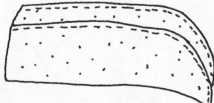

Stitch bottom seam in head bottom pieces.

Matching seams and raw edges, pin head bottom to head sides as shown. Stitch.

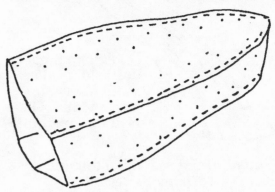

Install the safety eyes as instructed in chapter 1. Stuff head to about 1" from neck. Hand baste around opening with carpet thread. Insert stationary disk, post end out, into neck. Pull up on basting stitches. Baste around again, one or two times, until the opening is drawn tightly around the post. Knot the thread. Make a hole on the turtle shell bottom at marking and install the head as instructed in chapter 1.

6. Stuff the turtle's body, shaping him so the top of his shell is domed. Hand sew the opening in the turtle's side closed, as instructed in chapter 1.

7. Pin and stitch tail pieces, right sides facing, as shown.

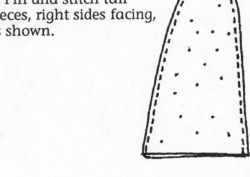

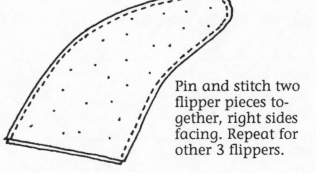

Pin and stitch two flipper pieces together, right sides facing. Repeat for other 3 flippers.

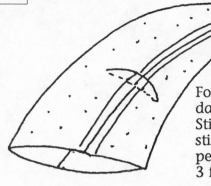

Fold along flipper dart foldline. Pin. Stitch along dart stitching lines. Repeat for remaining 3 flippers.

Trim seam allowances at tip of tail and flippers to ⅛". Turn right side out.

Turn raw ends of flippers and tail ¼" to inside. Pin. Whipstitch. Hand sew to seam along bottom shell and shell edge, between designated markings. Refer to the illustration and photographs to make sure the flippers point in the correct directions.

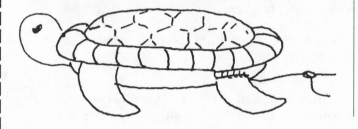

neck

stitch to Head Bottom

stitch to Head Gusset

LOGGERHEAD TURTLE
Head Side
cut 2
(reverse 2)

eye ●

A ●

LOGGERHEAD TURTLE
Shell Hexagon
(see cutting instructions on page 69)

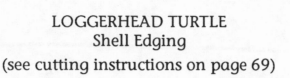

LOGGERHEAD TURTLE
Shell Edging
(see cutting instructions on page 69)

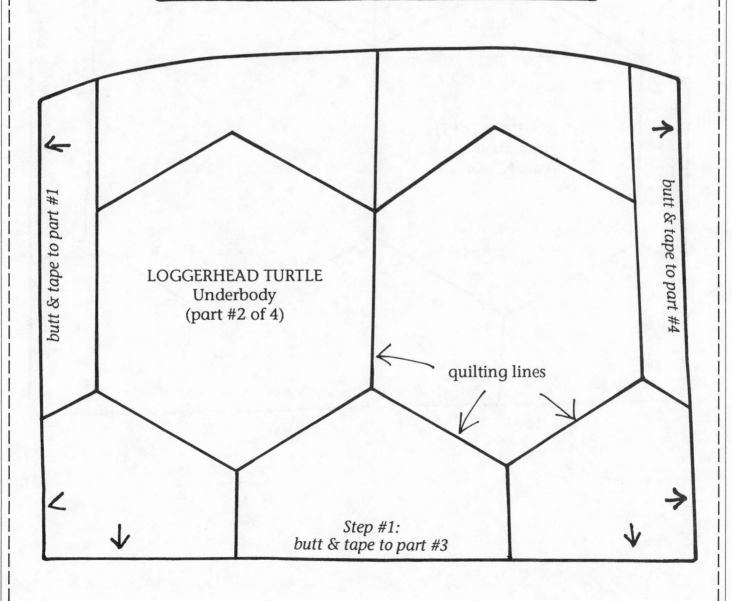

butt & tape to part #1

butt & tape to part #4

LOGGERHEAD TURTLE
Underbody
(part #2 of 4)

quilting lines

Step #1:
butt & tape to part #3

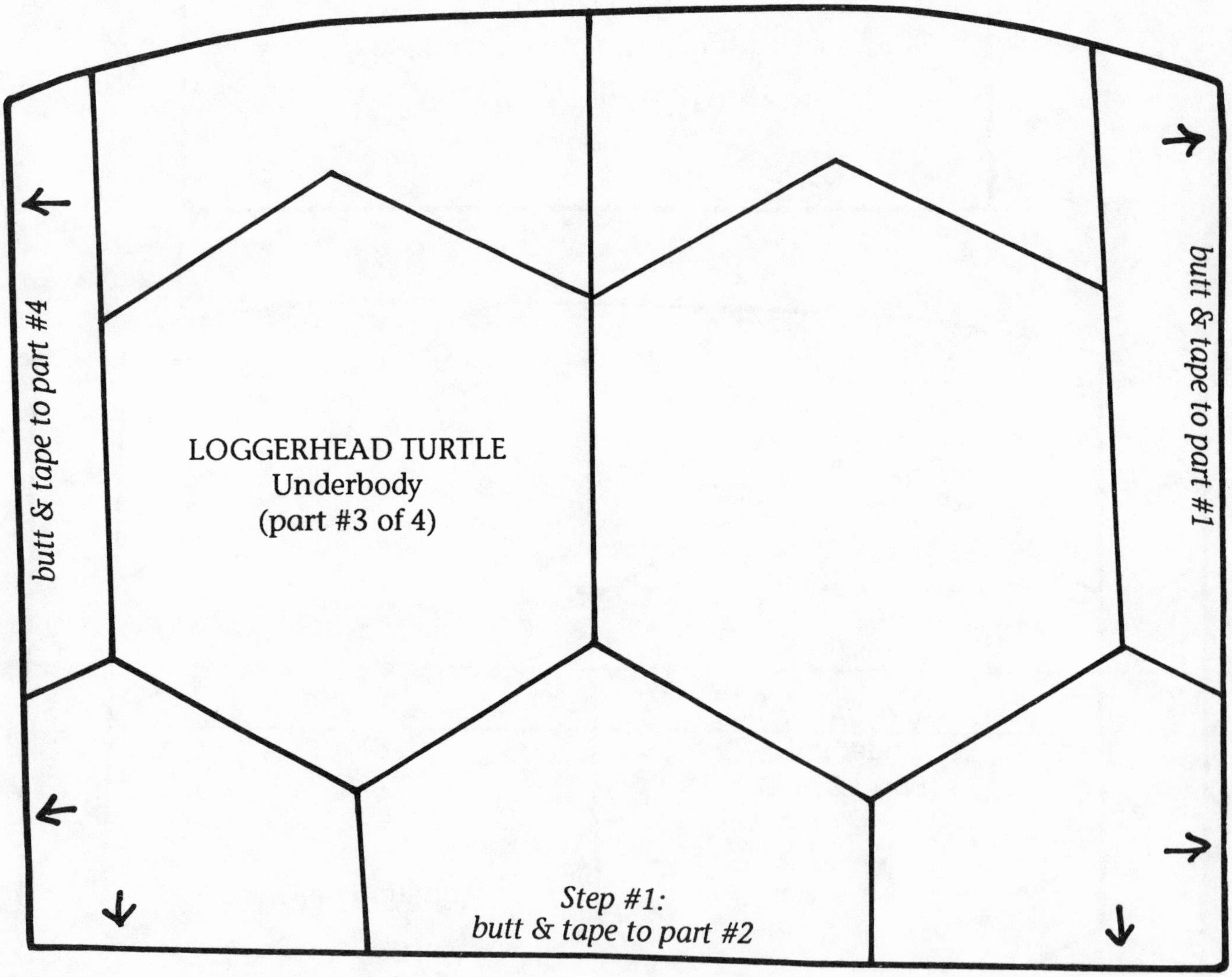

←

butt & tape to part #4

→

butt & tape to part #1

LOGGERHEAD TURTLE
Underbody
(part #3 of 4)

←

↓

→

↓

Step #1:
butt & tape to part #2

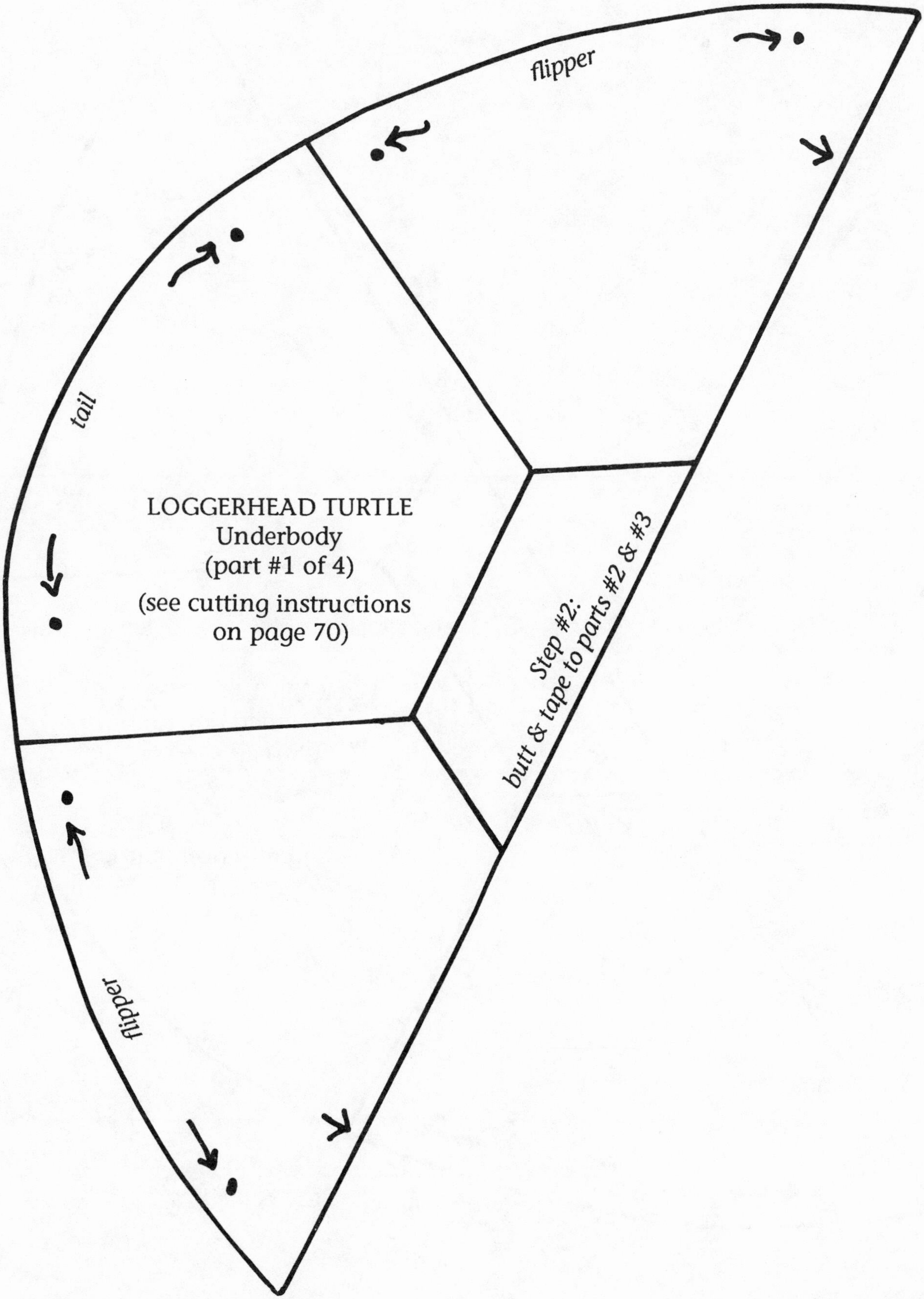

flipper

tail

LOGGERHEAD TURTLE
Underbody
(part #1 of 4)

(see cutting instructions
on page 70)

Step #2:
butt & tape to parts #2 & #3

flipper

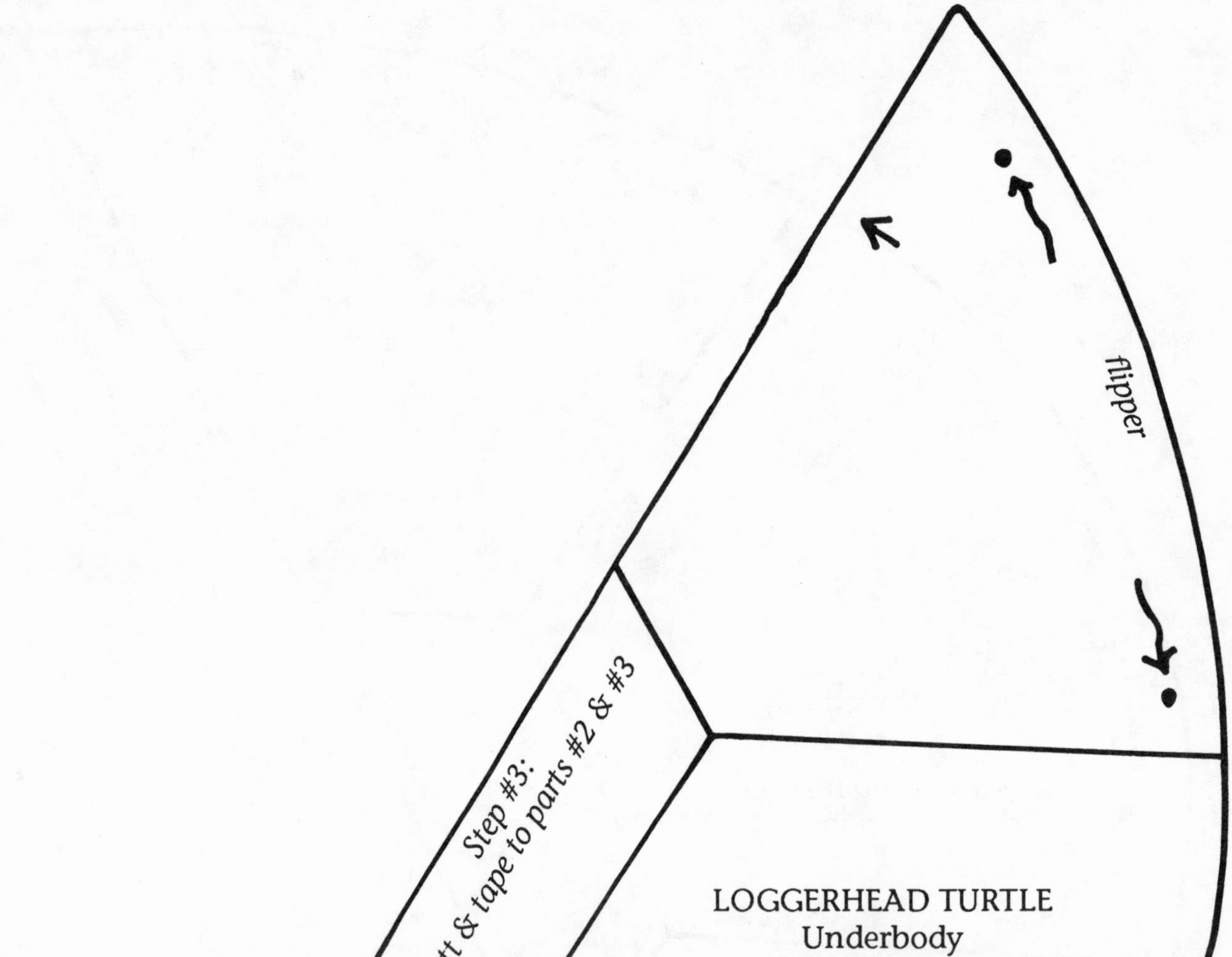

Step #3:
butt & tape to parts #2 & #3

flipper

LOGGERHEAD TURTLE
Underbody
(part #4 of 4)

head joint placement ●

flipper

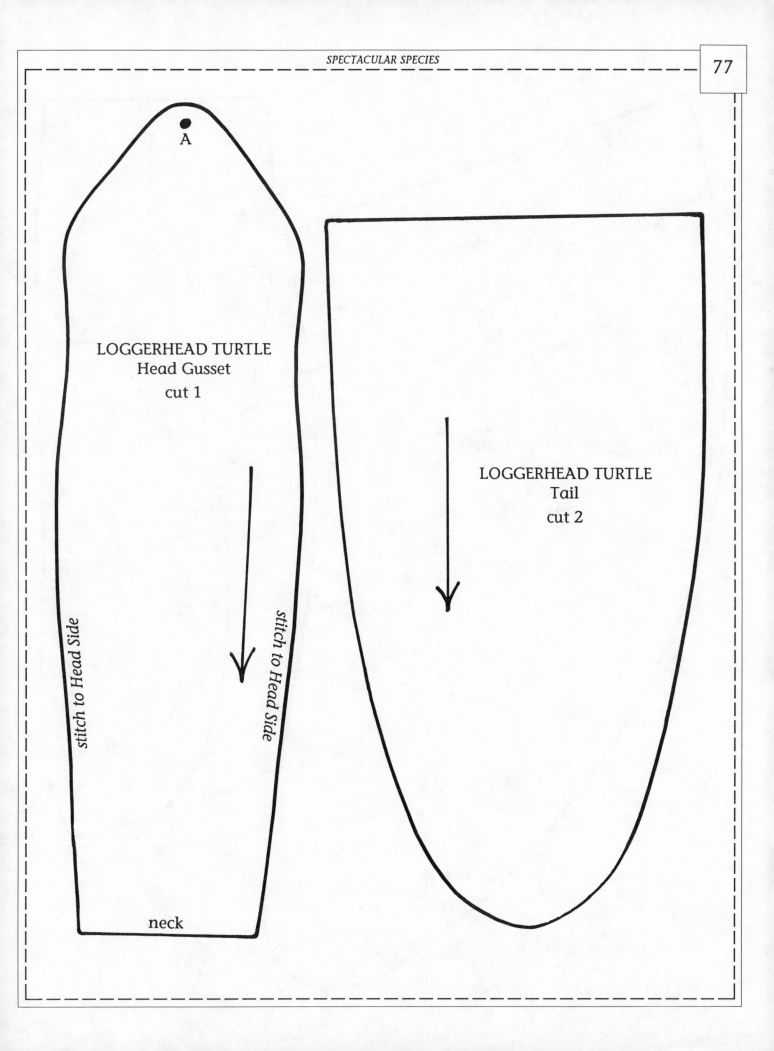

A

LOGGERHEAD TURTLE
Head Gusset
cut 1

LOGGERHEAD TURTLE
Tail
cut 2

stitch to Head Side

stitch to Head Side

neck

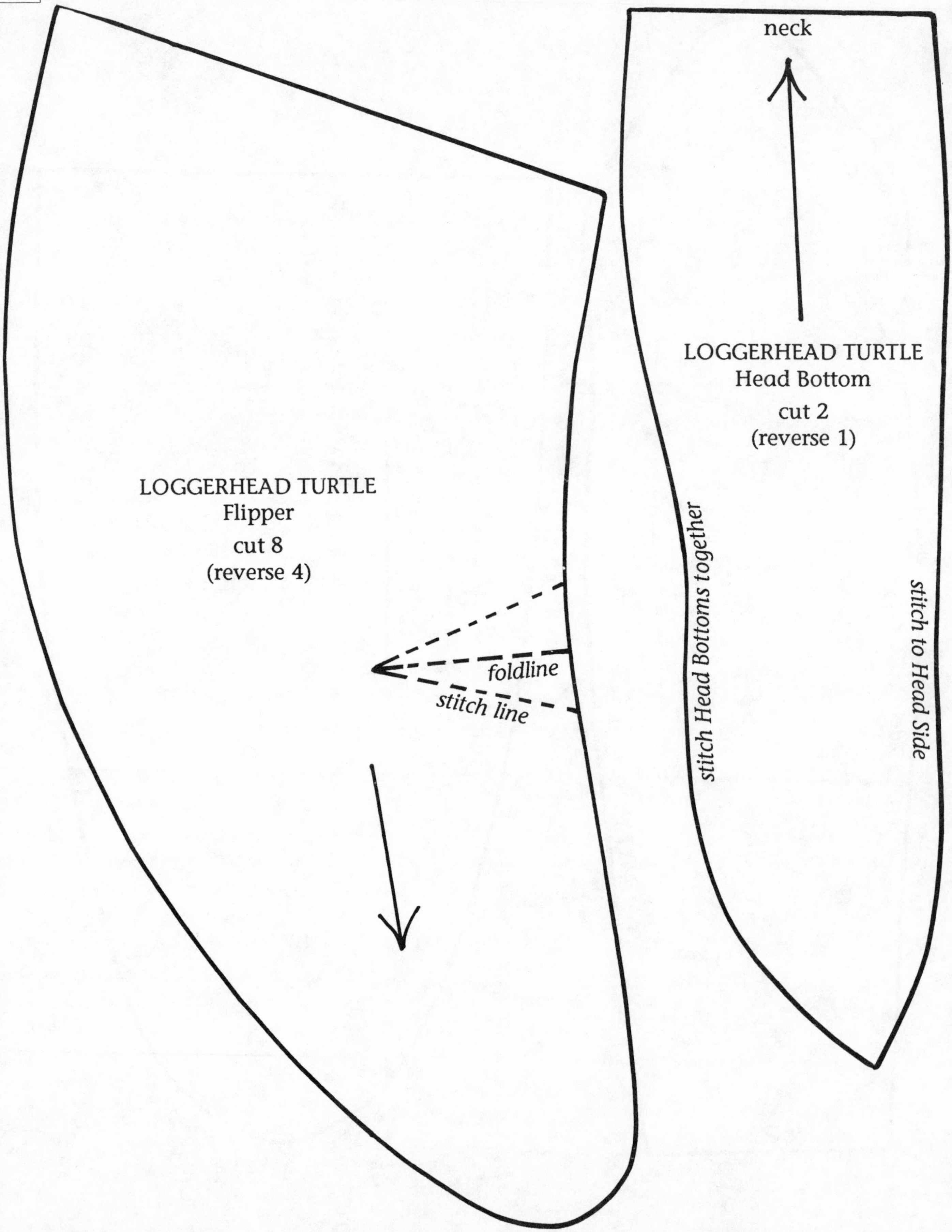

neck

LOGGERHEAD TURTLE
Head Bottom
cut 2
(reverse 1)

LOGGERHEAD TURTLE
Flipper
cut 8
(reverse 4)

foldline

stitch line

stitch Head Bottoms together

stitch to Head Side

♥ ♥ ♥

Big &
Beautiful
Animals

♥ ♥ ♥

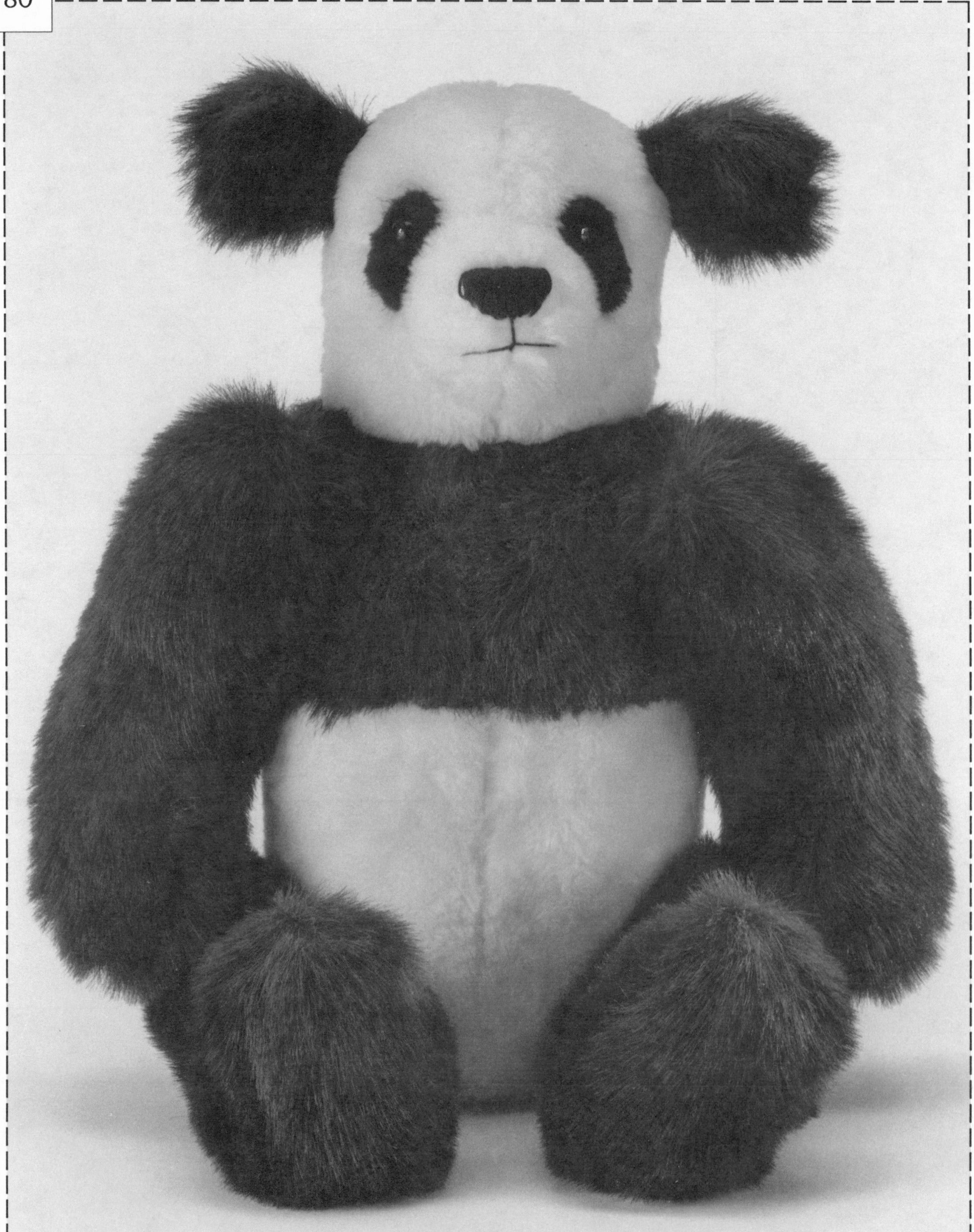

PANDA

Native to the mountains of central China, the giant panda is one of the world's rarest animals. In 1987, it was estimated that only 700 giant pandas existed. A newborn cub weighs a mere four ounces, but at maturity will be somewhat smaller than a black bear. Thanks to an extra digit on each front paw that functions much like a thumb, the giant panda can pick up and grip food much like apes and humans. Since they are herbivores, the giant pandas spend twelve hours a day eating bamboo shoots.

Your panda will be stuffed with fiberfill, not bamboo shoots. He has jointed arms and legs and stands 25" tall.

INSTRUCTIONS

Note: All seam allowances are ¼".

Prepare patterns, cut and mark fabric as instructed in chapter 1. On the wrong side of the body pieces mark "front" and "back" along edges as indicated on pattern, using a white pencil for the black fur and a dark pencil for the white fur.

1. Right sides facing, stitch two ear pieces together. Repeat for other ear. Trim seam allowances to ⅛". Turn right side out. Set aside.

2. Pin two head back pieces together along long, curved edges marked "center back." Stitch.

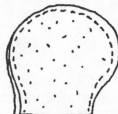

MATERIALS

½ yard white seal fur (available from by Diane and CR's Crafts, see Sources)

Matching thread

⅔ yard black seal fur (available from by Diane and CR's Crafts, see Sources)

Matching thread

Two 14 mm black safety eyes

One 30 mm animal nose

Carpet thread or waxed dental floss

Polyester fiberfill

Four 65 mm plastic joint sets and metal lockwashers

Black perle cotton or embroidery floss

3. Right side up, pin eye patches to right side of head fronts. Using a small zigzag stitch and black thread, applique all around the eye patches, just over the raw edges of the eye patches.

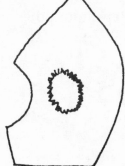

4. Pin two head front pieces together at forehead. Stitch.

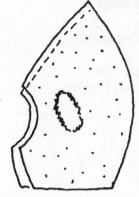

5. Pin ears to fur side of head fronts between dots, as shown. Make sure inside edges of ears point toward forehead. Baste.

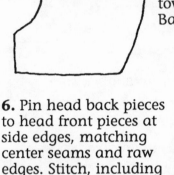

6. Pin head back pieces to head front pieces at side edges, matching center seams and raw edges. Stitch, including ears in the seam.

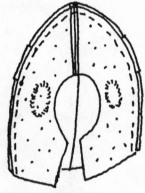

7. Fold one side of muzzle along foldline, matching two dots A. Stitch to center dot A.

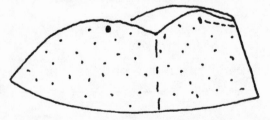

Repeat for other side of muzzle.

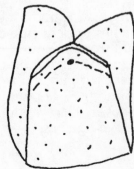

8. Right sides facing, pin muzzle to head fronts, matching center dot B on muzzle to center seam of head fronts at forehead and matching dots C. Ease muzzle between these points to fit head. Stitch.

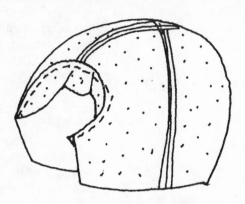

9. Pin chin/neck seam from dot A at nose on muzzle down to bottom edge of neck on head fronts, matching seams. Stitch.

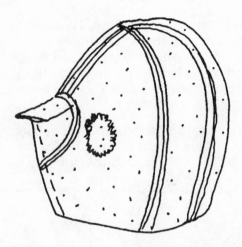

10. Install eyes and nose as instructed in chapter 1.

11. Pin black top body back pieces to black top body front pieces at sides with right sides facing. Stitch.

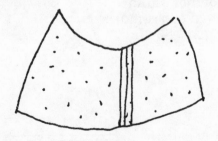

12. Right sides together, pin white bottom body back pieces to white bottom body front pieces at sides.

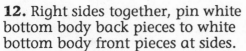
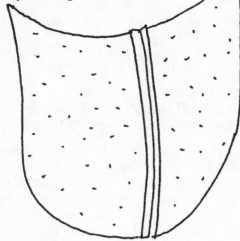

13. Pin one set of black top bodies to one set of white bottom bodies as shown. Make sure the edges marked "front" match, likewise those marked "back." Stitch. Repeat for the remaining sets.

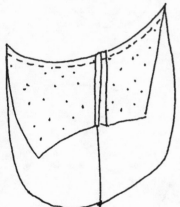

14. Pin the two body pieces together as shown. Stitch, leaving the neck edges open and leaving a gap between the dots on the back as marked for turning.

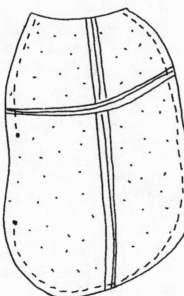

15. With head right side out and body inside out, pin head to body, matching chin seam to top center front body seam and head back seam to center body back seam. Stitch.

16. Make holes at markings on body for joints. Turn panda head/body right side out.

17. Pin two arm pieces together, right sides facing. Stitch, leaving an opening between the dots at the top of the arm. Repeat for second arm. Turn both arms right side out.

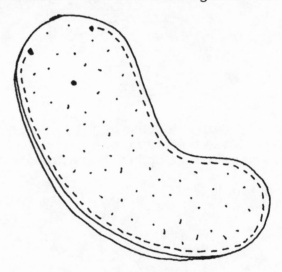

18. Pin two leg pieces together. Stitch, leaving an opening between the dots at the top of the leg. Leave the bottom of the foot open, too.

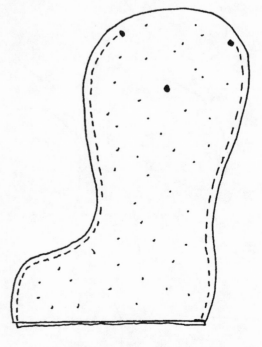

19. Pin foot pad to bottom of foot, matching large dot on pad to seam at front of leg and small dot on pad to back seam. Stitch.

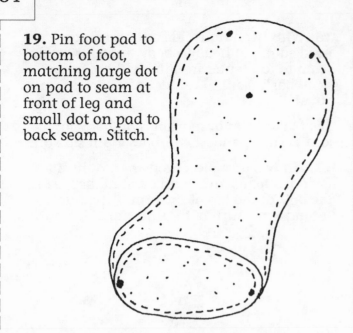

20. Set two arms together, side by side, as shown. Make holes at markings on side of arms that face each other. This will make a right and left arm. Do the same for the legs.

Insert the stationary disks into the arms and legs and install them on the panda as instructed in chapter 1.

21. Stuff arms and legs, following the instructions in chapter 1. When the limbs are fully stuffed, ladder stitch the openings closed as instructed in chapter 1.

Starting with small pieces of stuffing in the nose, stuff the panda's head and then body. Ladder stitch the opening in the back closed.

22. To embroider the mouth: Thread an embroidery needle with the perle cotton or embroidery floss. Make a knot in the end. Push the needle into the fabric a needle's length below the nose. Come up at the center bottom of the nose. The knot will be hidden by the fur.

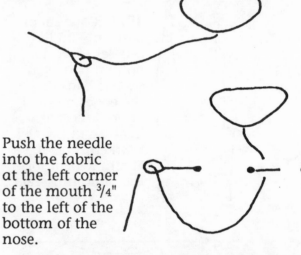

Push the needle into the fabric at the left corner of the mouth 3/4" to the left of the bottom of the nose.

Come out 3/4" below the nose on the seam, looping the thread behind the needle.

It will look like this:

Go back into the fur 3/4" to the right and 3/4" below the nose to form the right side of the mouth.

Come out somewhere in the neck, make a knot, and hide it in the fur.

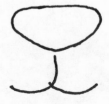

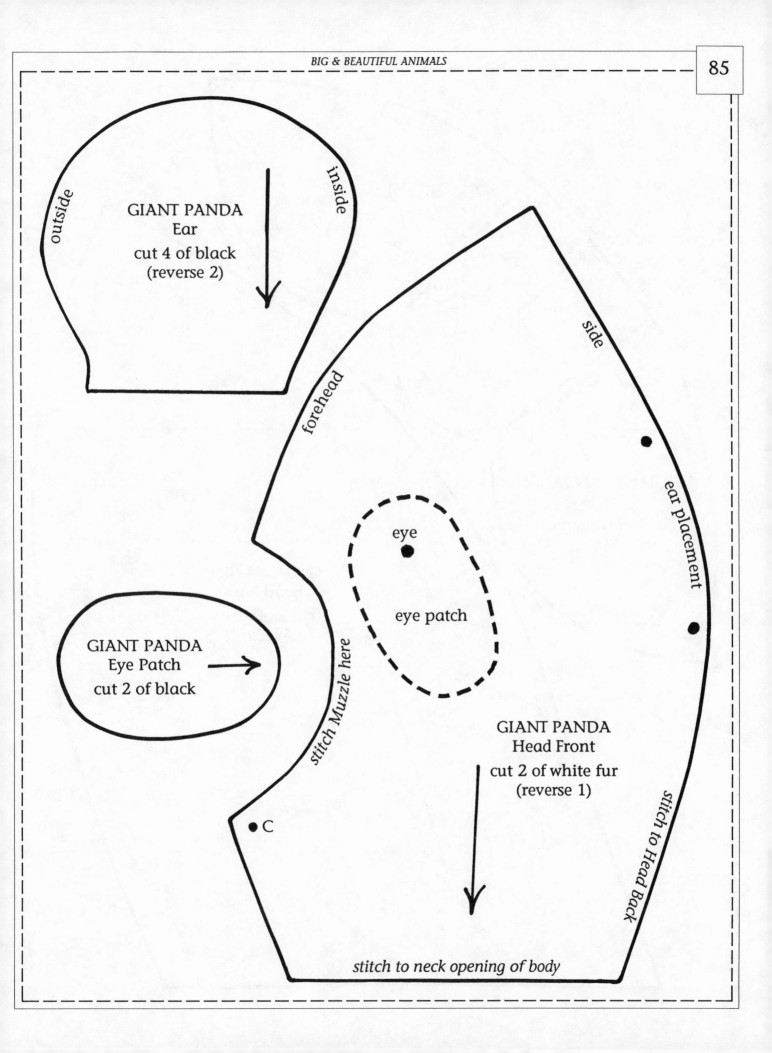

GIANT PANDA
Ear
cut 4 of black
(reverse 2)

outside

inside

forehead

side

ear placement

stitch to Head Back

GIANT PANDA
Eye Patch
cut 2 of black

stitch Muzzle here

eye

eye patch

• C

GIANT PANDA
Head Front
cut 2 of white fur
(reverse 1)

stitch to neck opening of body

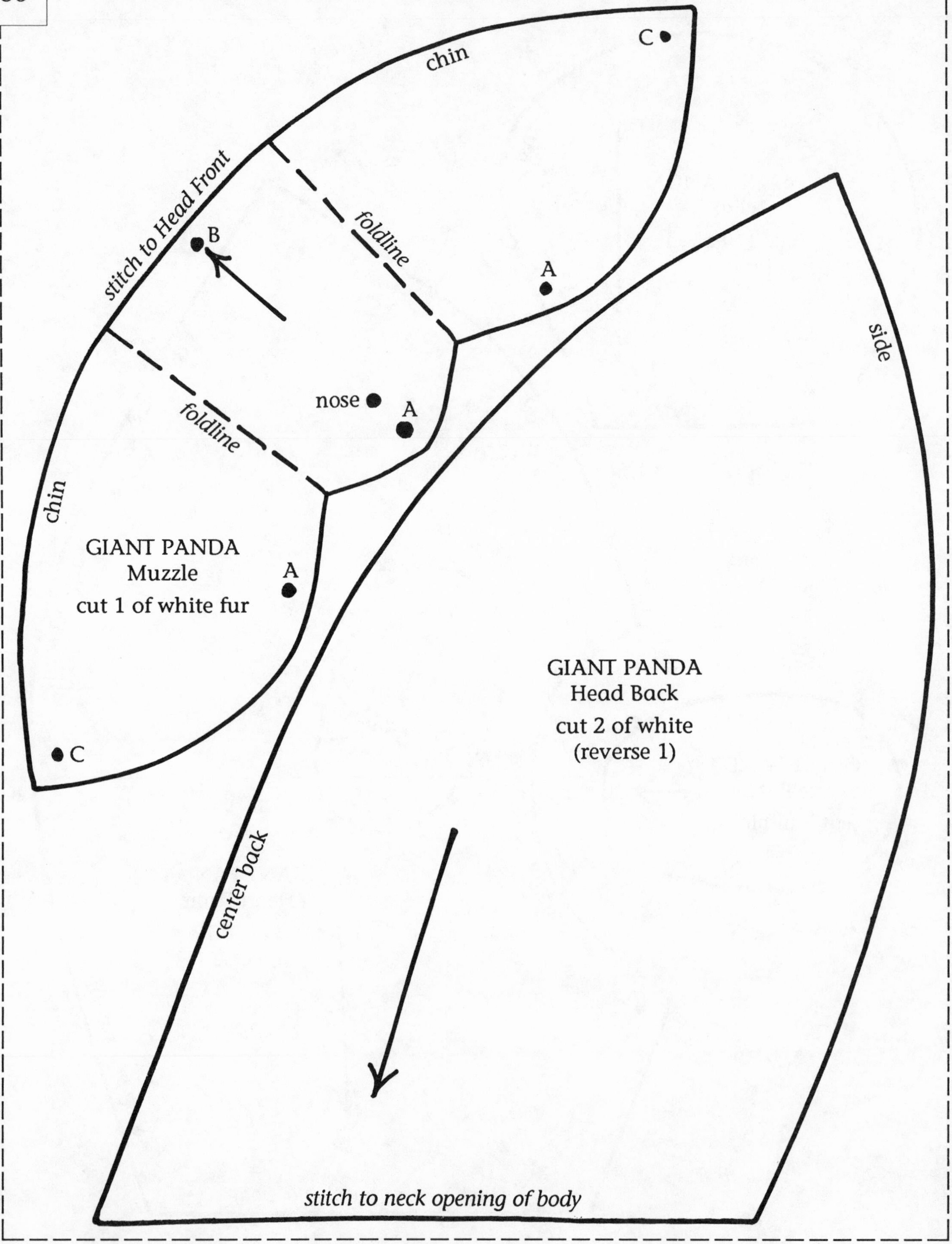

chin

C

stitch to Head Front

B

foldline

A

chin

nose ● A

A

foldline

side

GIANT PANDA
Muzzle
cut 1 of white fur

A

C

GIANT PANDA
Head Back
cut 2 of white
(reverse 1)

center back

stitch to neck opening of body

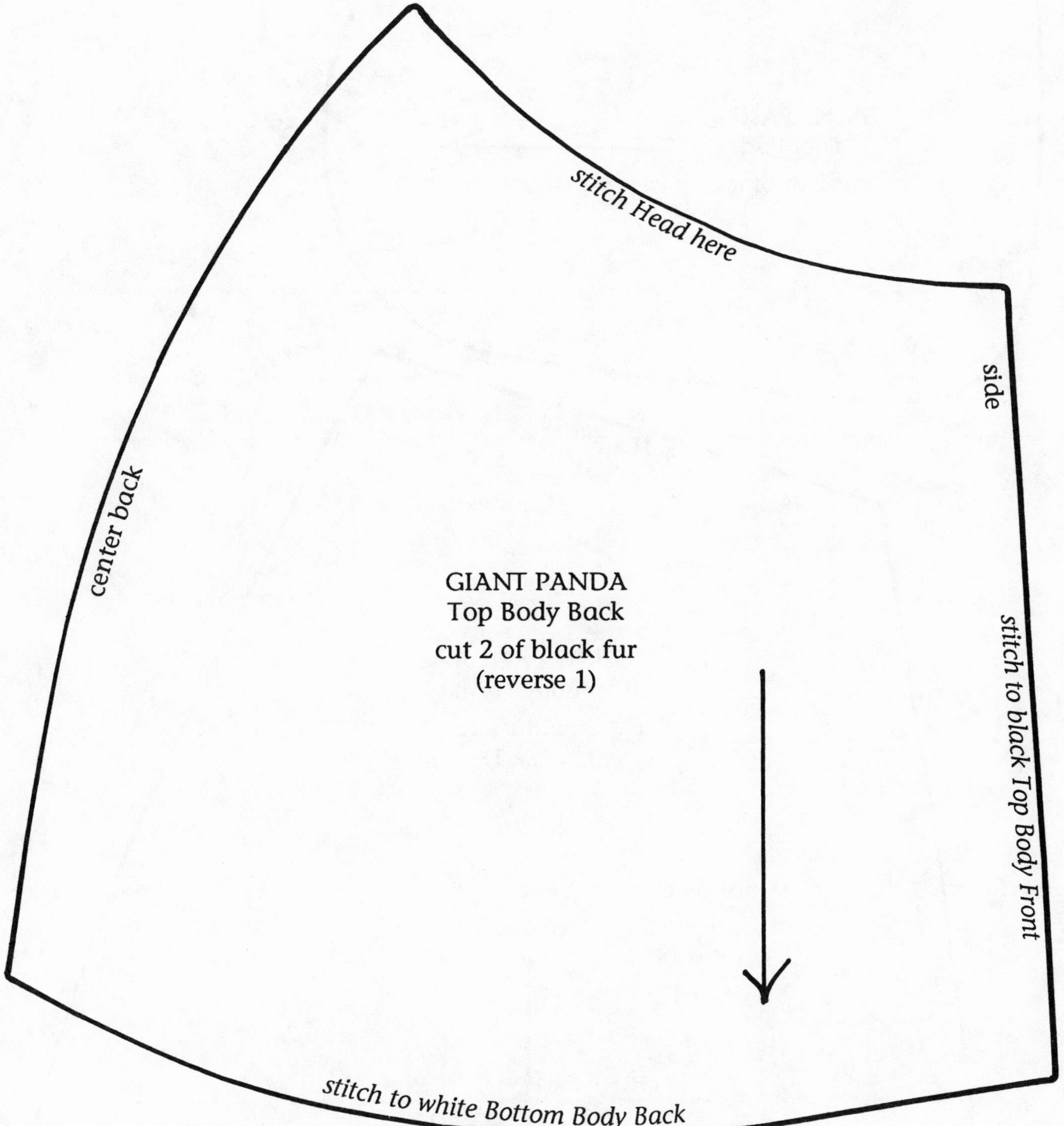

stitch Head here

side

center back

GIANT PANDA
Top Body Back
cut 2 of black fur
(reverse 1)

stitch to black Top Body Front

stitch to white Bottom Body Back

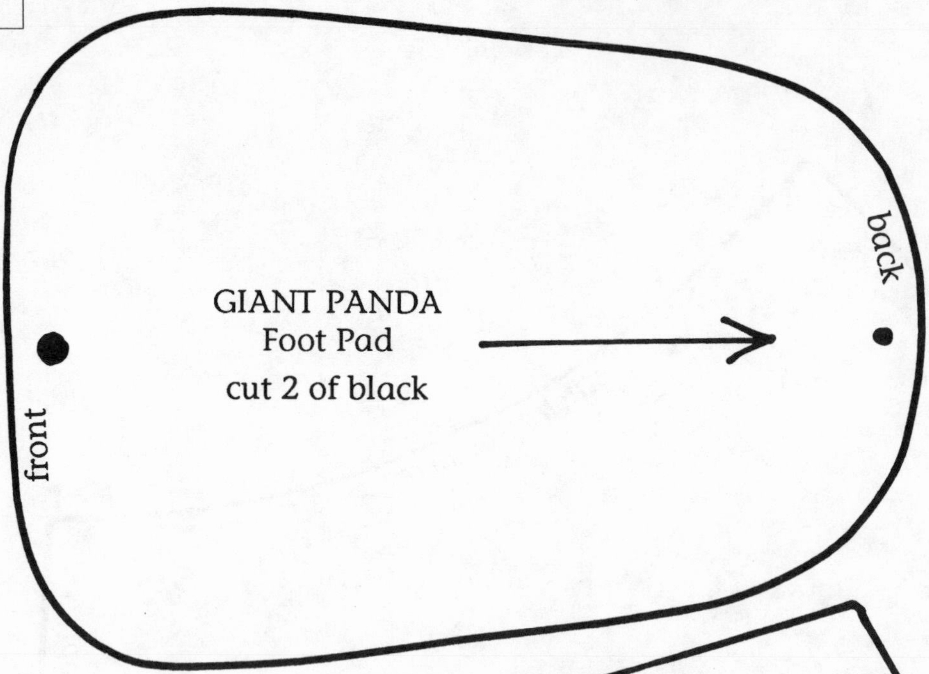

GIANT PANDA
Foot Pad
cut 2 of black

front

back

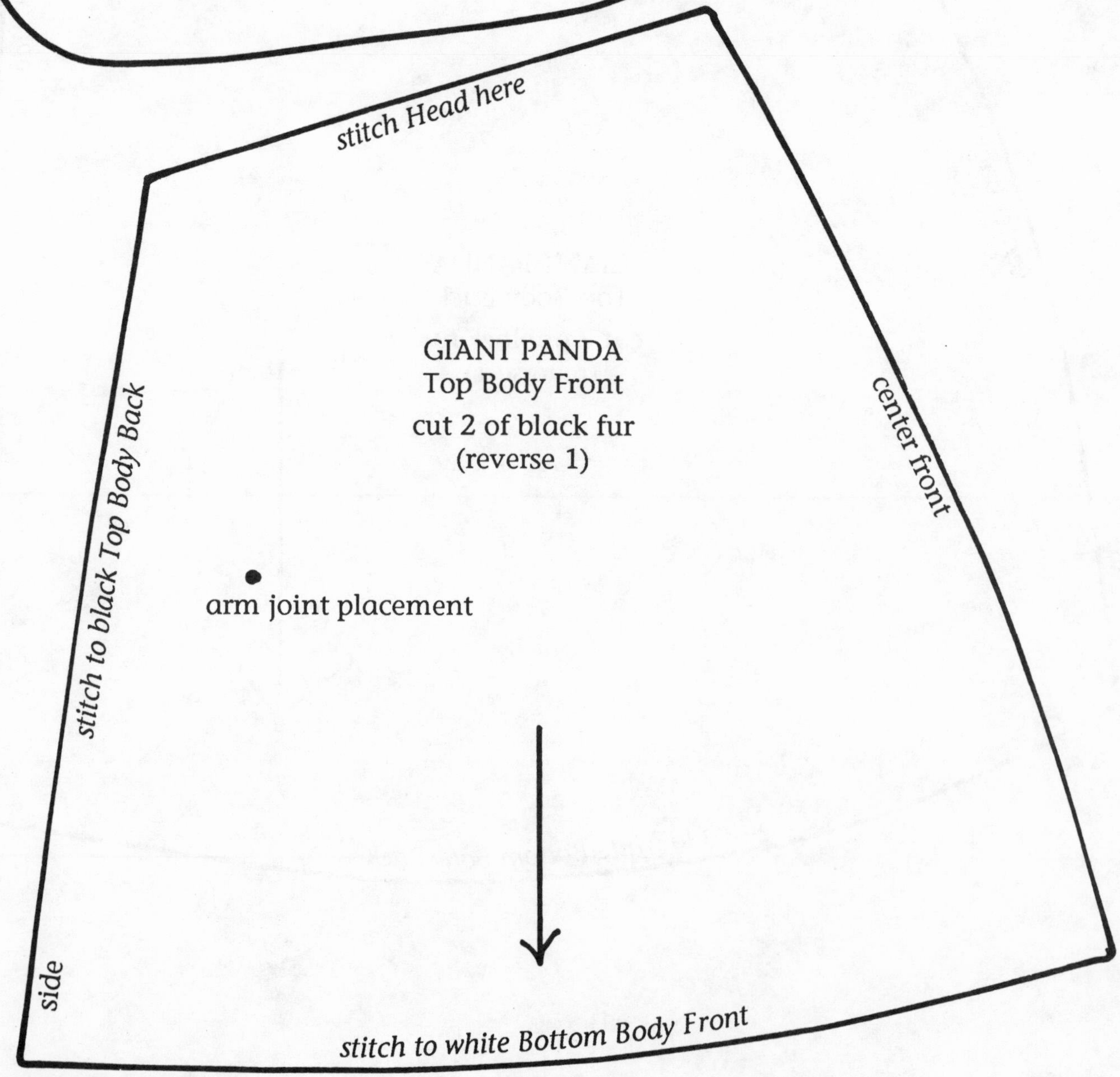

stitch Head here

GIANT PANDA
Top Body Front
cut 2 of black fur
(reverse 1)

stitch to black Top Body Back

arm joint placement

center front

side

stitch to white Bottom Body Front

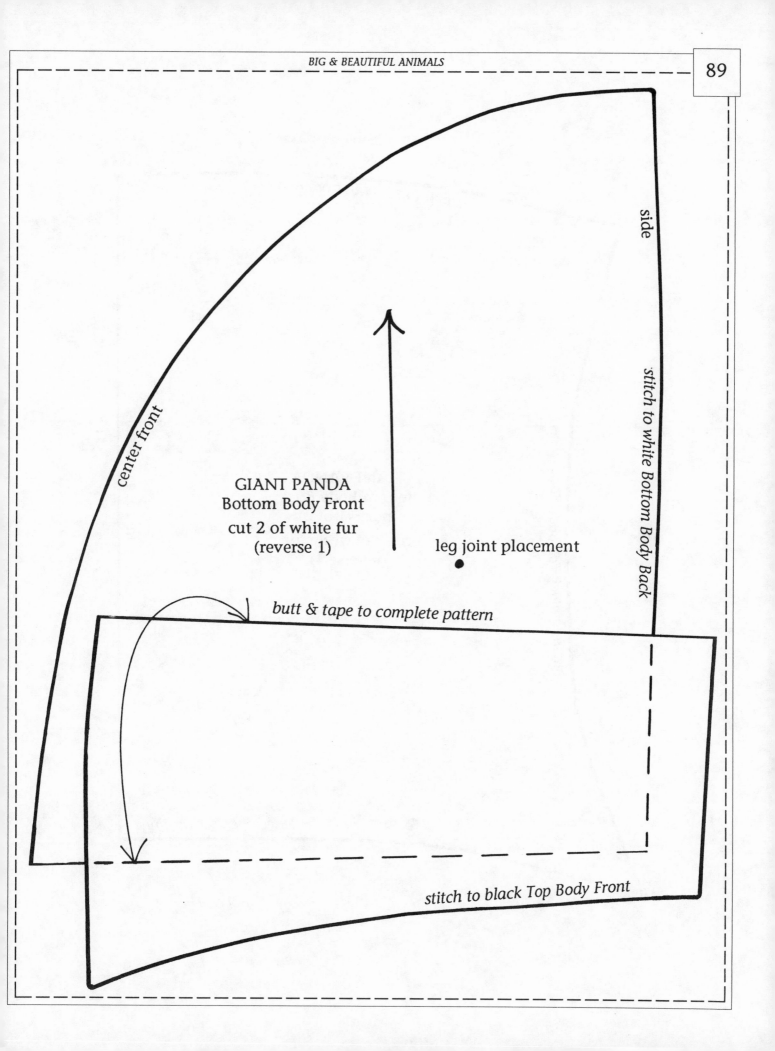

side

stitch to white Bottom Body Back

center front

GIANT PANDA
Bottom Body Front
cut 2 of white fur
(reverse 1)

leg joint placement

butt & tape to complete pattern

stitch to black Top Body Front

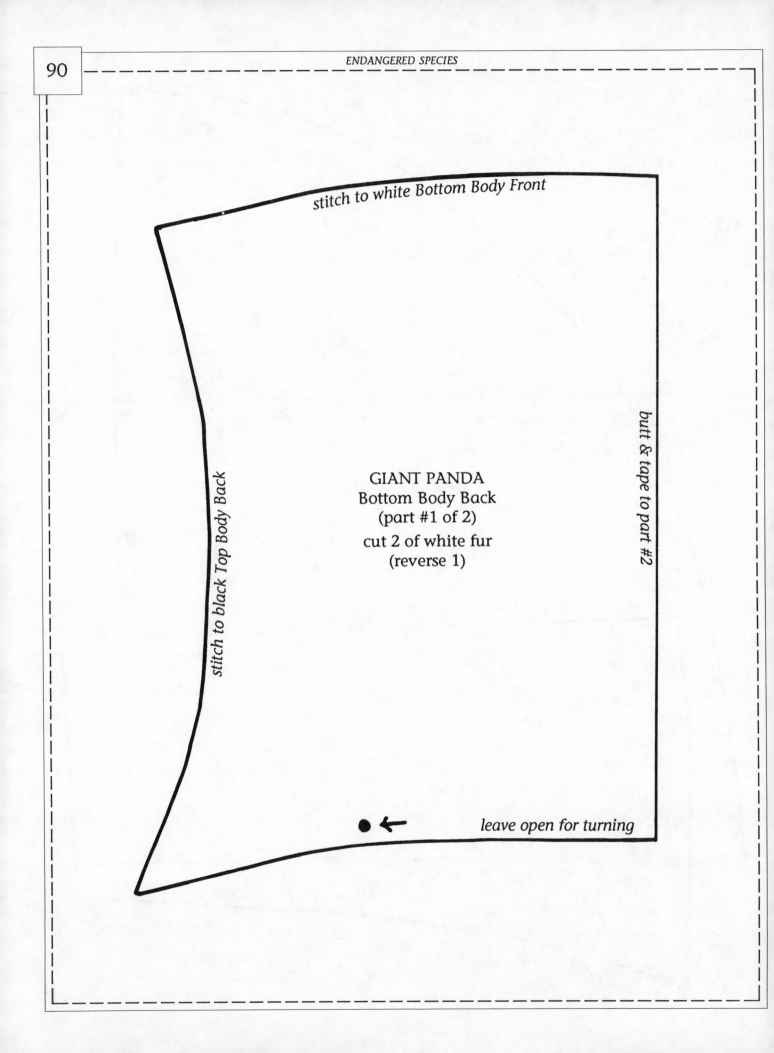

stitch to white Bottom Body Front

butt & tape to part #2

stitch to black Top Body Back

GIANT PANDA
Bottom Body Back
(part #1 of 2)

cut 2 of white fur
(reverse 1)

leave open for turning

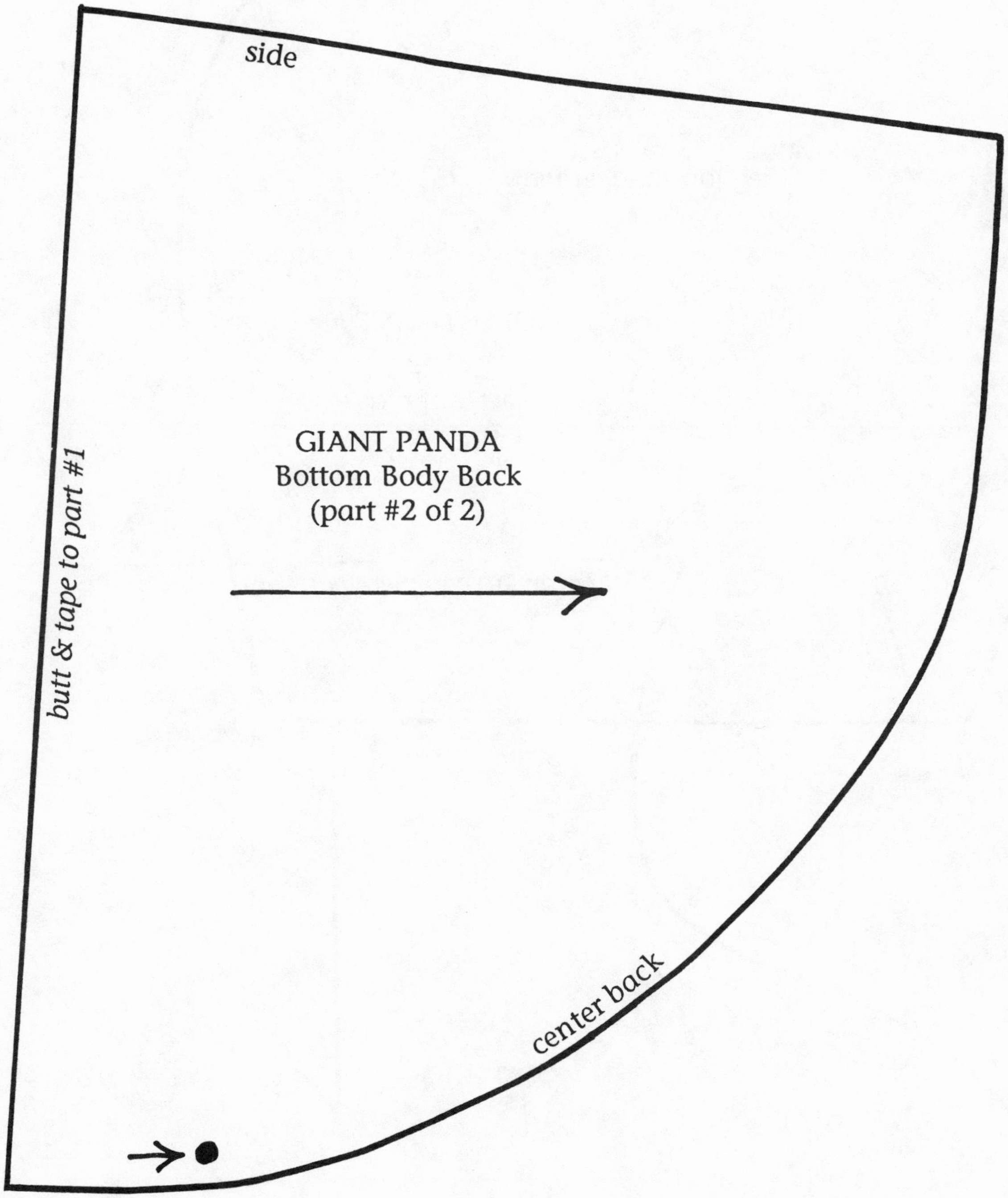

side

butt & tape to part #1

GIANT PANDA
Bottom Body Back
(part #2 of 2)

center back

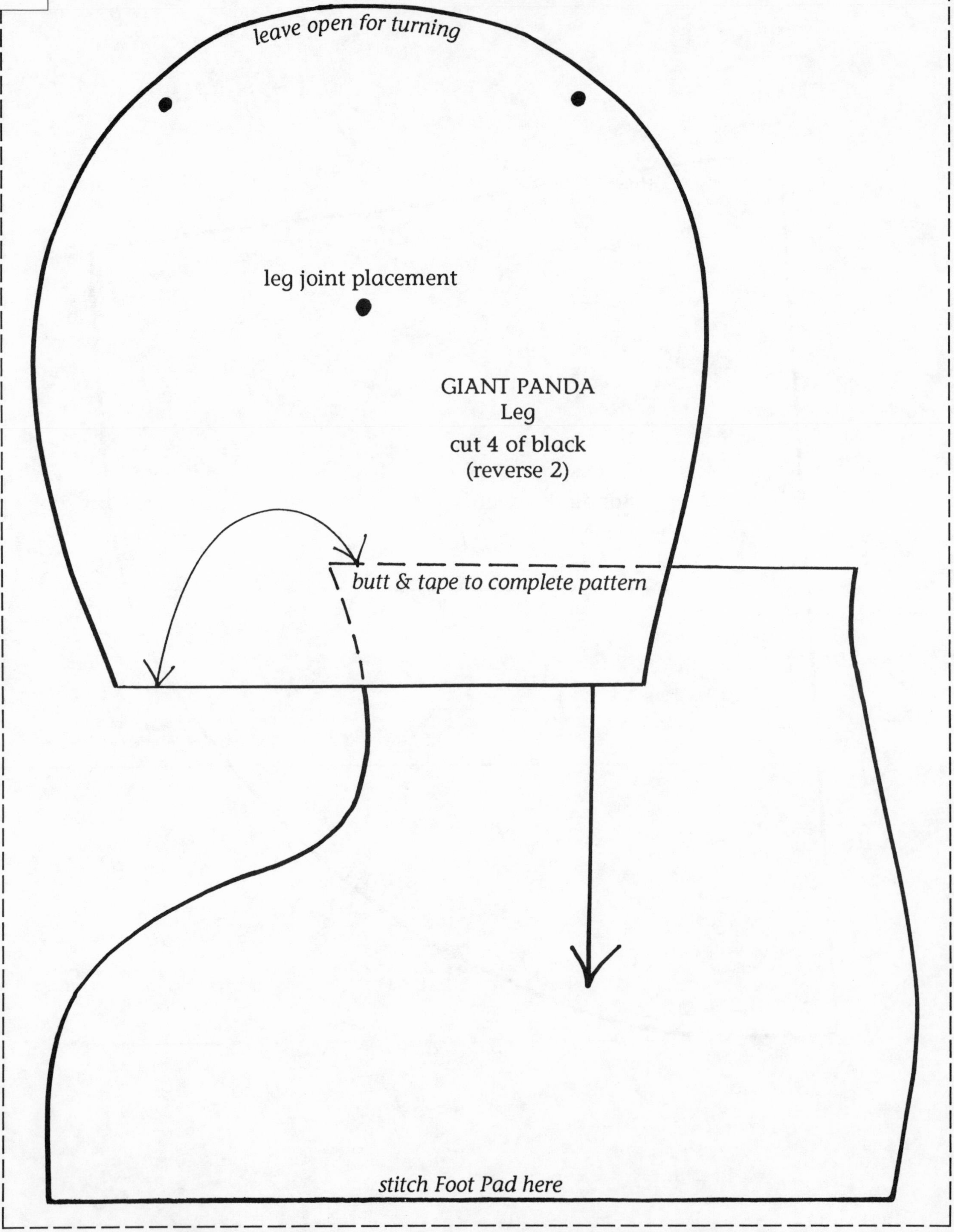

leave open for turning

leg joint placement

GIANT PANDA
Leg
cut 4 of black
(reverse 2)

butt & tape to complete pattern

stitch Foot Pad here

leave open for turning

arm joint placement

GIANT PANDA
Arm
cut 4 of black
(reverse 2)

butt & tape to complete pattern

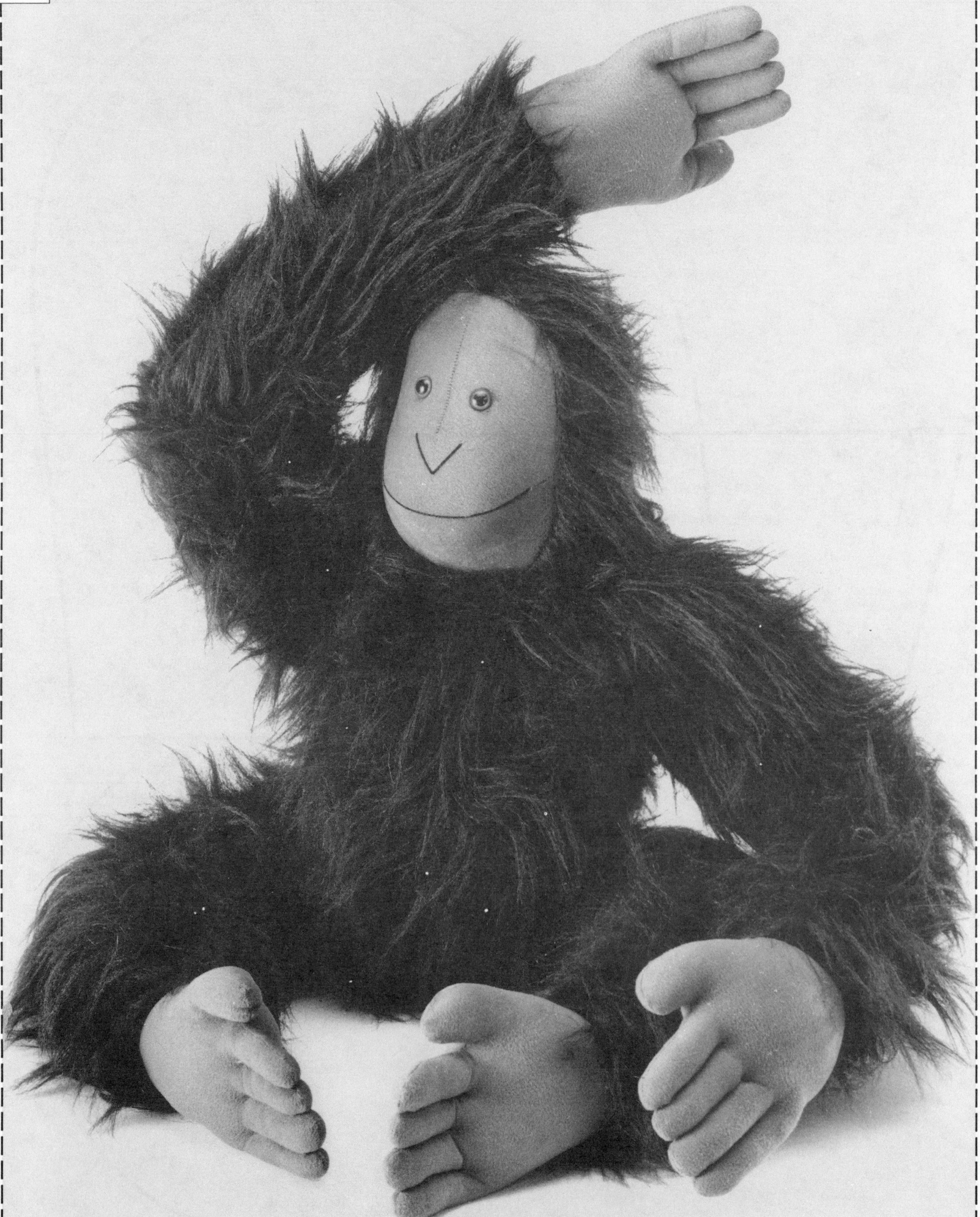

ORANGUTAN

Natives of Borneo and Sumatra call him the "man of the forest." The orangutan is also called the Red Ape. Orangutans may live 25 to 40 years in the wild, but today they face habitat depletion and poaching. The orangutan lives in the tree canopy of the forest, moving among the limbs in search of food. The largest fruit-eating animal in the world, the orangutan relies on its memory to find the enormous amount of food necessary to sustain its 150-200 pounds.

Your orangutan will be a lightweight, measuring three feet tall — about the actual size of a grown female orangutan. Fully jointed, she will love monkeying around — hanging from beams or ficus trees, or hugging a young friend.

MATERIALS

1 yard brown "fun fur," 3" pile length (from CR's Crafts, see Sources)
Matching thread
½ yard warm brown doe suede or felt
Two 14 mm brown safety eyes with black pupils (from CR's Crafts, see Sources)
Polyester fiberfill
Five 65 mm joint sets and metal washers
Brown carpet thread
Black embroidery floss or perle cotton

INSTRUCTIONS

Note: All seam allowances are ¼" unless noted otherwise.

Prepare patterns, cut and mark fabric as instructed in chapter 1.

1. Pin and stitch dart in face top.

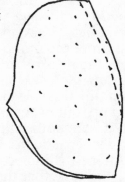

2. Pin face bottom to face top, matching dots A and matching sides marked "mouth edge." Stitch all the way to the raw edges.

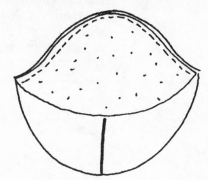

3. Pin the two fur head sides together at chin and back of head, right sides facing, as shown. Stitch back of head from top to bottom. Stitch together at chin.

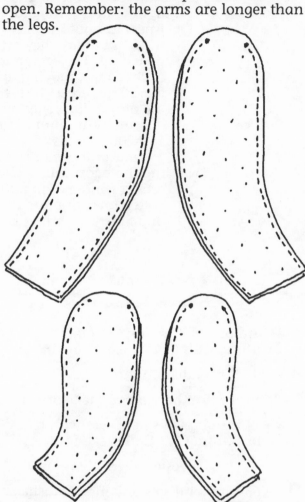

4. With fur head sides still wrong side out, pin face to head, right sides facing, matching dart at top of face to seam at top of head sides, and dot B at bottom of face bottom to the short seam at the bottom of the head sides. Stitch.

5. Turn head right side out. Make holes for the eyes at markings, then install safety eyes as instructed in chapter 1.

6. Stuff the head firmly, making sure the muzzle points out and is firmly stuffed. Don't worry if the eye area is wrinkled — these character lines are part of the natural expression of the orangutan. Stuff to about 1/2" from the neck opening. With the head upside down, place a stationary disk in the opening, the flat side on the fiberfill, the post sticking up, out of the opening. Using strong carpet thread, gather the neck edge with long (1/2" or so) stitches 1/4" from the raw edge. After stitching around once, pull up on the stitches to gather the fabric at the neck. Stitch around the edge once or twice more, pulling up on the thread as you go, until the fur fabric is gathered tightly around the post. Neatness isn't necessary since this stitching will not show once the head is installed on the body.

7. Stitch two sets of arm pieces and two sets of leg pieces together, right sides facing, leaving the bottom, straight edges and between the dots at the top of the limbs open. Remember: the arms are longer than the legs.

8. Right sides facing, pin and stitch two sets of hands/feet pieces together (hands and feet are the same pattern), leaving the straight edges at the wrists open. Repeat for other three pairs.

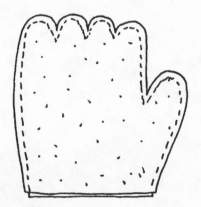

9. Turn hands and feet right side out. To form fingers, topstitch along marked lines. Rather than use a bulky backstitch to secure the threads at the beginning and end of the stitching, start and finish the stitching with several very short stitches.

10. With arm or leg wrong side out and hand or foot right side out, put hand or foot inside bottom arm or leg opening, right sides facing. Pin: for arms match seams in hands to seams in arms; for feet match dots C on hands to seams in legs. Be sure to make a left and right arm and a left and right leg as shown. The bend in the elbows point to the back, the bends in the knees, forward. Make holes for joints at markings. Put stationary disks into "body side" of arms and legs, and poke the posts out of the holes in the limbs.

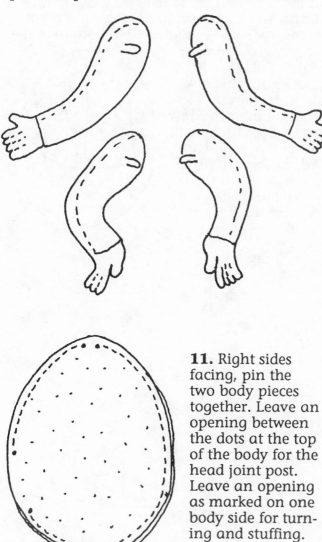

11. Right sides facing, pin the two body pieces together. Leave an opening between the dots at the top of the body for the head joint post. Leave an opening as marked on one body side for turning and stuffing.

12. Turn the body right side out. As instructed in chapter 1, install the head, arms, and legs. Double check that the longer limbs, the arms, are at the top, and that the arms and legs point in the correct directions. Refer to the picture of the orangutan and to your own body. Remember to pound the metal lockwashers in place before preceding to the next step.

13. Take your time stuffing the hands and feet. Use small pieces of stuffing to stuff each finger of the arms and legs. A Stuff-It™ tool (check your local crafts store) makes the job much easier. Stuff the arms, legs, and body to a medium firmness. Close the openings. Mold the hands into a natural position.

14. Needle sculpting uses the tension of thread to pull facial features into more natural expressions. For our orangutan, we will use needle sculpting to sink the eyes into the head.

Note: Right and left of the head are from your perspective as you look at the animal's face from the front. The right eye is the eye to your right.

To needle sculpt the eyes, thread a long dollmaking needle (5") with brown doubled carpet thread. Knot the ends. Start with the right eye. Push the point of the needle into the left side of the head somewhere in the neck. Emerge at about five o'clock, close to the right side of the metal lockwasher (shown as dotted circle in illustrations) which is inside the head, behind the eye.

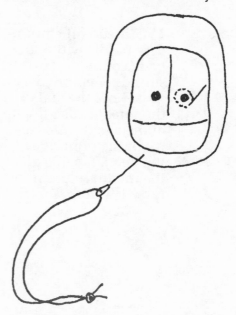

Go back in the very same hole the needle just emerged from. Come out as close to three o'clock as possible, against the eye. (Had the metal lockwasher not been in the way, we could have gone directly from the entry in the neck to three o'clock.)

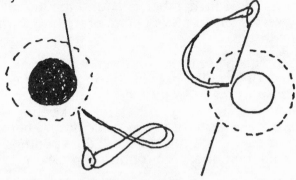

Go back in at the left side of the eye, at nine o'clock against the edge of the eye, and come out at about seven o'clock, just off the edge of the metal lockwasher. Make sure the threads loop evenly around the top of the eye. When tightened (in a few steps), the threads will slide under the eye and pull the eye down, into the head.

Go back into the very same hole the needle just made as it came out of the fabric. Emerge at the left side of the neck again, about where you first went in. Pull on the threads very tightly, so that the eye is pulled into the head. Knot and trim the thread. The knots will be hidden by the fur.

Repeat for the left eye.

15. Thread an embroidery needle with black perle cotton or six strands of embroidery floss. Knot the end of the thread. Push the tip of the needle into the fur at the right side of the head. Emerge along the mouth seam in the face, 1¼" from the fur.

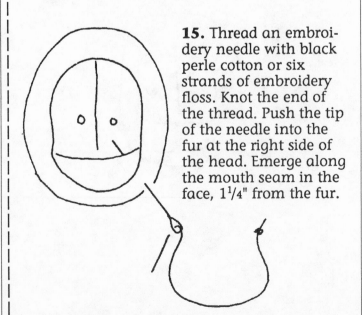

Go back into the face, again along the mouth seam, 1¼" from the fur on the left side of the face. Emerge in the fur on the left side of the head. Pull the thread just enough to make it lie on the mouth seam.

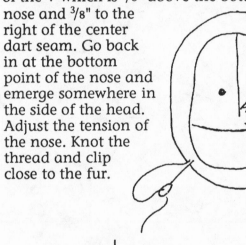

To make the nose, which is a V: Go back into the fur near where the thread just emerged. Come up at the bottom point of the nose, which is on the face dart (center seam), 1½" above the mouth. Go back in at the top left point of the V which is ⅜" above the bottom of the nose and ⅜" to left of the center face dart seam. Come out at the top right point of the V which is ⅜" above the bottom of the nose and ⅜" to the right of the center dart seam. Go back in at the bottom point of the nose and emerge somewhere in the side of the head. Adjust the tension of the nose. Knot the thread and clip close to the fur.

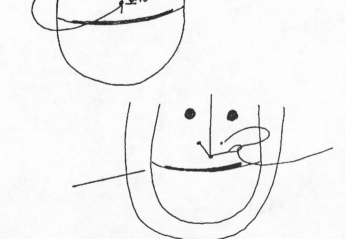

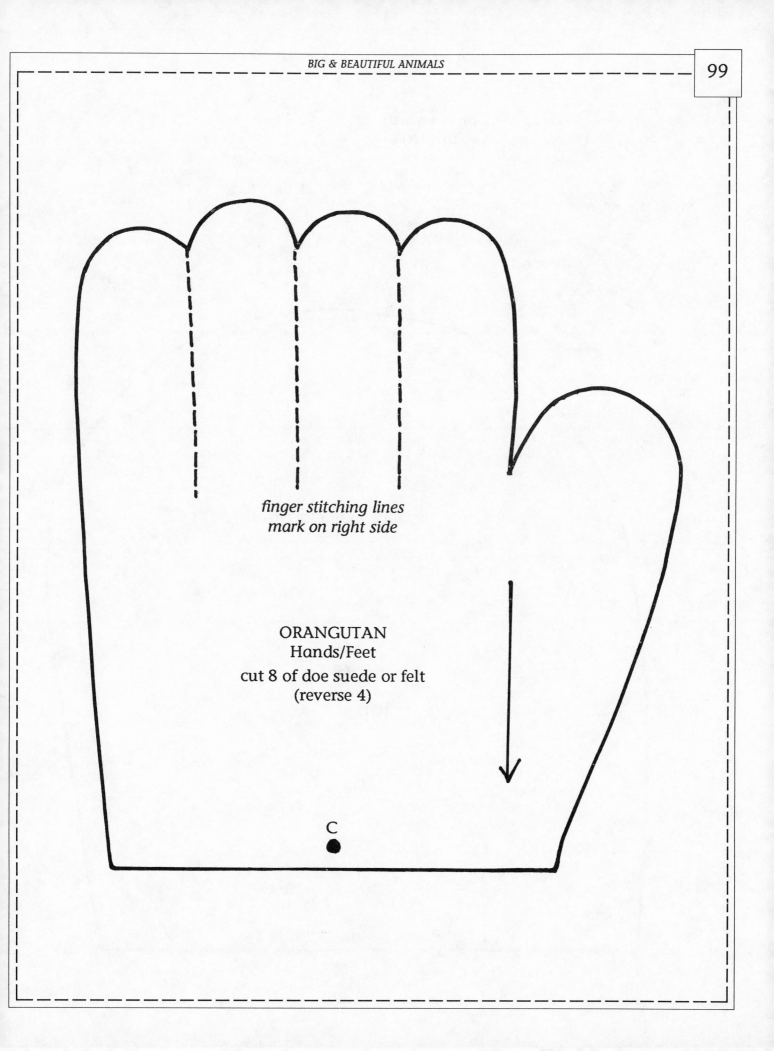

finger stitching lines
mark on right side

ORANGUTAN
Hands/Feet
cut 8 of doe suede or felt
(reverse 4)

C
●

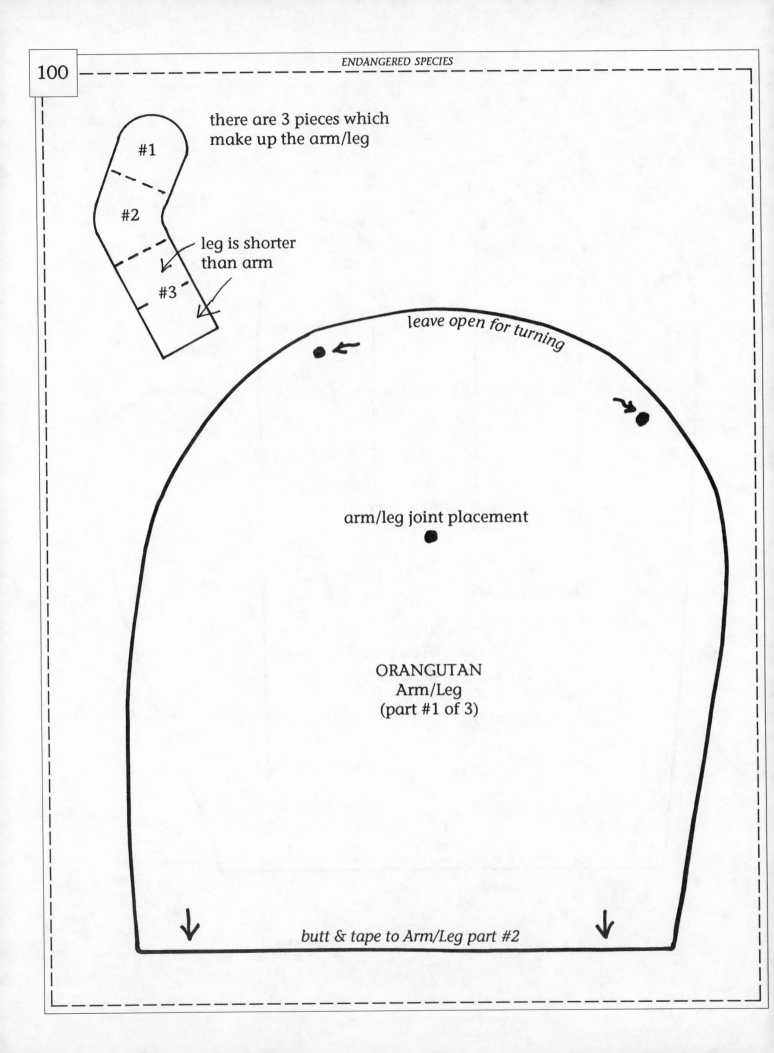

there are 3 pieces which
make up the arm/leg

#1

#2

leg is shorter
than arm

#3

leave open for turning

arm/leg joint placement

ORANGUTAN
Arm/Leg
(part #1 of 3)

butt & tape to Arm/Leg part #2

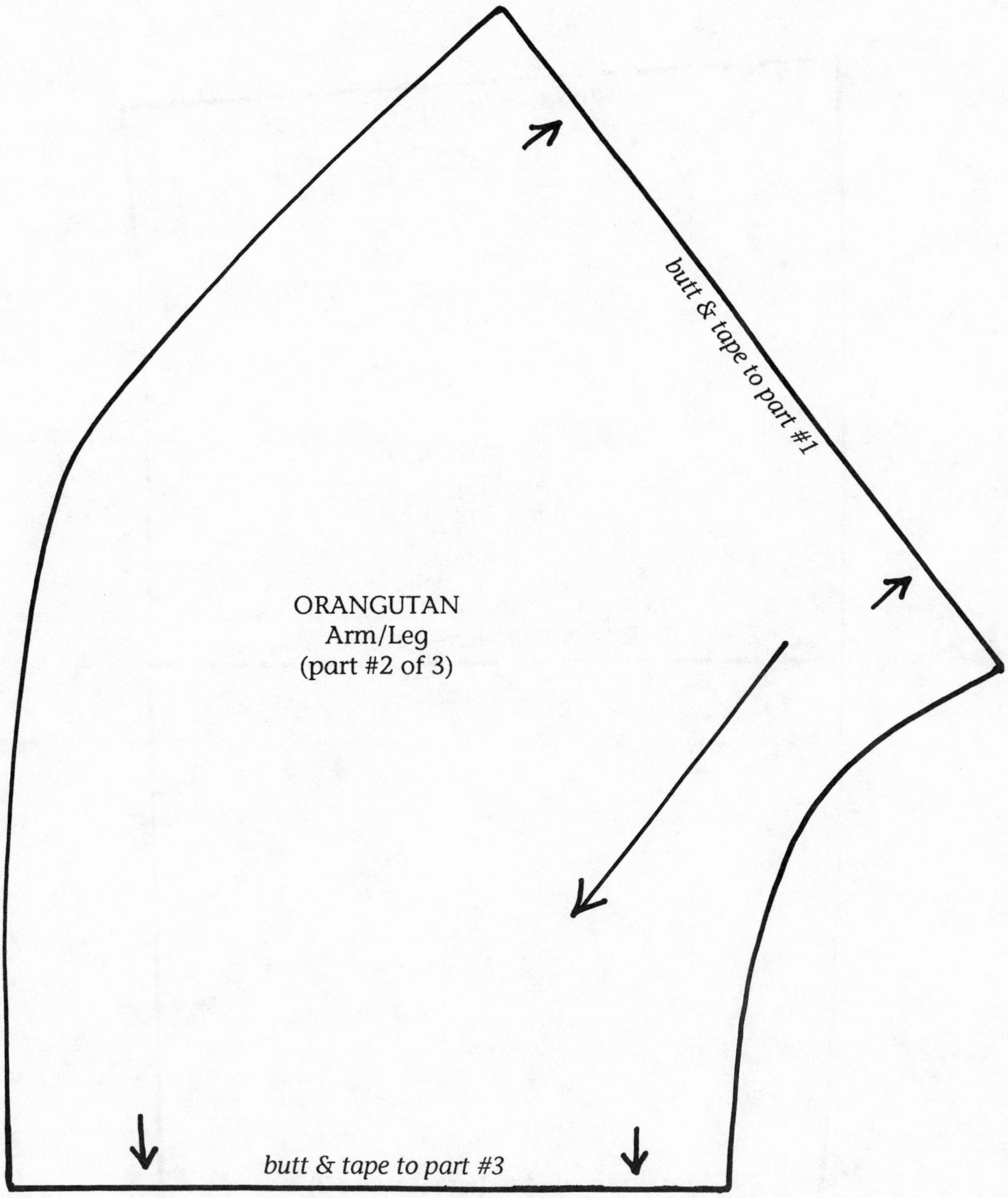

butt & tape to part #1

ORANGUTAN
Arm/Leg
(part #2 of 3)

butt & tape to part #3

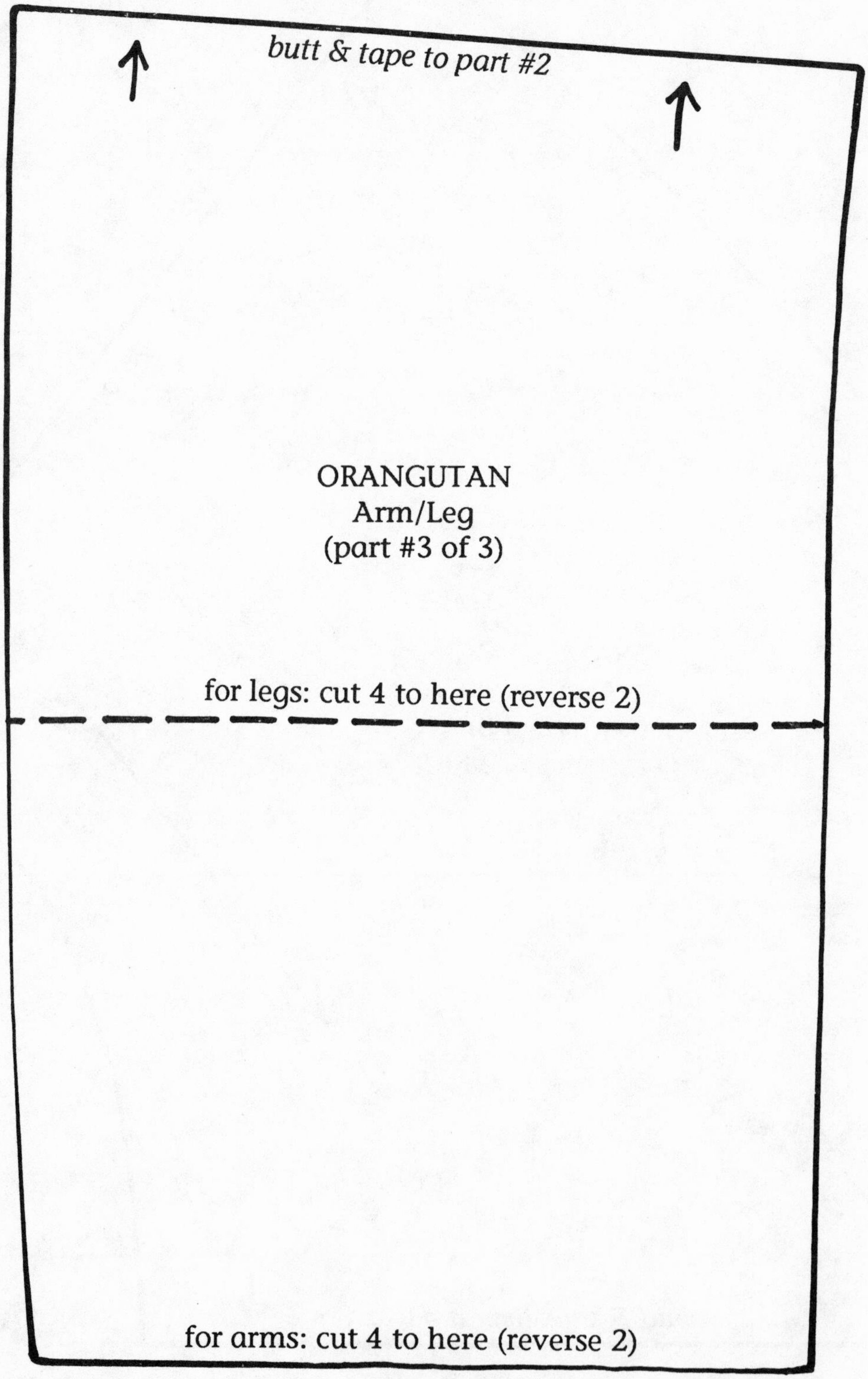

↑ *butt & tape to part #2* ↑

ORANGUTAN
Arm/Leg
(part #3 of 3)

for legs: cut 4 to here (reverse 2)

for arms: cut 4 to here (reverse 2)

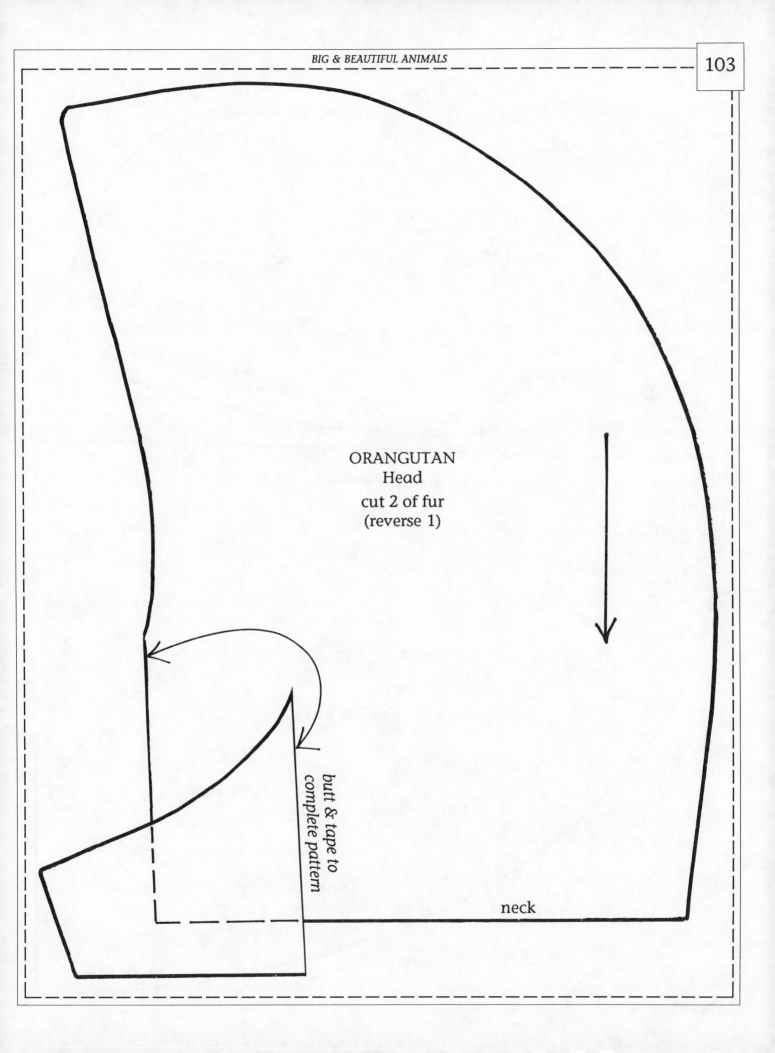

ORANGUTAN
Head
cut 2 of fur
(reverse 1)

butt & tape to
complete pattern

neck

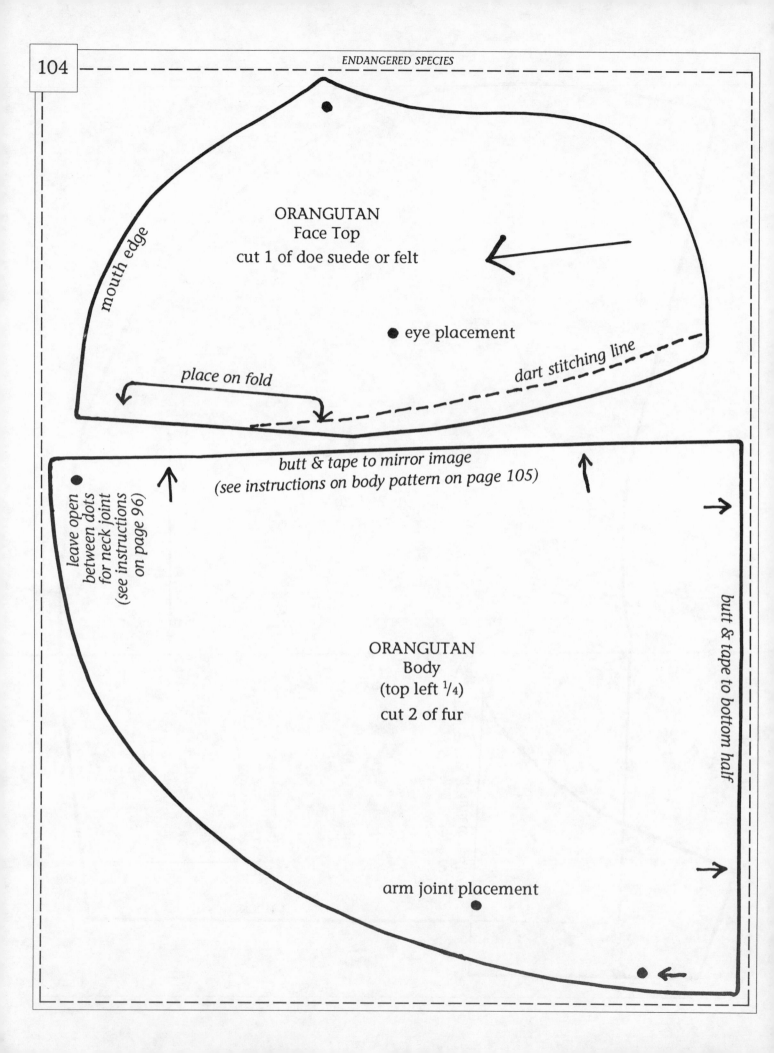

ORANGUTAN
Face Top
cut 1 of doe suede or felt

mouth edge

● eye placement

place on fold

dart stitching line

butt & tape to mirror image
(see instructions on body pattern on page 105)

leave open between dots for neck joint (see instructions on page 96)

ORANGUTAN
Body
(top left ¼)
cut 2 of fur

butt & tape to bottom half

arm joint placement

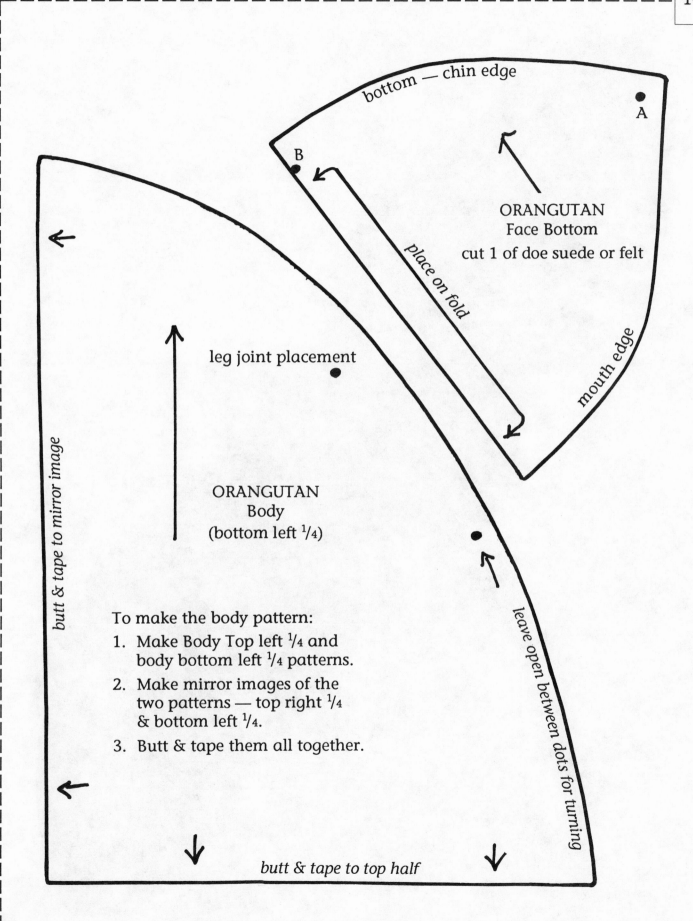

bottom — chin edge

A

B

ORANGUTAN
Face Bottom
cut 1 of doe suede or felt

place on fold

mouth edge

leg joint placement •

ORANGUTAN
Body
(bottom left ¼)

butt & tape to mirror image

leave open between dots for turning

To make the body pattern:

1. Make Body Top left ¼ and
   body bottom left ¼ patterns.

2. Make mirror images of the
   two patterns — top right ¼
   & bottom left ¼.

3. Butt & tape them all together.

butt & tape to top half

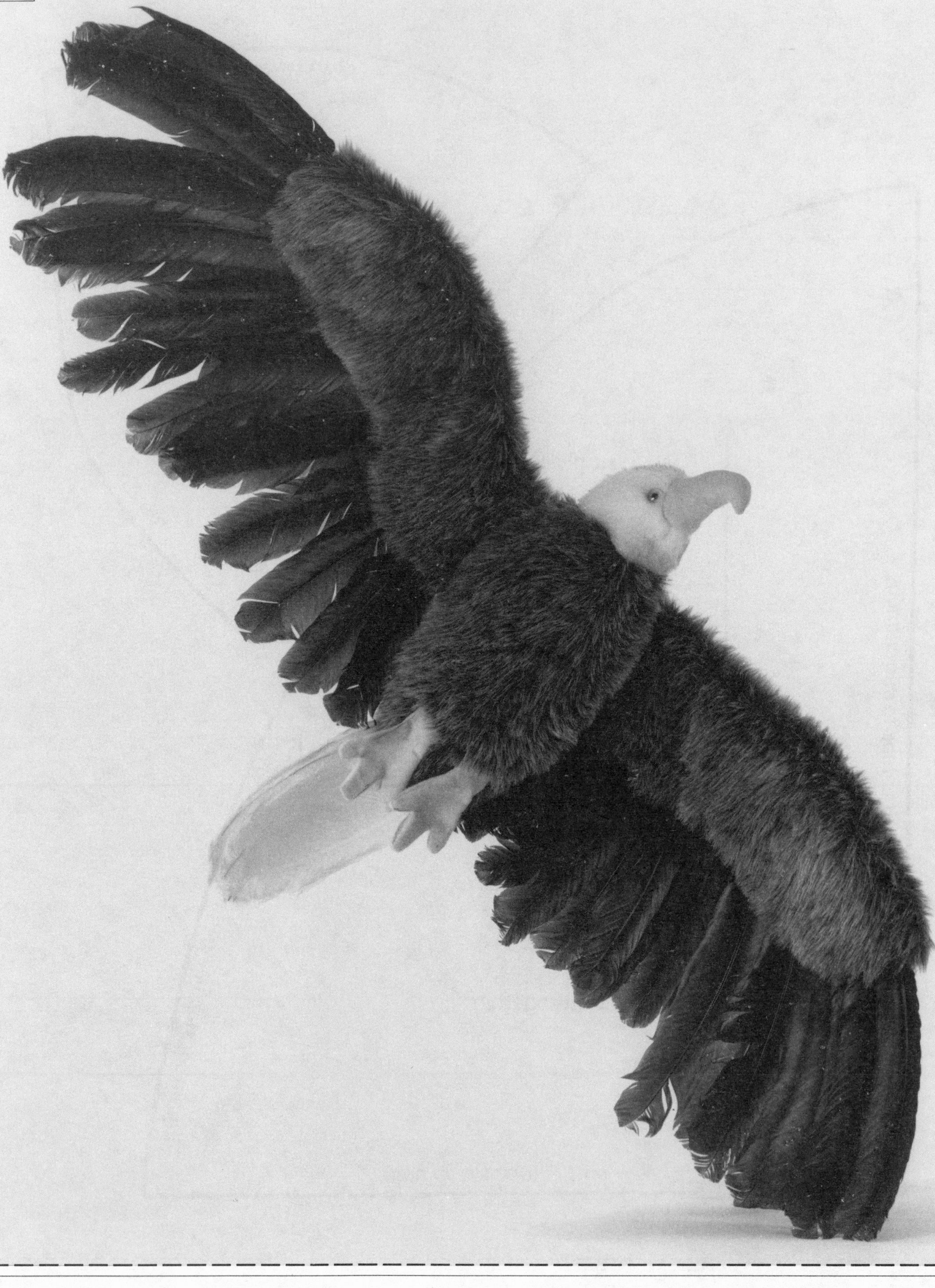

BALD EAGLE

Symbolic of the American spirit, the bald eagle soars into our imagination as a regal bird. He is making a triumphant come back all across the country, nesting again where his numbers had dwindled to nil.

The eagle nesting at your house will measure 20" from beak to tail. This eagle's wing span is reduced from his natural 6 to 7½ feet to a more manageable wingspan of 4 feet.

INSTRUCTIONS

Note: All seam allowances are ¼" except a ⅛" seam allowance for the felt beak and feet.

Prepare patterns, cut and mark the fabric by following the instructions in chapter 1.

1. Pin and stitch one long edge of the felt beak gusset to one beak piece from dot A through dot B.

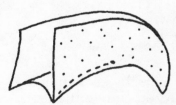

Pin and stitch the remaining beak piece to other side of beak gusset from dot A through dot B.

Stitch beak pieces together from dot A, around tip of beak, through dot C, as shown.

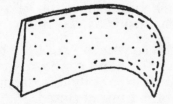

Trim seam allowances at tip of beak. Turn beak right side out. Set aside.

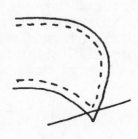

MATERIALS

⅝ yard fur (905Y Medium Brown Cubby Bear Fur from Carver's Eye Co., see Sources)
Matching thread
¼ yard white seal fur (or use a leftover scrap)
Bone-colored felt
Matching thread
Two 14 mm yellow glass bird eyes (style #10140 from Carver's Eye Co., see Sources)
64" of 18-gauge wire
Polyester fiberfill stuffing
14 or 15 left and 14 or 15 right black "wing" feathers, 10" to 12" long
5 left and 5 right white "wing" feathers
Craft glue
Fishing line for hanging

Stitch two bone-colored felt foot pieces together, leaving the short, straight edges open. Repeat for two remaining foot pieces. Turn right side out. Set aside.

2. Pin one long edge of the head gusset to one head side piece, matching dots D and dots E. Stitch.

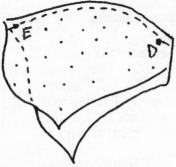

Pin the remaining head side piece to other side of head gusset matching dots D and dots E.

Pin head side pieces together at dots F and G. Stitch.

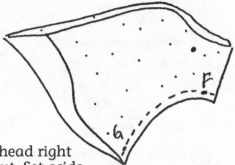

Turn head right side out. Set aside.

3. Right sides facing, pin the two body bottom pieces together, matching dots G and H. Stitch, leaving an opening between the marked dots.

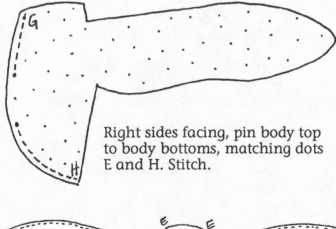

Right sides facing, pin body top to body bottoms, matching dots E and H. Stitch.

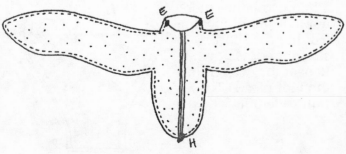

4. Put the eagle's head, which is right side out, inside the body, which is wrong side out. Match and pin dots G and E. Stitch the head to the body.

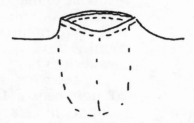

5. Turn the entire eagle right side out. Cut a piece of wire about 64" long. Twist the last inch or so of the ends together. Insert into the body as shown so it creates a big loop inside the body from wing to wing. To hold the stuffing in the body and to secure the wire so it won't twist, topstitch two seams along an imaginary dividing line between the body and wings as illustrated. Be careful not to stitch over the wire.

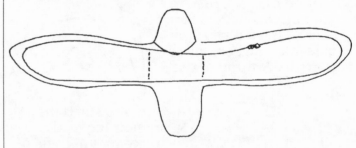

6. Stuff the head through the beak opening. Working from the outside, match the seam at the top of the beak to dot C at the center of the head gusset and dot K at the center bottom of the beak gusset to dot F at the center bottom seam of the head. Hand stitch the beak to the head, turning the 1/4" seam allowance to the inside as you stitch.

Unstuff the head so you can stuff the beak. Again, stuff the head and continue, carefully stuffing the bird's body. Ladder stitch the opening at the tummy closed.

7. For glass eyes (one eye on each end of a wire), cut the wire with wire cutters about 1" from each eye. Use needle-nose pliers to bend the last third of the wire back on itself and bend it down again.

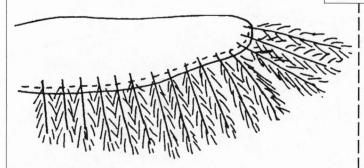

With an awl or a seam ripper, make holes at the markings for the eyes. Remove the colored thread markings. Apply a drop of Fray Check™ and leave to dry. Double thread and knot a long dollmaker's needle with heavy thread or waxed dental floss. Push the needle through the fabric under the neck (the fur will hide the knot) and come out the eye hole. It will take a few stabs to get the needle to come out exactly in the hole.

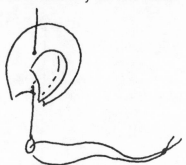

For the white tail feathers, make 10 holes in the top side of the eagle's rump above the seam as illustrated. Trim the feathers to 7" or 8" in length. Apply glue and insert all 10 of them in place, right facing feathers on the left and left facing feathers on the right.

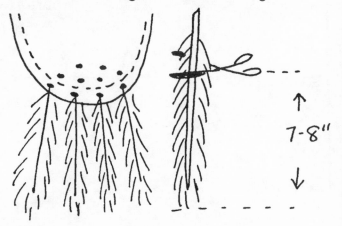

Put the needle through the loop in the eye wire (or, if the needle is too large for the hole in the loop, just work the thread onto the loop as you would if linking one paper clip to another) and push the needle back into the eye hole. Push the needle out through the base of the neck near where you started it.

Pull the thread very tightly, seating the eye flatly and firmly against the head. Pull again to be sure the eye is secure. Install the second eye as above. Be sure both eyes are tight before knotting the thread at the neck.

8. Starting at the far end of one wing, make a hole with a seam ripper above the back seam of the wing, insert a feather. You will see why some are right- and others are left-facing. Check it for fit, then remove it. Cover the quill with glue and insert it back into the hole. Spacing the feathers 1" to 1½" apart, repeat this until the wing is complete with 14 or 15 feathers. You will need to trim the length of the last half of the feathers by cutting the quill ends. Repeat for the second wing.

9. Turn the raw edges of the openings of the feet ¼" so they are inside. Whipstitch closed. Hand stitch feet to eagle's body bottom as shown.

10. To hang the eagle, thread a needle with the fishing line. Take a stitch at one of the points on the top side of the eagle as shown. Cut the fishing line to the desired length. Knot the ends together. Repeat for two remaining points.

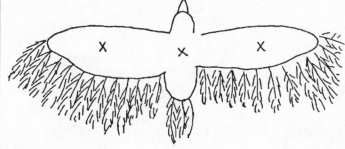

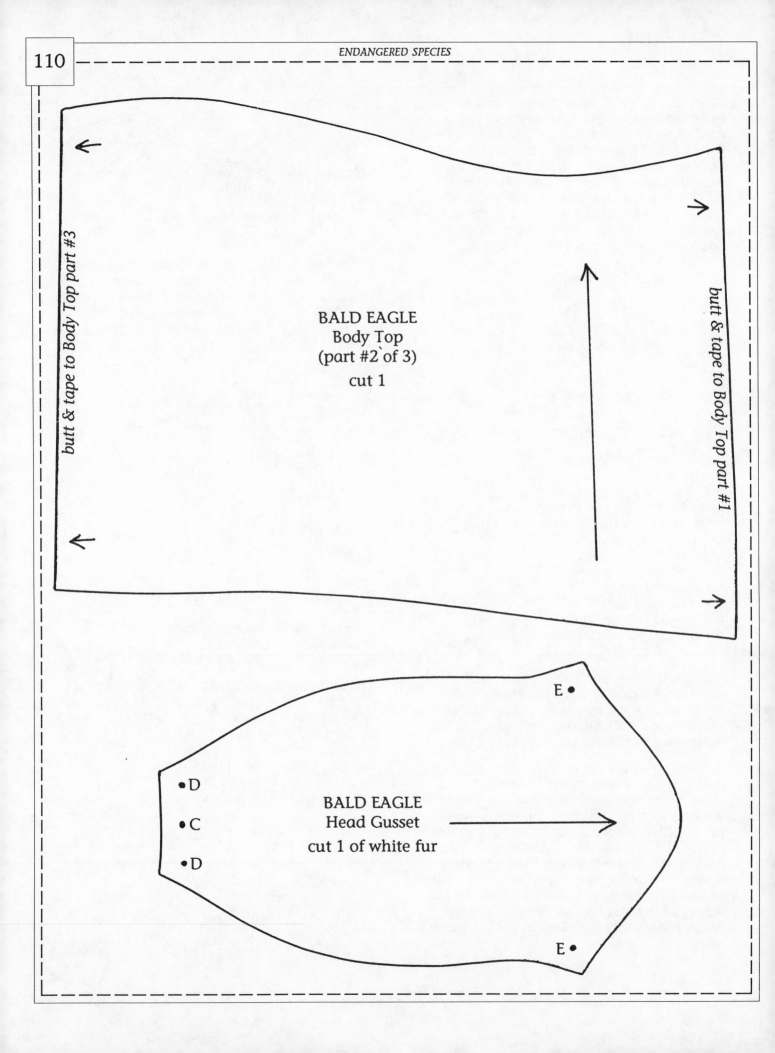

butt & tape to Body Top part #3

BALD EAGLE
Body Top
(part #2 of 3)
cut 1

butt & tape to Body Top part #1

E •

• D
• C
• D

BALD EAGLE
Head Gusset
cut 1 of white fur

E •

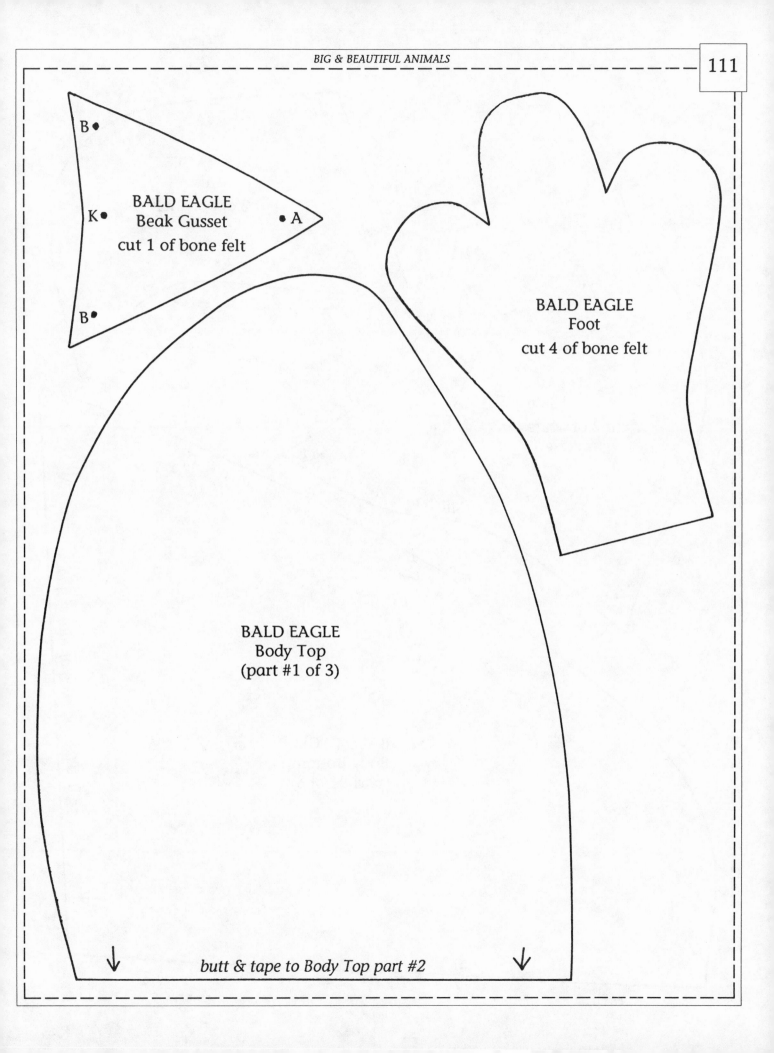

B •

K •   **BALD EAGLE**
         Beak Gusset   • A
         cut 1 of bone felt

B •

BALD EAGLE
Foot
cut 4 of bone felt

BALD EAGLE
Body Top
(part #1 of 3)

↓   *butt & tape to Body Top part #2*   ↓

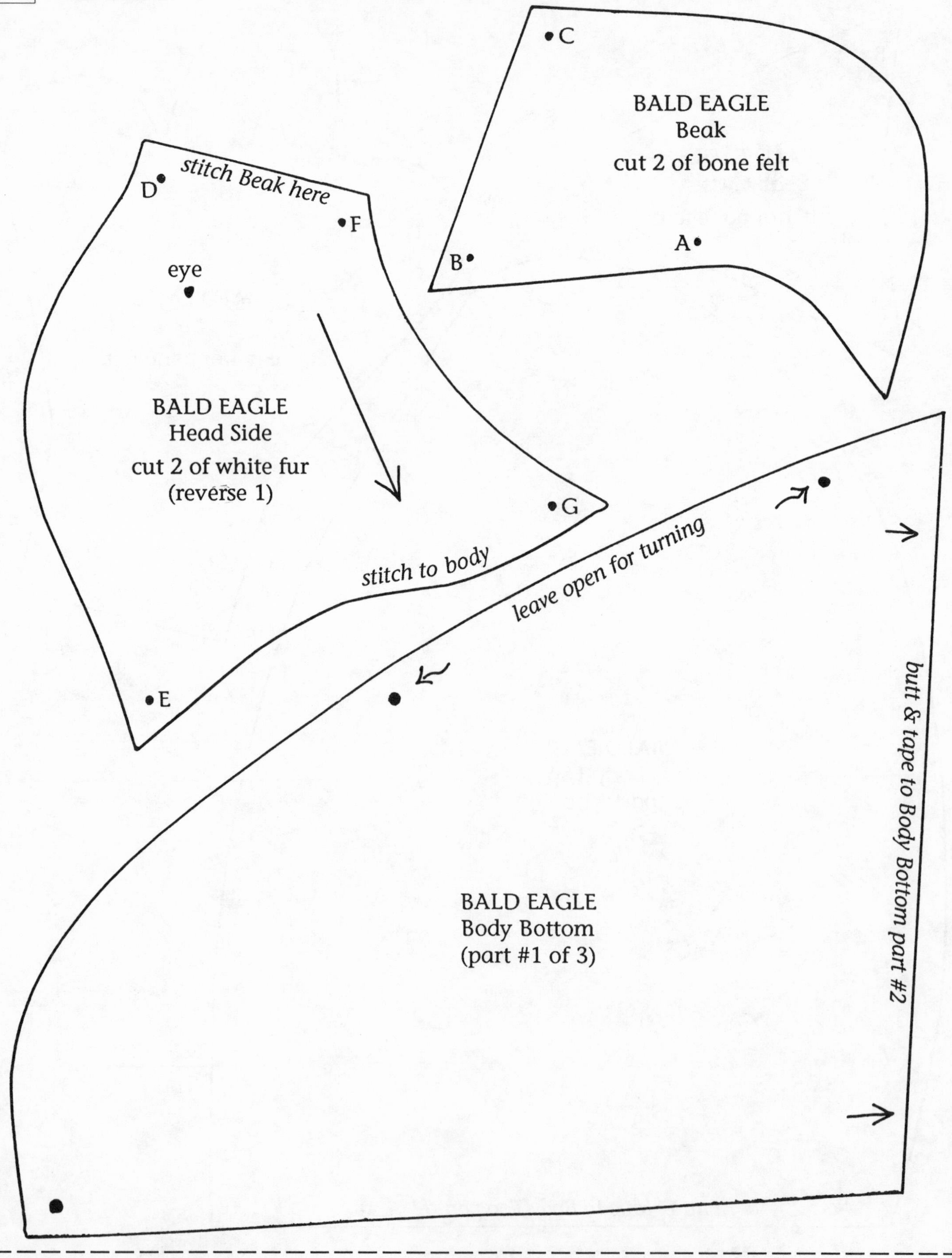

•C

BALD EAGLE
Beak
cut 2 of bone felt

D• *stitch Beak here*

•F

eye

•A

B•

BALD EAGLE
Head Side
cut 2 of white fur
(reverse 1)

•G

stitch to body

leave open for turning

•E

BALD EAGLE
Body Bottom
(part #1 of 3)

butt & tape to Body Bottom part #2

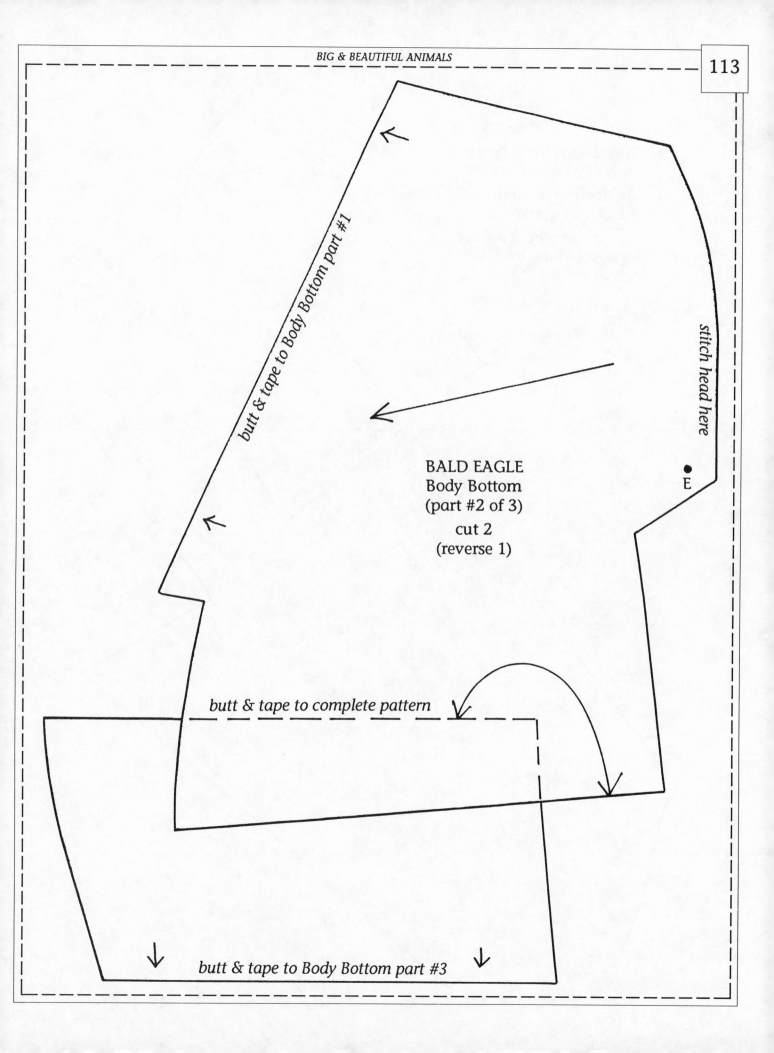

butt & tape to Body Bottom part #1

stitch head here

BALD EAGLE
Body Bottom
(part #2 of 3)

cut 2
(reverse 1)

E

butt & tape to complete pattern

butt & tape to Body Bottom part #3

To make the body top pattern:

1. Butt & tape the 3 parts of the body top pattern together.

2. Make a mirror image of the body top pattern.

3. Butt & tape the 2 halves together along the center top line.

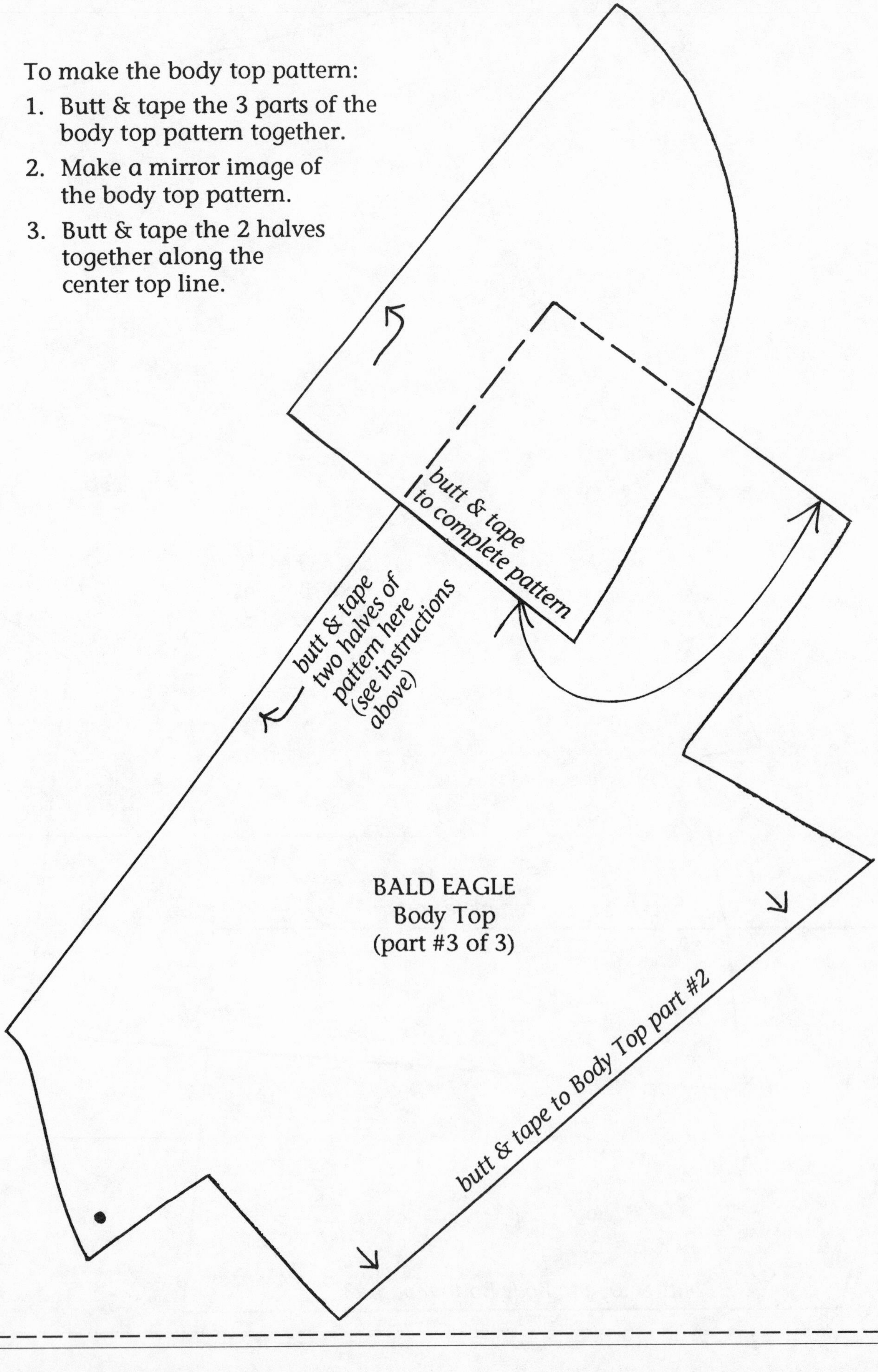

butt & tape to complete pattern

butt & tape two halves of pattern here (see instructions above)

BALD EAGLE
Body Top
(part #3 of 3)

butt & tape to Body Top part #2

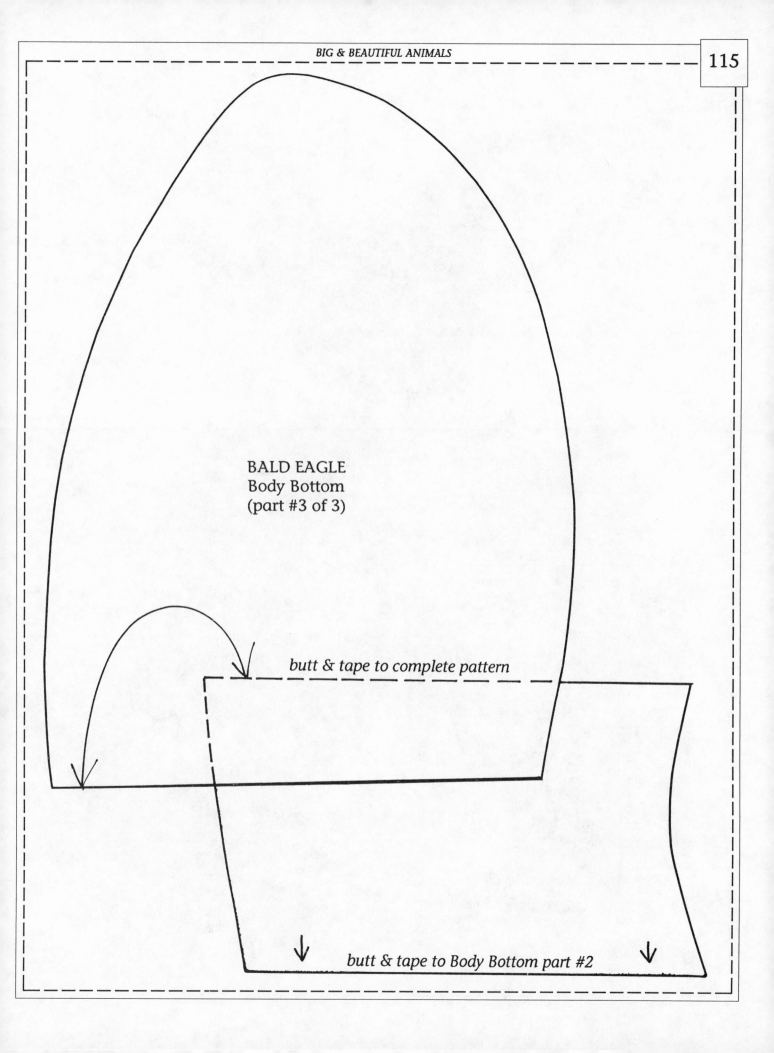

BALD EAGLE
Body Bottom
(part #3 of 3)

butt & tape to complete pattern

butt & tape to Body Bottom part #2

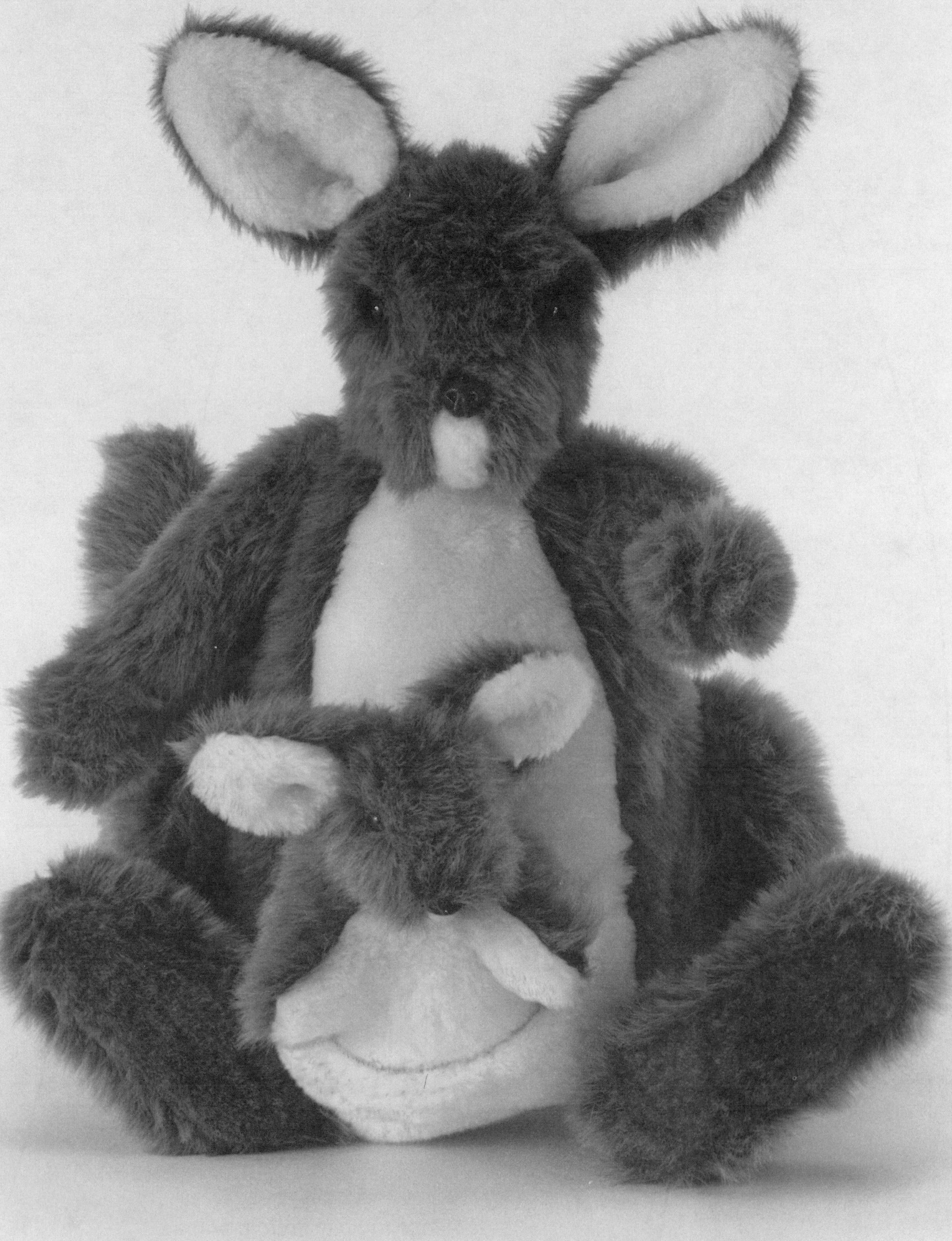

K A N G E R O O & J O E Y

At birth, the kangaroo is barely an inch long but matures to the height of man and weighs 100 to 170 pounds. At high speeds, the kangaroo can cover 20 feet or more in a single bound, traveling at about 35 miles per hour. Kangaroos come in two colors; red and gray. Your scaled-down kangaroo can only hop with human assistance. He stands 31 inches at the tip of his ears. The joey, or baby kangaroo, is 12 inches long — just the right size to fit in his mother's elasticized pouch.

MATERIALS

1²/₃ yards fur fabric (available from by Diane as kodiak or CR's Crafts as 905K Koala, see Sources)
Matching thread
³/₄ yard white seal fur (available from by Diane or CR's Crafts, see Sources)
Scrap of 1" long pile black fur for eye backing
6¹/₂" of ¹/₄" wide elastic
One pair 14 mm black safety eyes
One 25 mm nose
Two 65 mm plastic bear joints and metal washers
Polyester fiberfill stuffing
Carpet thread or waxed dental floss
One pair 12 mm eyes for joey
One 20 mm nose for joey

INSTRUCTIONS

Note: All seam allowances are ¹/₄" unless noted otherwise.

Prepare patterns, cut and mark the fabric as instructed in chapter 1.

Mother Kangaroo

1. Turn and pin top 1" of straight edge of white pouch to wrong side. Stitch. Pin ends of elastic to wrong side of pouch over stitching as shown. From

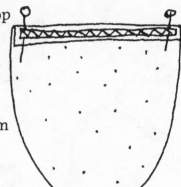

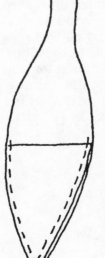

the wrong side of the pouch, zigzag stitch the elastic to the pouch, stretching the elastic as you stitch.

2. With the wrong side of pouch facing right side of underbody gusset, pin pouch to underbody gusset, matching top folded edge of pouch to placement line on underbody gusset. Baste.

3. Pin and stitch short, straight edge of underbody gusset to matching edge of head gusset as marked.

4. Right sides facing, pin one side of gussets to one body side, matching dots A at back of head on body side and on head gusset, dots C at bottom of body and on underbody gusset, and matching seam in gussets to dot B at nose on body side. Pin between these points. Stitch from A to B to C.

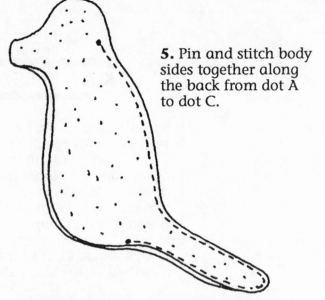

5. Pin and stitch body sides together along the back from dot A to dot C.

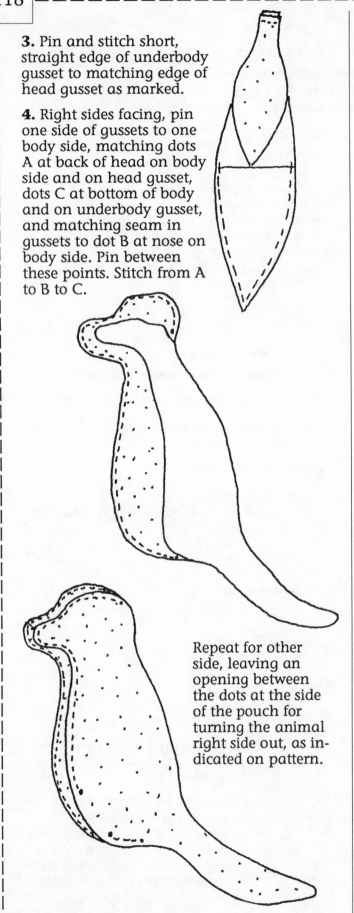

Repeat for other side, leaving an opening between the dots at the side of the pouch for turning the animal right side out, as indicated on pattern.

6. As marked on the patterns, make holes in the head for the eyes and in the underbody gusset for the nose. Also make holes for the arms.

Make a hole in the eye backings at the markings. From the fur side of the eye backings, insert the post of the eyes into the holes. Install the eyes as instructed in chapter 1. Install the nose at the marking on the underbody gusset.

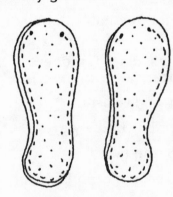

7. Pin two arm pieces together, fur sides facing. Stitch, leaving the tops of the arms open between the dots as marked. Repeat for the other arm. Turn right side out.

8. Hold two arms together as shown. Make holes at markings on facing sides of the arms. Put a stationary disk into each arm. Poke the posts out of the arms. Install the arms in the body as instructed in chapter 1. Check the picture of the kangaroo to be sure the arms point in the correct direction. Stuff the arms and ladder stitch the openings closed.

9. Stuff the kangaroo's tail, then the nose and head. Stuff the remainder of the body. Ladder stitch the opening at the pouch closed.

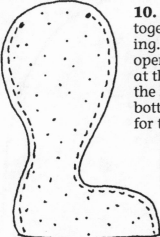

10. Pin two leg pieces together, right sides facing. Stitch, leaving an opening between the dots at the top of the leg and the straight edges at the bottom of the leg. Repeat for the second leg.

11. Trim the fur of the foot sole as instructed in chapter 1. Pin one foot sole to the bottom of one leg, matching the large dot to the leg's front seam and the small dot to the leg's back seam. Stitch. Repeat for second leg.

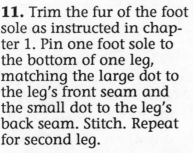

12. Turn legs right side out. Stuff. As instructed in chapter 1, ladder stitch openings closed. Hand stitch legs to body, following colored thread guidelines. For added strength, stitch around a second time.

13. Pin a white and a brown ear piece together. Stitch, leaving the straight edges at the bottom unstitched. Repeat for second ear. Turn right side out. Brush fur out of seams. Turn bottom edge of one ear ½" to inside. Whipstitch. Fold ear in half, with white, inner side of ear to the inside. Whipstitch. Sew to head as shown, between markings. Repeat for second ear.

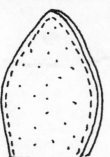

14. Trim any long hairs of the fur poking out from below the eyes. Leave the long black fur above the eyes. Comb these hairs with a needle or small brush to form eyelashes.

Baby Joey

1. Pin the two body sides together, right sides facing, from dot A at back of head to dot B under tail. Stitch between the dots.

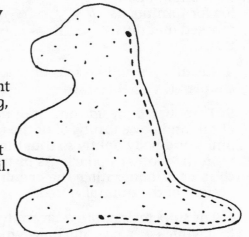

2. Pin short straight ends of head gusset to underbody gusset as marked on patterns. Stitch.

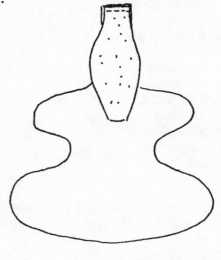

3. Match and pin dots A and C on head/underbody gusset to dots A and C on one body side, right sides facing. Pin between these two points, matching seam in gussets to dot B at body sides nose. Stitch from dots A to B to C.

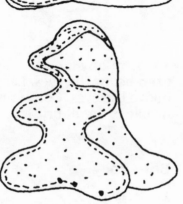

Repeat for other side of gussets/body side, this time leaving an opening between the dots at the bottom of one leg for turning, as marked and illustrated.

4. Install eyes and nose as instructed in chapter 1.

5. Turn joey right side out. Stuff nose, end of tail and paws firmly. Stuff the rest of the limbs and body lightly so that the baby will fit in the mother's pouch. As instructed in chapter 1, ladder stitch the opening at the bottom of the animal closed.

6. Fur sides facing, pin a brown fur ear piece to a white ear piece. Stitch, leaving the bottom straight edges open. Turn right side out. Brush fur out of seam.

Turn bottom edge of ear ¼" to inside. Whipstitch. Fold ear in half with the inner white ear to the inside. Whipstitch. Sew to head, centering the ears over the gusset/head side seam at markings. Repeat for second ear.

7. Trim fur between the eyes and nose and across the bridge of the nose so the baby can see.

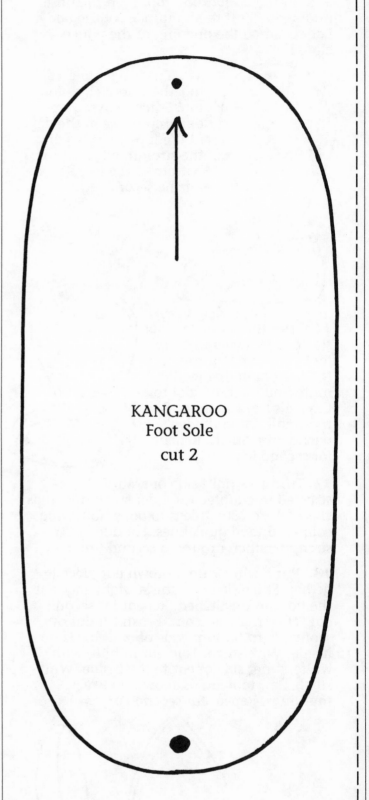

KANGAROO
Foot Sole
cut 2

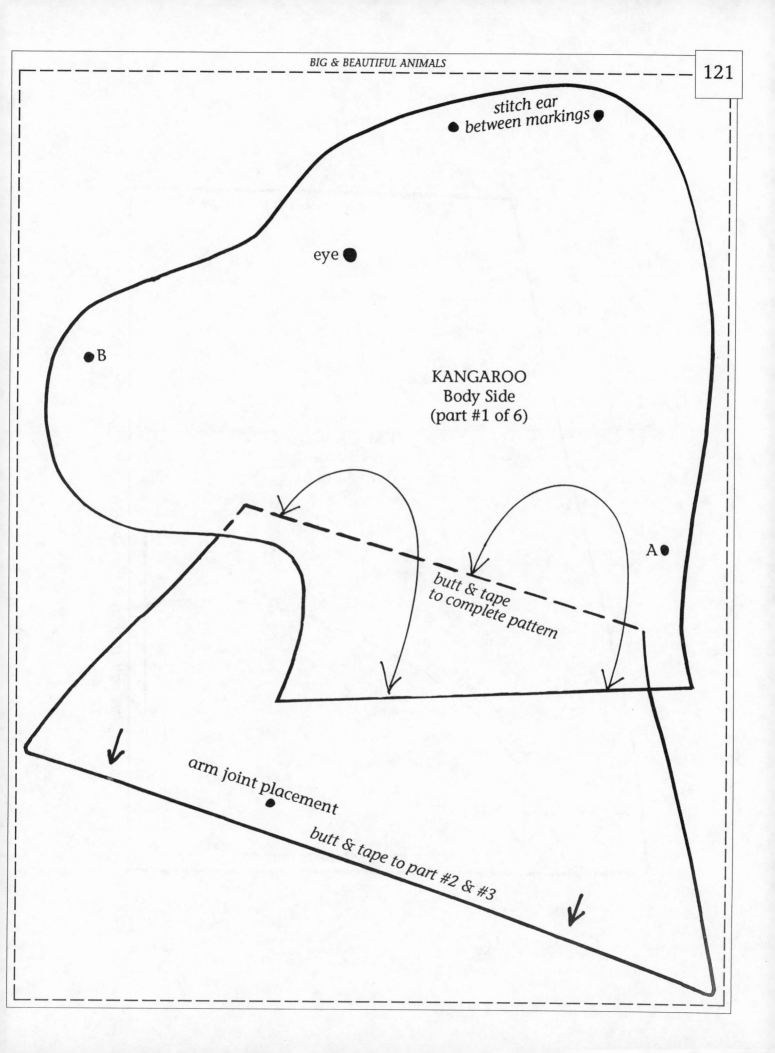

stitch ear
between markings

eye

B

KANGAROO
Body Side
(part #1 of 6)

A

butt & tape
to complete pattern

arm joint placement

butt & tape to part #2 & #3

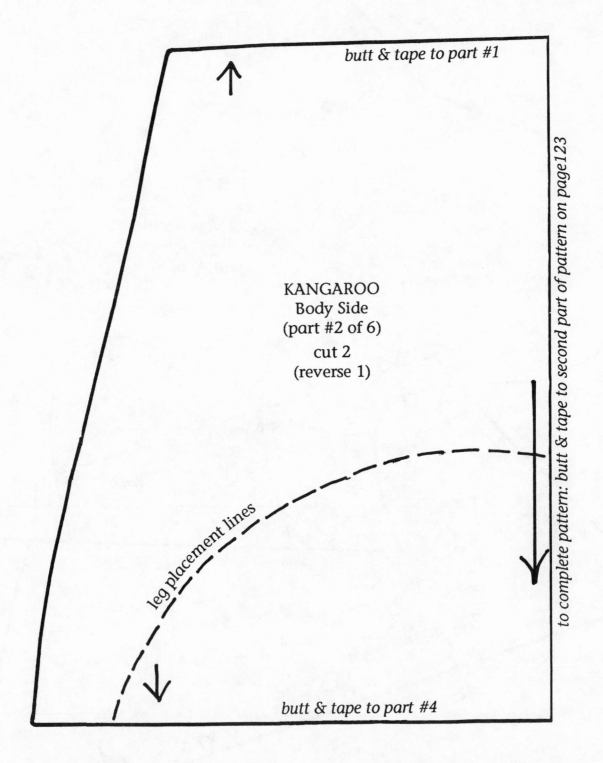

butt & tape to part #1

KANGAROO
Body Side
(part #2 of 6)

cut 2
(reverse 1)

leg placement lines

to complete pattern: butt & tape to second part of pattern on page123

butt & tape to part #4

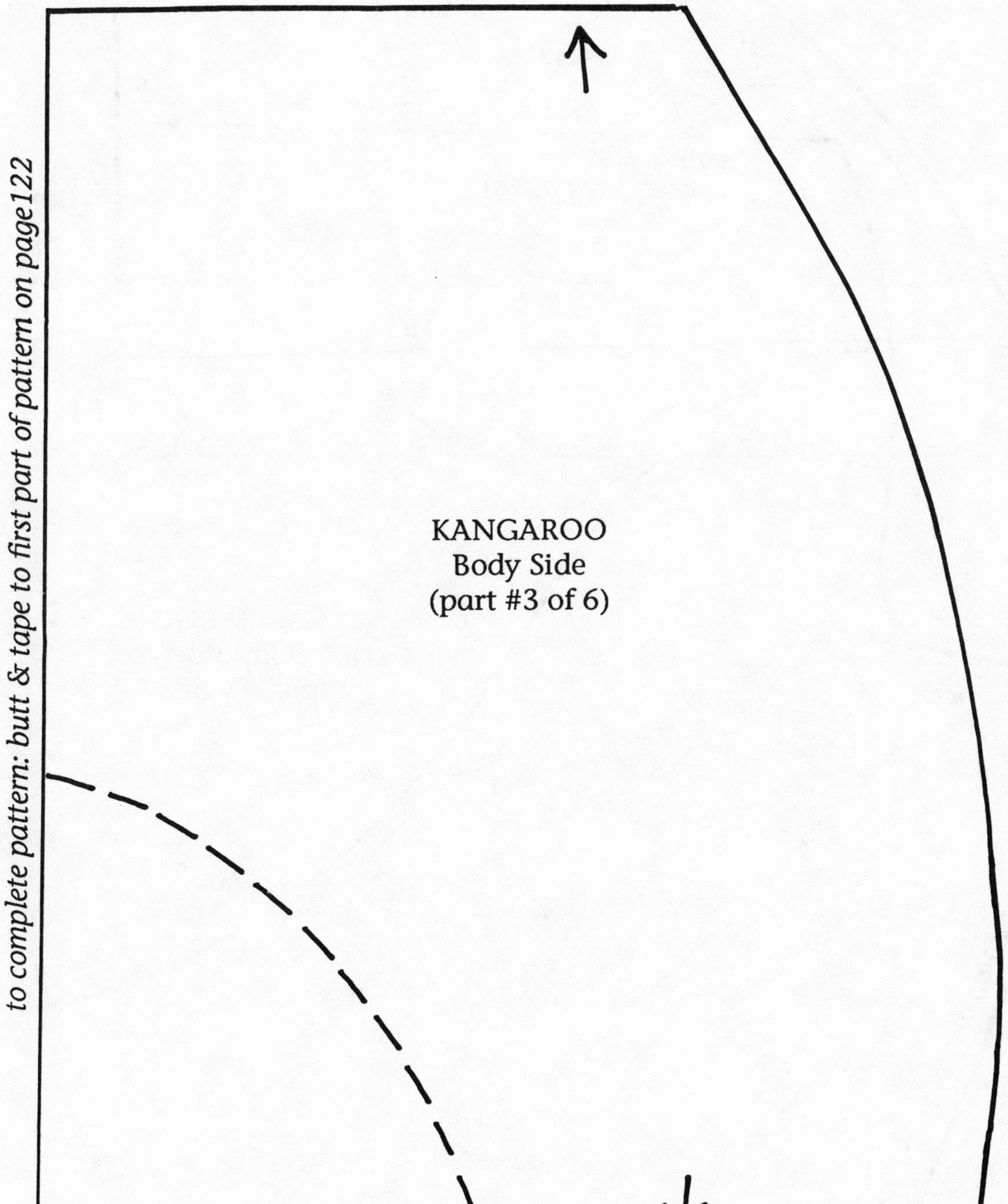

to complete pattern: butt & tape to first part of pattern on page122

KANGAROO
Body Side
(part #3 of 6)

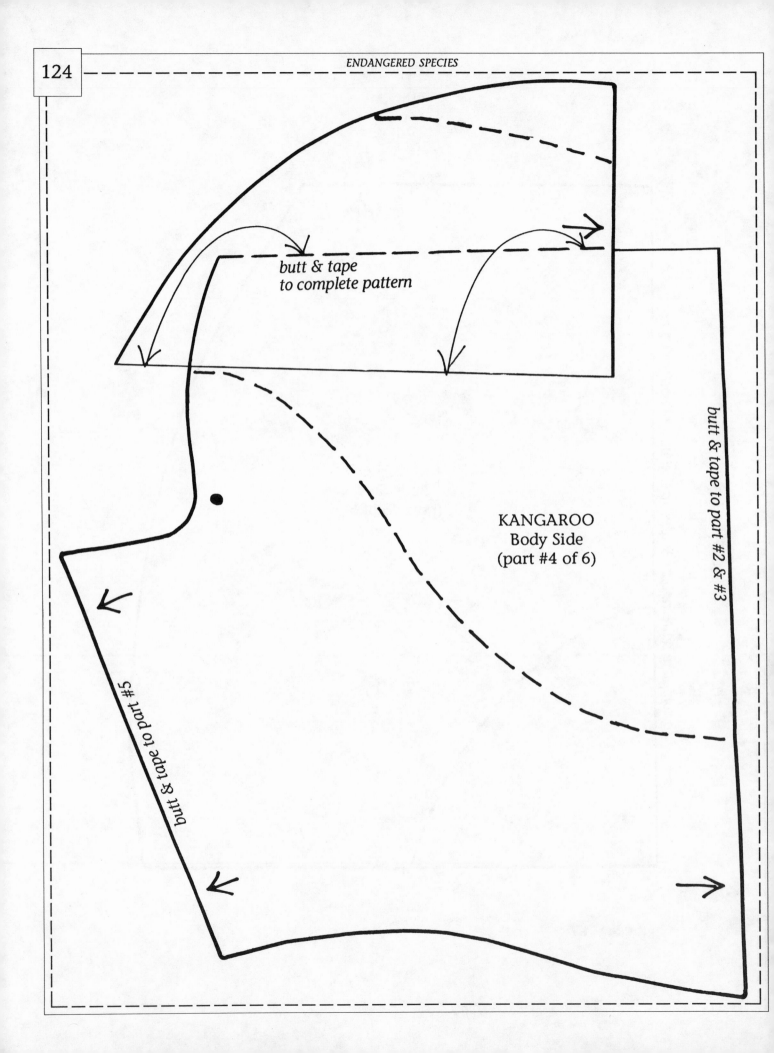

*butt & tape
to complete pattern*

KANGAROO
Body Side
(part #4 of 6)

butt & tape to part #2 & #3

butt & tape to part #5

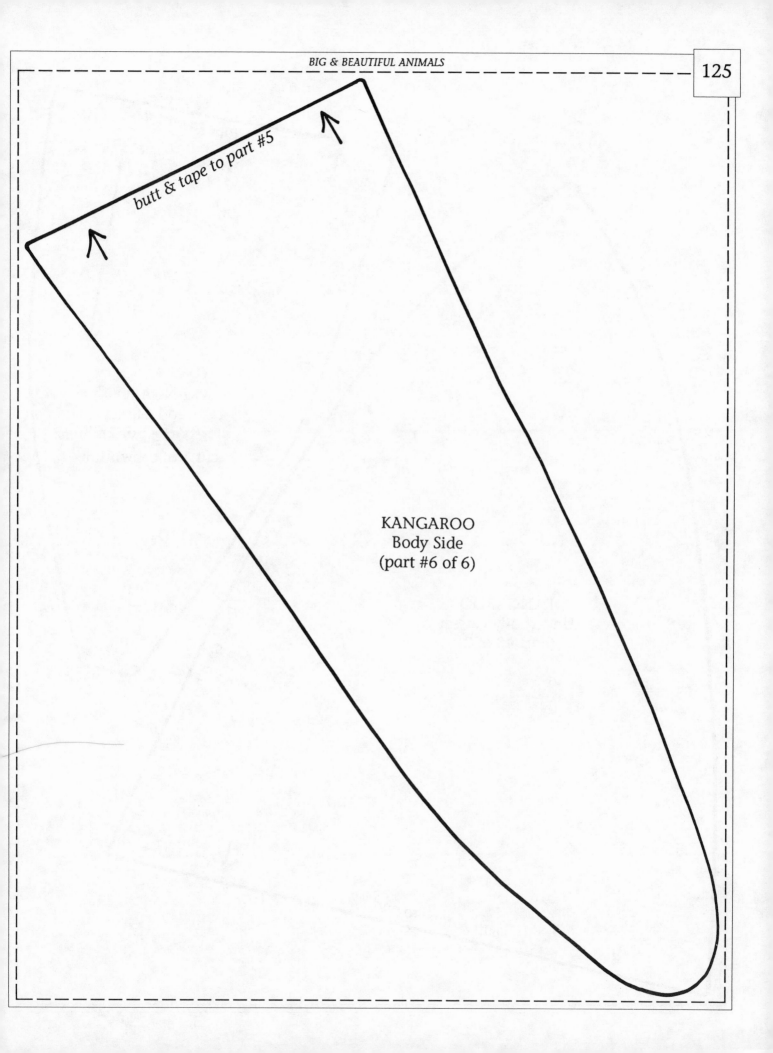

butt & tape to part #5

KANGAROO
Body Side
(part #6 of 6)

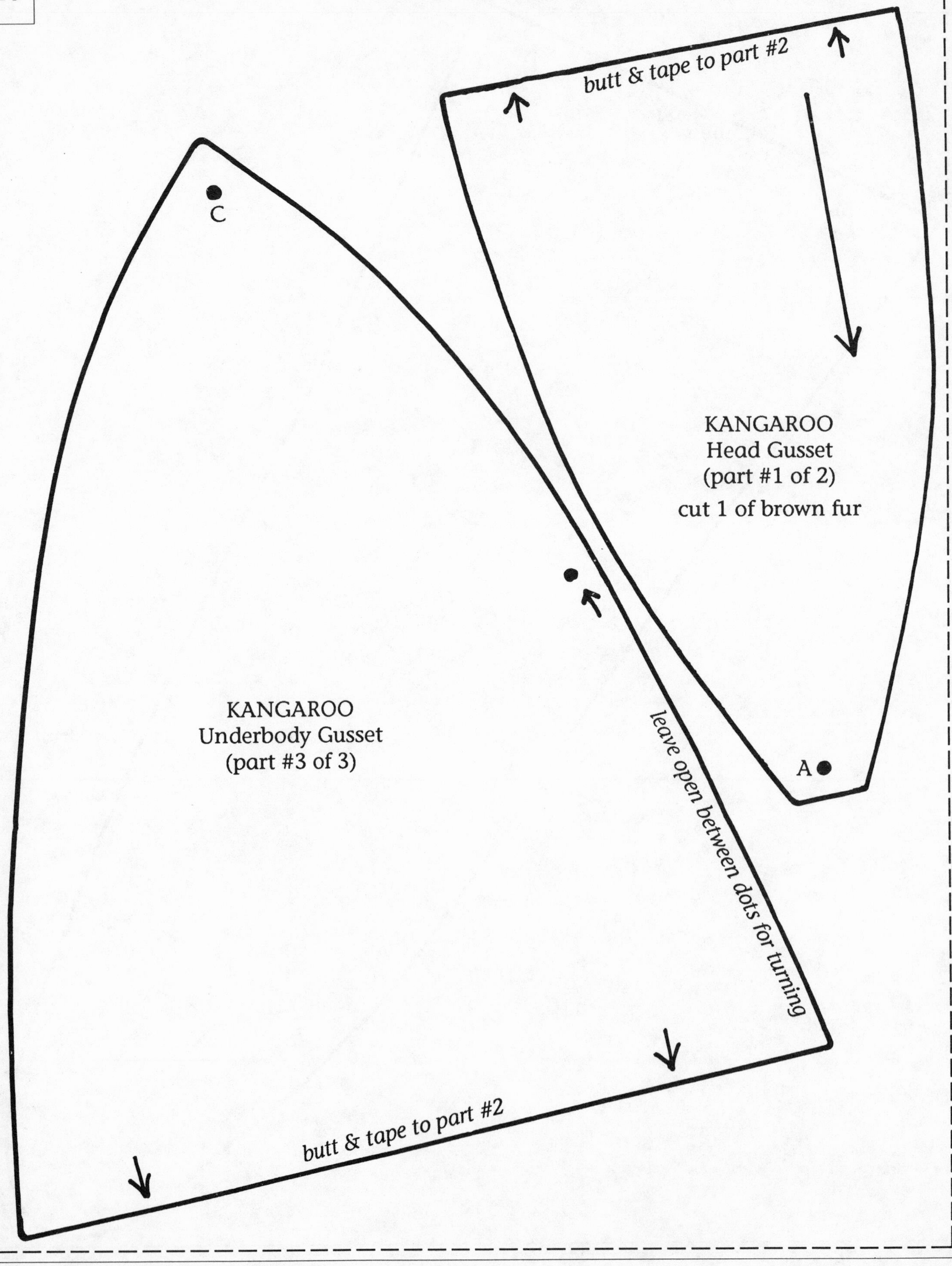

butt & tape to part #2

KANGAROO
Head Gusset
(part #1 of 2)

cut 1 of brown fur

A ●

leave open between dots for turning

C ●

KANGAROO
Underbody Gusset
(part #3 of 3)

butt & tape to part #2

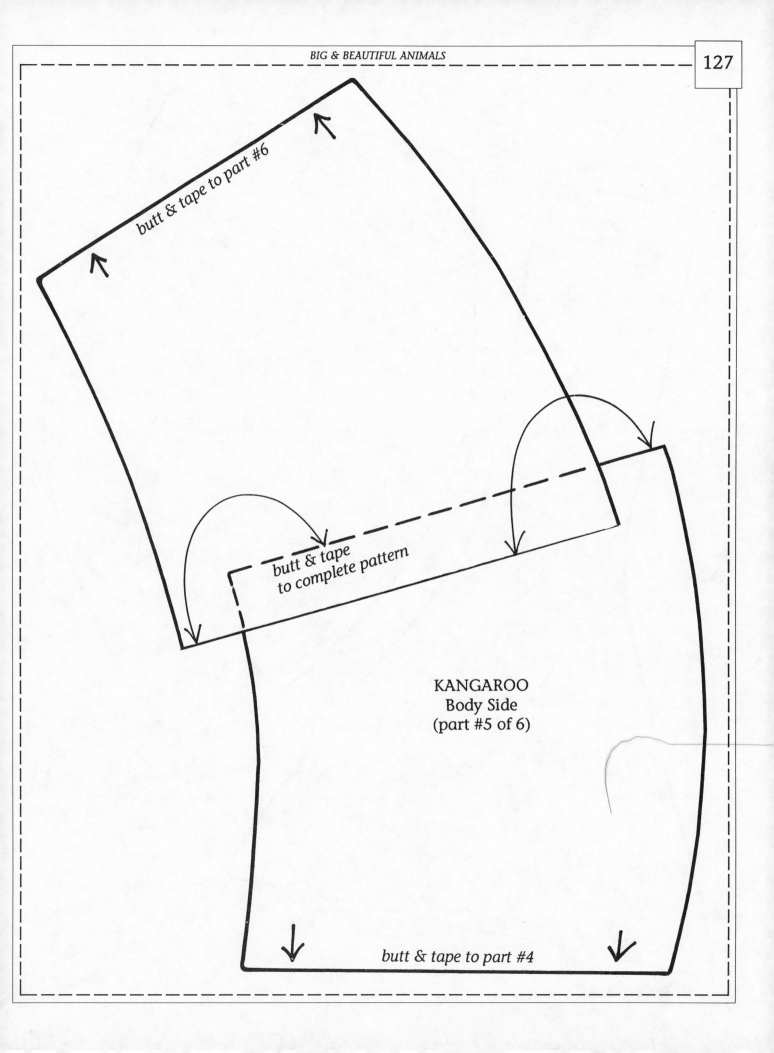

butt & tape to part #6

butt & tape
to complete pattern

KANGAROO
Body Side
(part #5 of 6)

butt & tape to part #4

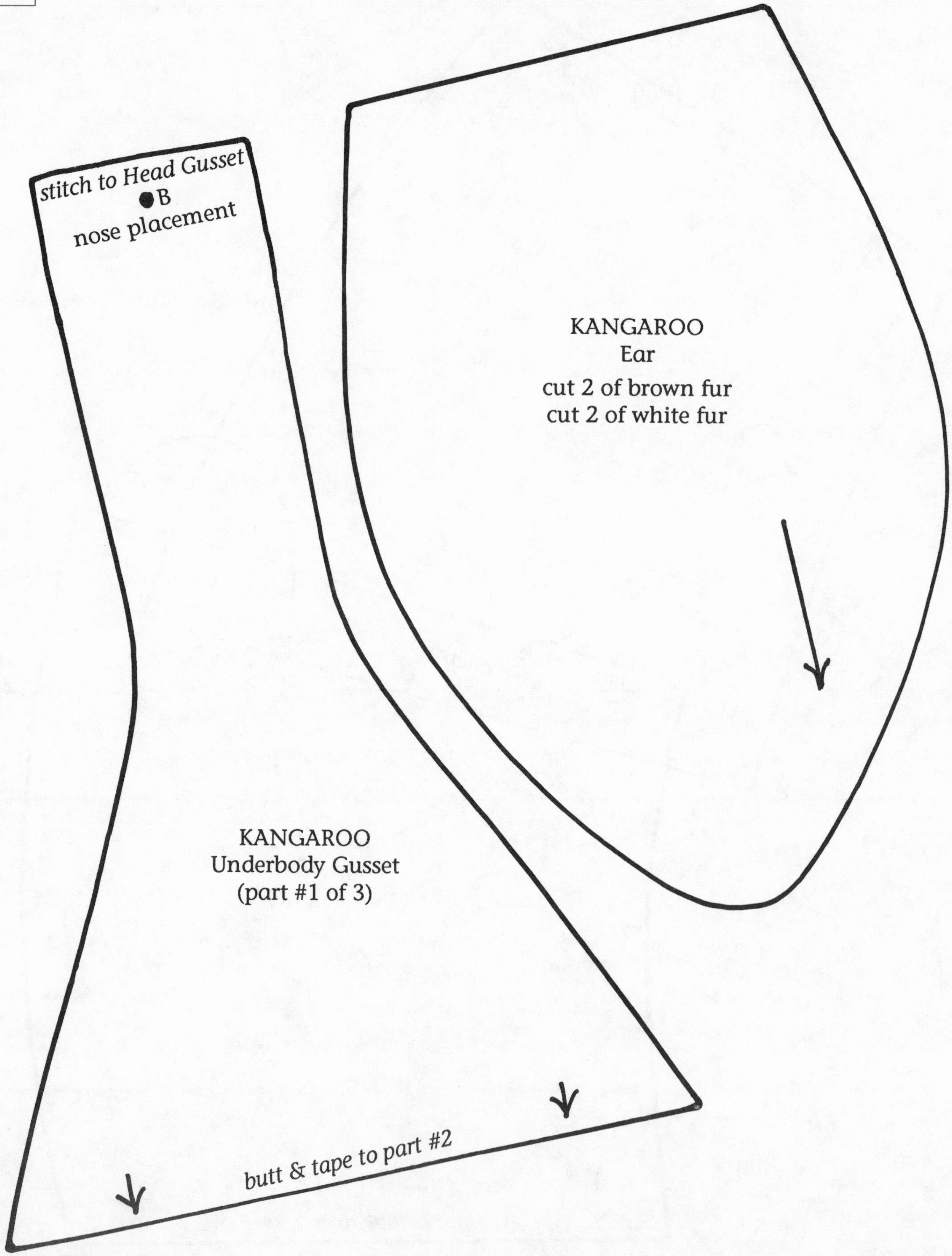

stitch to Head Gusset
● B
nose placement

KANGAROO
Ear
cut 2 of brown fur
cut 2 of white fur

KANGAROO
Underbody Gusset
(part #1 of 3)

butt & tape to part #2

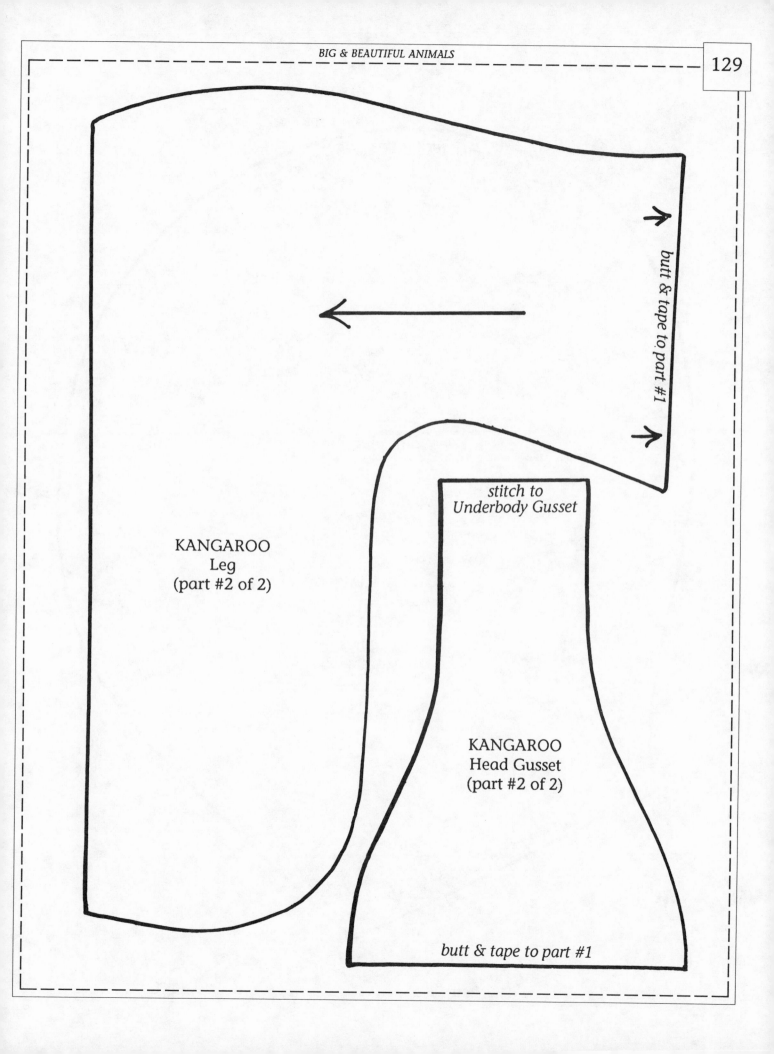

butt & tape to part #1

stitch to
Underbody Gusset

KANGAROO
Leg
(part #2 of 2)

KANGAROO
Head Gusset
(part #2 of 2)

butt & tape to part #1

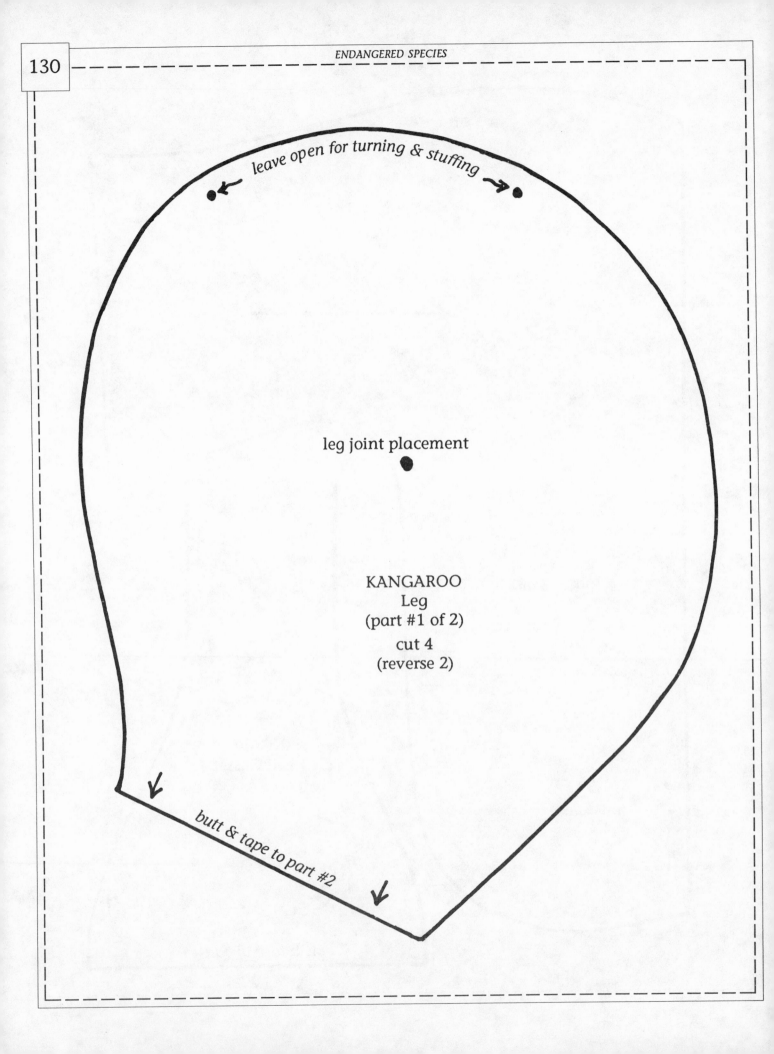

leave open for turning & stuffing

leg joint placement

KANGAROO
Leg
(part #1 of 2)

cut 4
(reverse 2)

butt & tape to part #2

leave open for
turning & stuffing

leg joint placement

KANGAROO
Arm
cut 4
(reverse 2)

butt & tape
to complete pattern

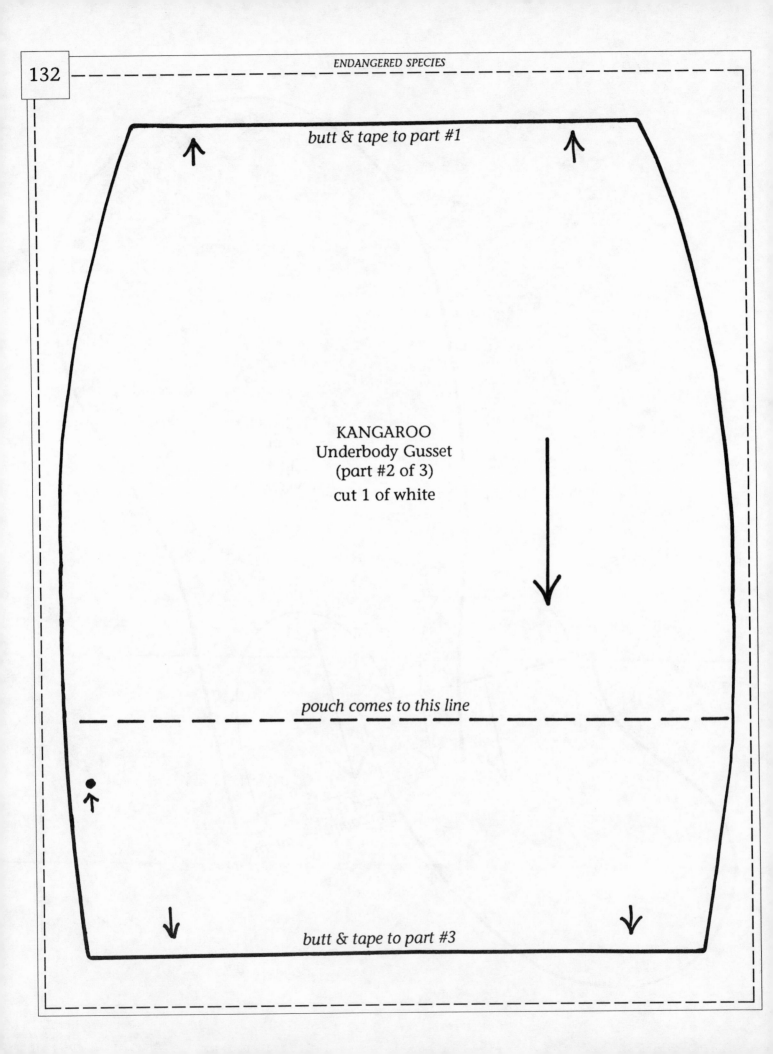

butt & tape to part #1

KANGAROO
Underbody Gusset
(part #2 of 3)
cut 1 of white

pouch comes to this line

butt & tape to part #3

KANGAROO
Pouch
cut 1 of white

leave open between dots for turning

place on fold

butt & tape
to complete pattern

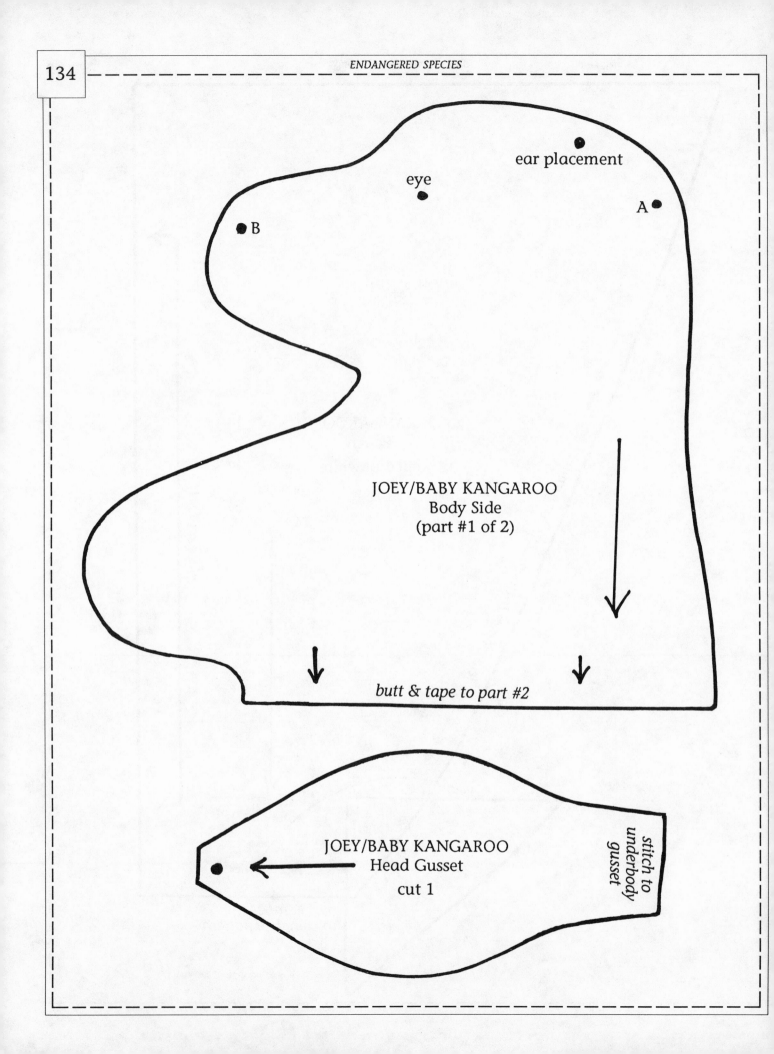

eye

ear placement

A

B

JOEY/BABY KANGAROO
Body Side
(part #1 of 2)

butt & tape to part #2

JOEY/BABY KANGAROO
Head Gusset
cut 1

stitch to underbody gusset

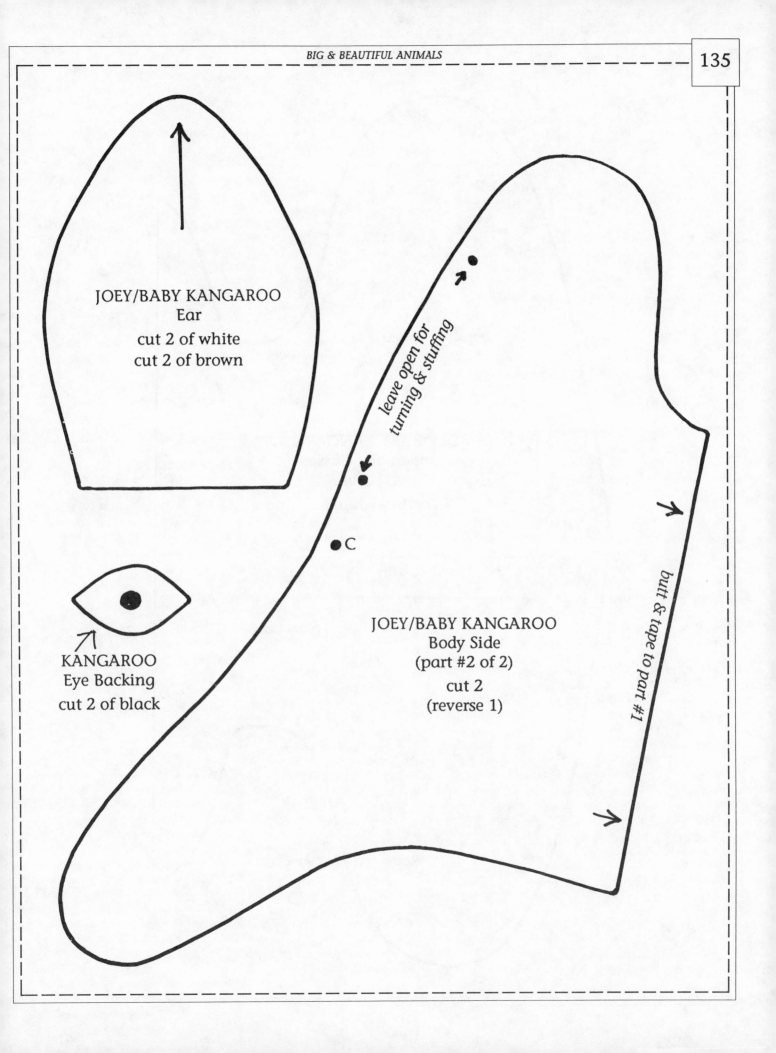

JOEY/BABY KANGAROO
Ear
cut 2 of white
cut 2 of brown

leave open for
turning & stuffing

• C

KANGAROO
Eye Backing
cut 2 of black

JOEY/BABY KANGAROO
Body Side
(part #2 of 2)
cut 2
(reverse 1)

butt & tape to part #1

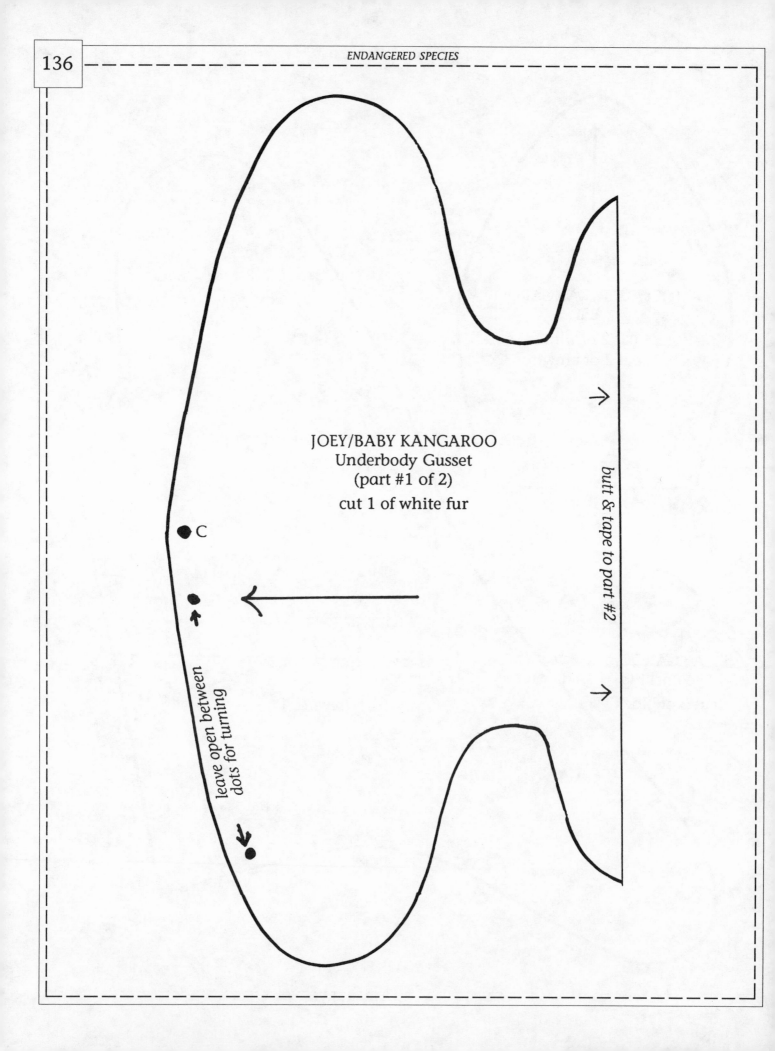

JOEY/BABY KANGAROO
Underbody Gusset
(part #1 of 2)
cut 1 of white fur

● C

leave open between
dots for turning

butt & tape to part #2

JOEY/BABY KANGAROO
Underbody Gusset
(part #2 of 2)

butt & tape to part #1

nose ● B

stitch to head gusset

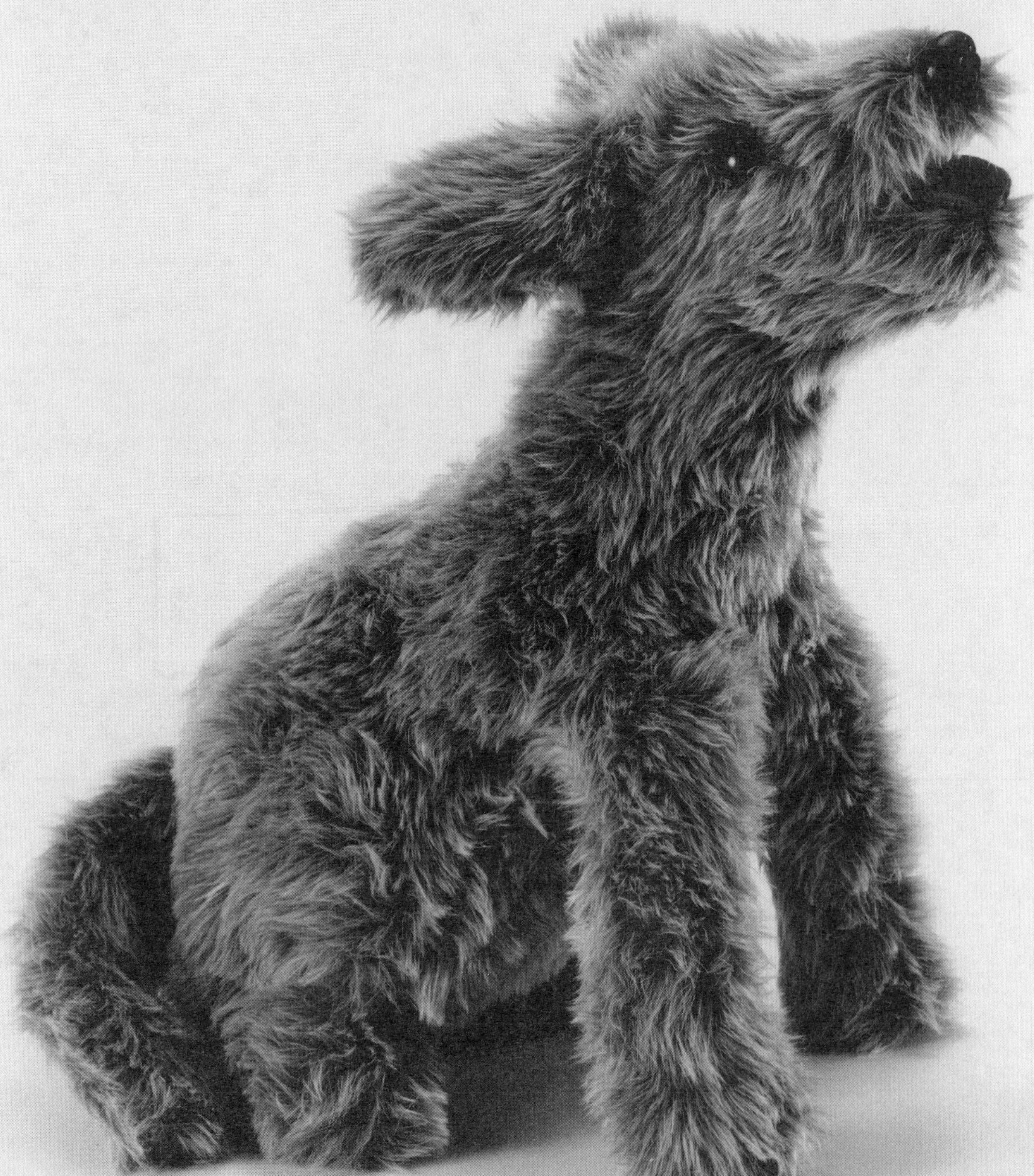

WOLF

The wolf is yet another animal who suffers when his lifestyle clashes with the needs of humans.
Here is an American emblem, the howling wolf, 17" tall and made of a variegated gray/brown fur.

MATERIALS

³/₄ yard fur (904P gray brown frost cubby bear fur from CR's Crafts, see Sources)

Matching thread

One pair 18 mm black safety eyes

One 30 mm black bear nose (from CR's Crafts or Carver's Eye, see Sources)

Beige felt

Red felt

Polyester fiberfill stuffing

INSTRUCTIONS

Note: All seam allowances are ¼".

Prepare, cut and mark the patterns as instructed in chapter 1.

1. Right sides facing, pin and stitch long center seam of the two underbody gusset pieces together.

2. Right sides together, pin inside front legs to underbody gusset as shown, matching dots L and M. Stitch.

3. Right sides facing, pin inside hind legs to underbody gusset, matching dots P and C. Stitch.

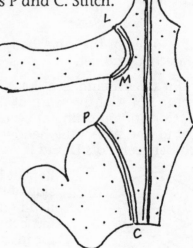

4. Right sides facing, pin and stitch the two body side pieces from dot A at nose down to mouth . . . . and from dot B at chin up to mouth.

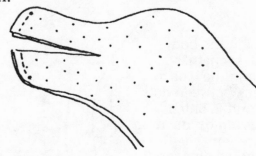

5. Right sides facing, pin one side of underbody gusset to one body side from dot B at chin, down the front of the front leg, up the back of the front leg, under the belly, around the back leg to dot C under tail. Stitch.

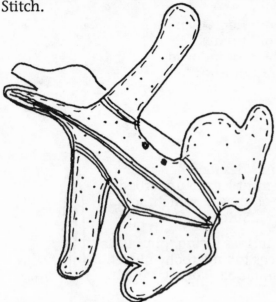

Do the same for the other body side/side of underbody gusset.

6. Right sides facing, pin dot A on head gusset to dot A at the seam at the wolf's nose. Continue pinning one side of the head gusset to one side of the head to dots E. Stitch between dots D and E.

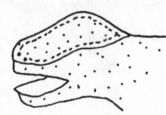

Repeat for the other side of the body side/head gusset. The gap left between dots D is for insertion of the nose.

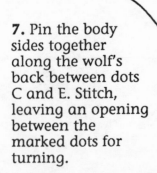

7. Pin the body sides together along the wolf's back between dots C and E. Stitch, leaving an opening between the marked dots for turning.

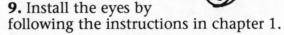

8. Matching dots on beige felt mouth to seams, pin felt mouth piece to the mouth opening. Stitch.

9. Install the eyes by following the instructions in chapter 1.

10. Starting with the front legs, stuff the wolf. Pay careful attention to the tops of the front legs. This tends to be a weak spot that seems to resist firm stuffing.

11. Right sides facing, pin two ear pieces together. Stitch, leaving the straight edges open. Repeat for the other two ear pieces. Turn right side out.

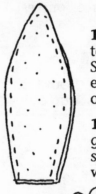

12. Pin the two tail pieces together, right sides facing. Stitch, leaving the straight edges open. Turn right side out.

13. Referring to the photograph and illustration, hand stitch the ears to the wolf's head.

14. Hand stitch the tail to the place where the underbody gusset comes to a point above the hind legs as shown.

15. Pin the two red felt tongue pieces together. Stitch, leaving the straight edges open. Turn right side out.

Turn ¼" at the straight edges to the inside. Whipstitch. Hand stitch to the crease at the back of the mouth.

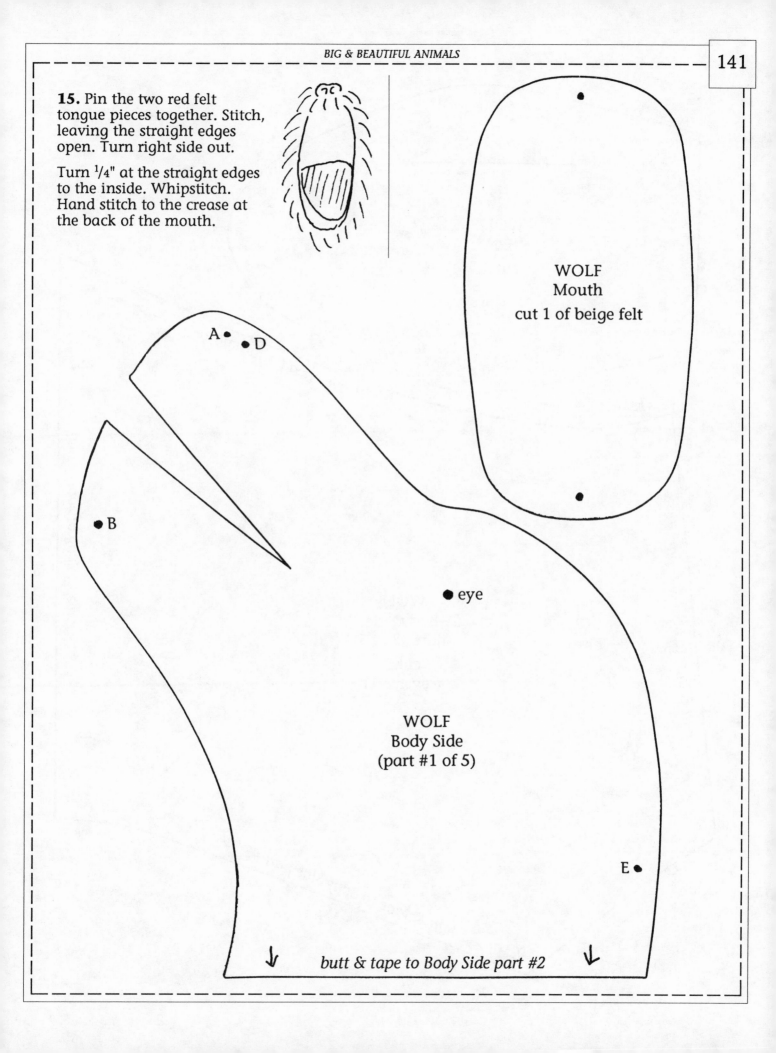

WOLF
Mouth
cut 1 of beige felt

A • • D

• B

• eye

WOLF
Body Side
(part #1 of 5)

E •

↓   *butt & tape to Body Side part #2*   ↓

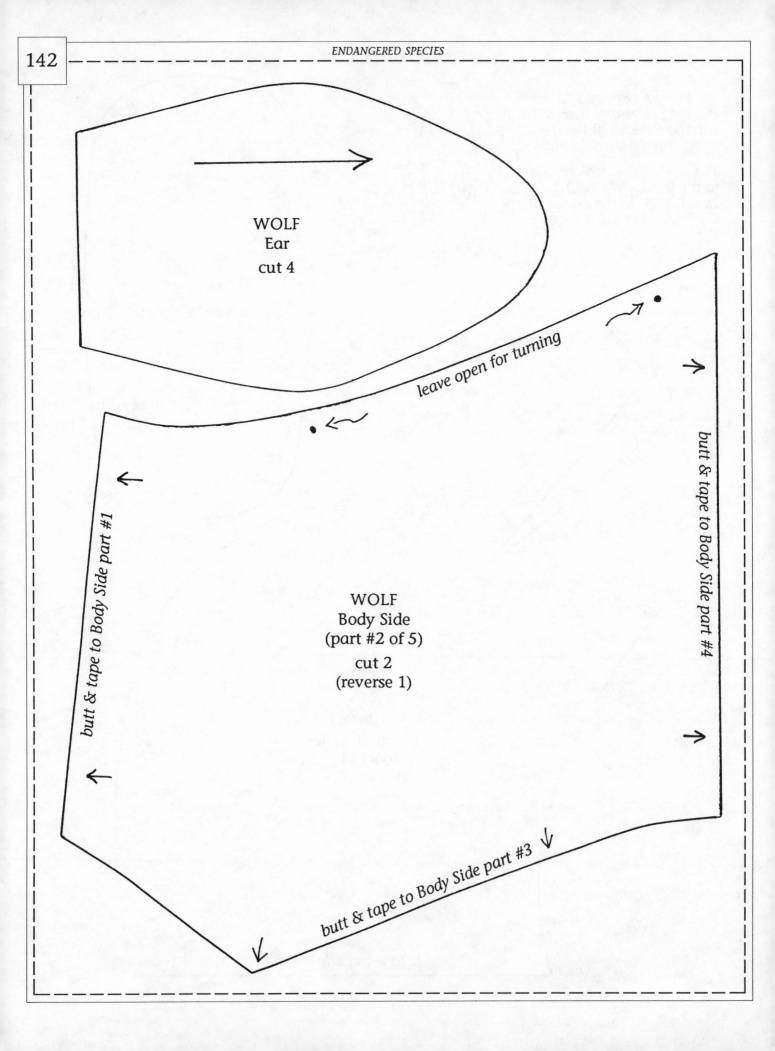

WOLF
Ear
cut 4

leave open for turning

butt & tape to Body Side part #1

butt & tape to Body Side part #4

WOLF
Body Side
(part #2 of 5)

cut 2
(reverse 1)

butt & tape to Body Side part #3

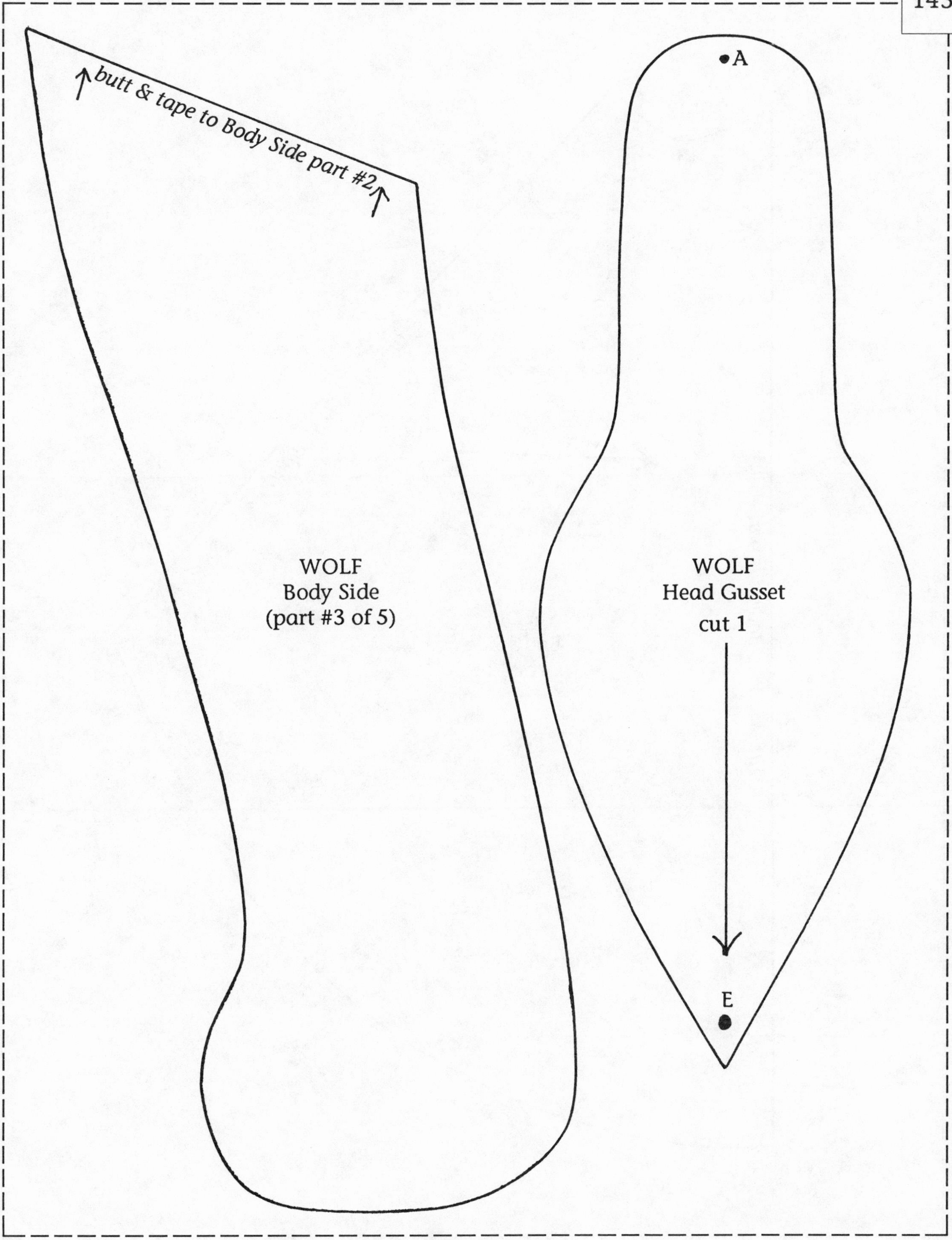

↑ *butt & tape to Body Side part #2* ↑

WOLF
Body Side
(part #3 of 5)

• A

WOLF
Head Gusset
cut 1

E
•

butt & tape to Body Side part #2

butt & tape to Body Side part #5

WOLF
Body Side
(part #4 of 5)

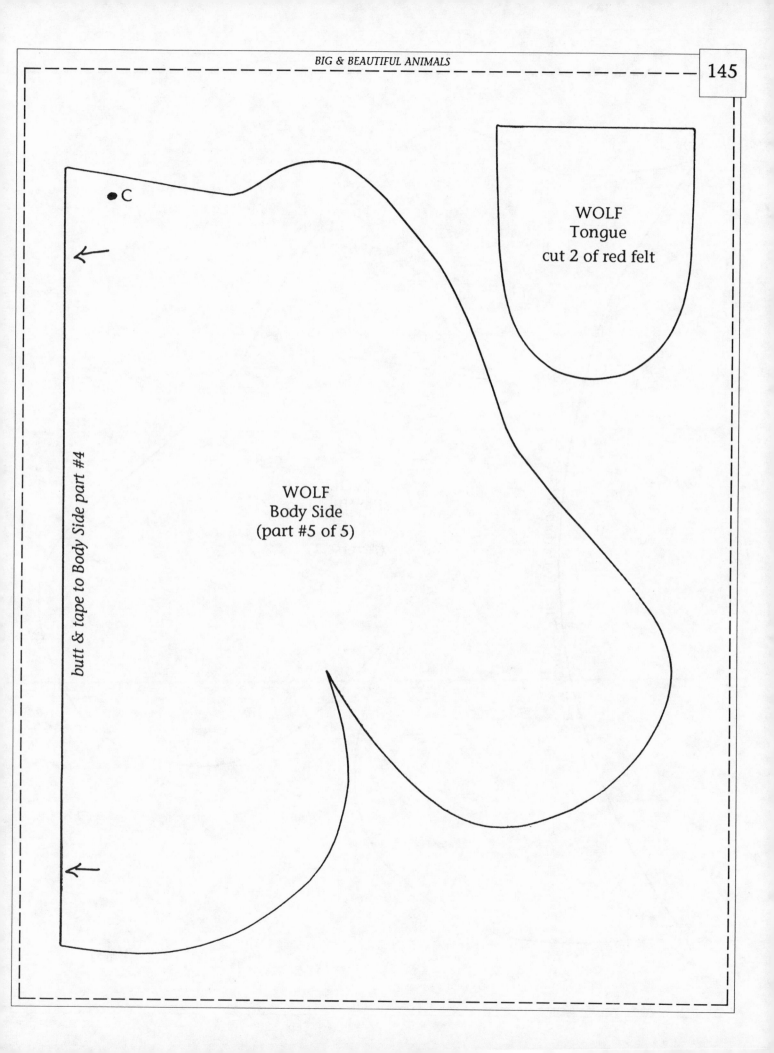

● C

butt & tape to Body Side part #4

WOLF
Tongue
cut 2 of red felt

WOLF
Body Side
(part #5 of 5)

• C

ease to fit — stitch to Underbody Gusset

WOLF
Inside Hind Leg
cut 2
(reverse 1)

• P

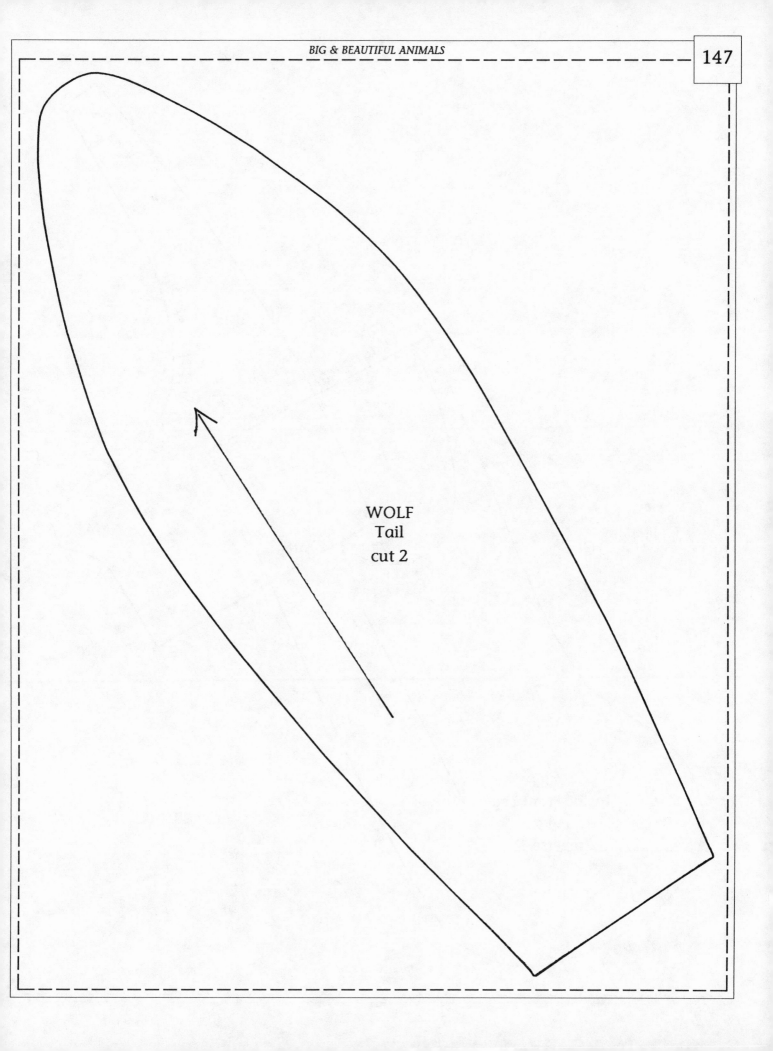

WOLF
Tail
cut 2

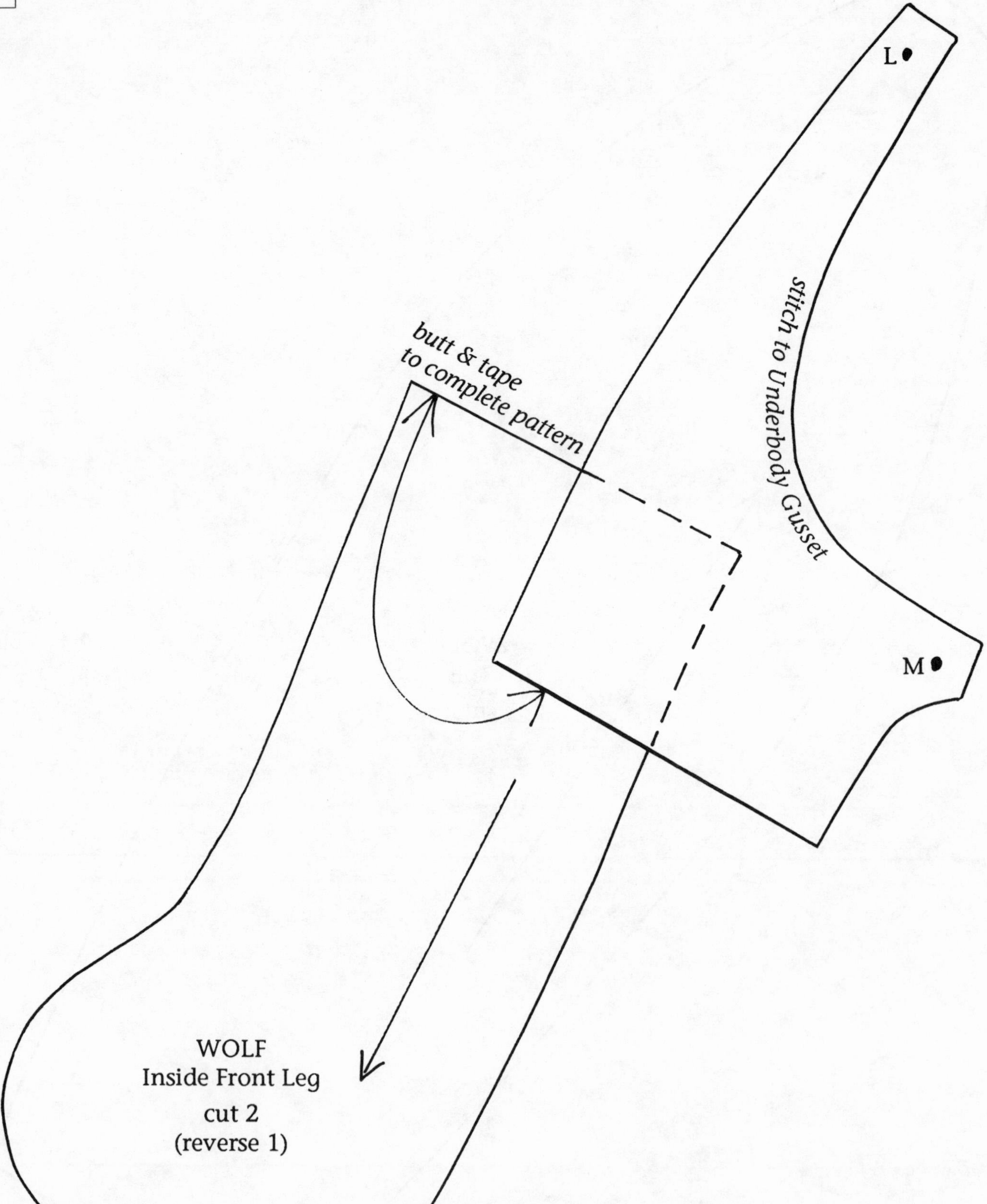

148

L ●

stitch to Underbody Gusset

butt & tape
to complete pattern

M ●

WOLF
Inside Front Leg
cut 2
(reverse 1)

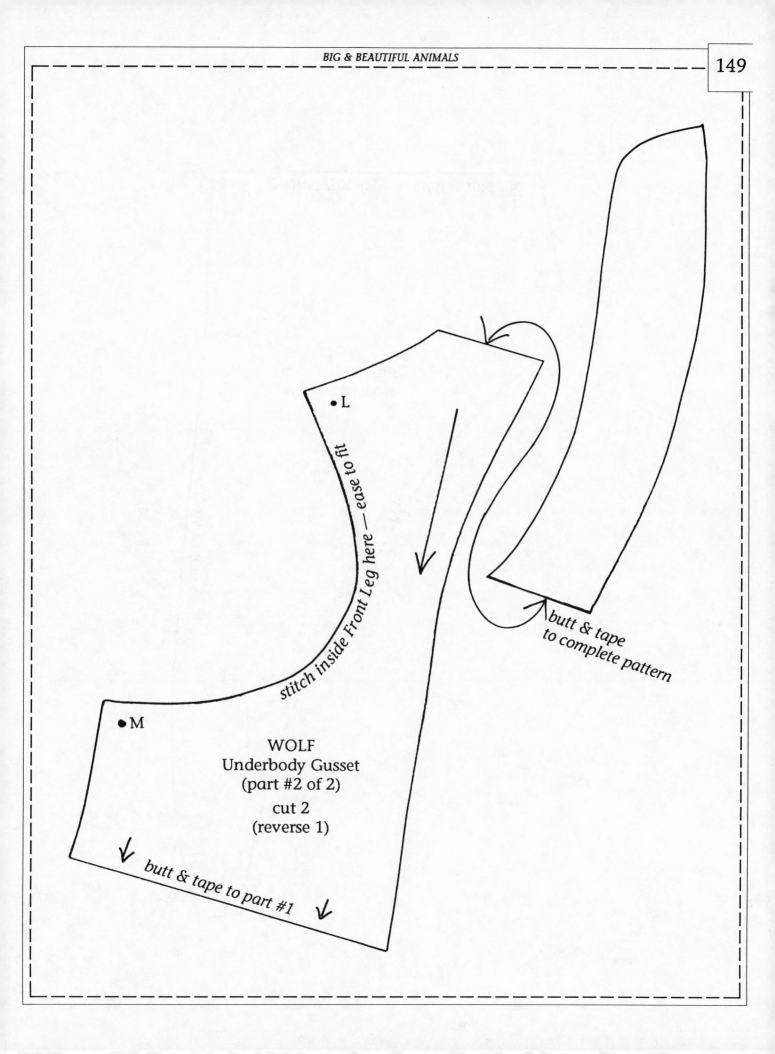

• L

stitch inside Front Leg here — ease to fit

butt & tape to complete pattern

• M

WOLF
Underbody Gusset
(part #2 of 2)
cut 2
(reverse 1)

butt & tape to part #1

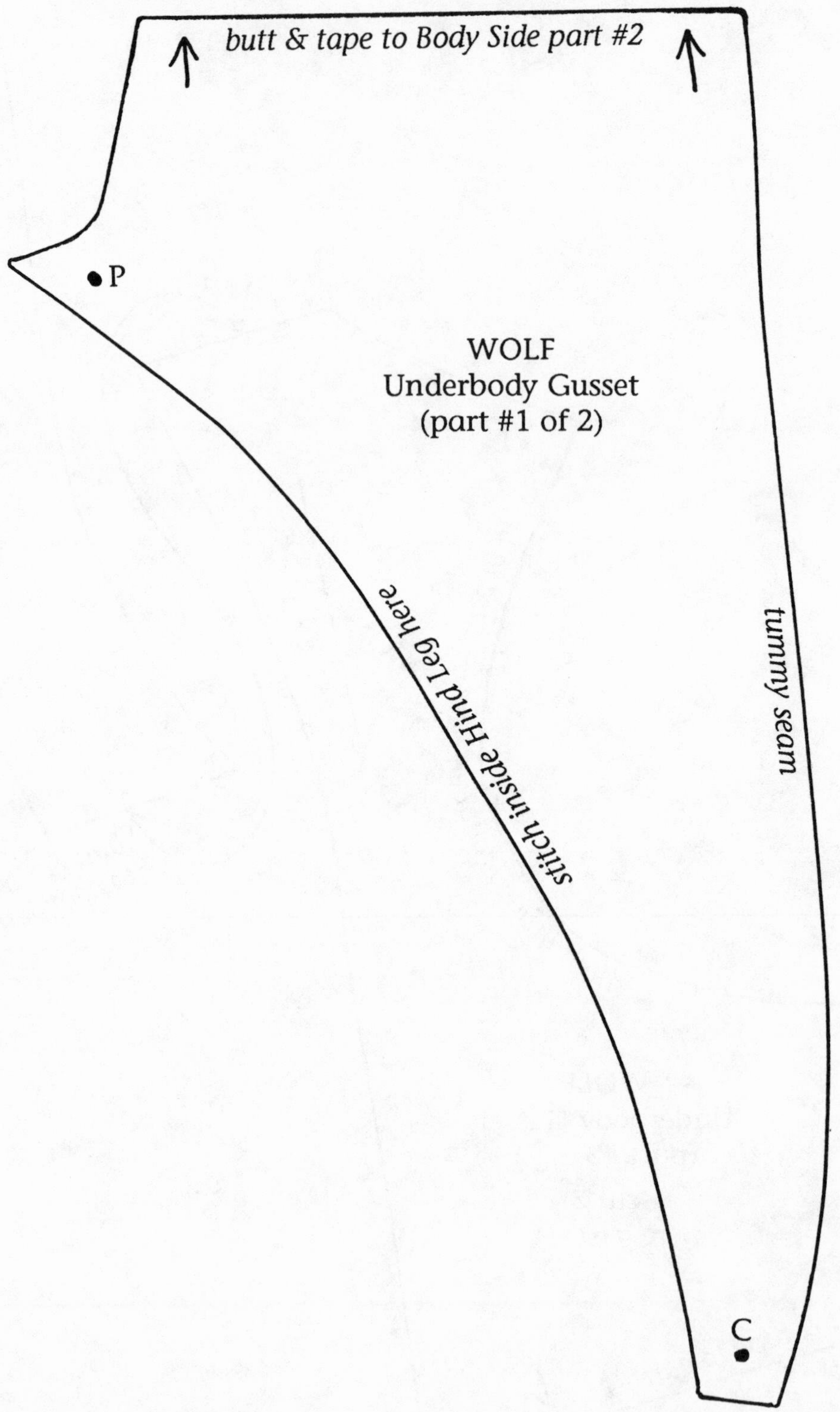

butt & tape to Body Side part #2

●P

WOLF
Underbody Gusset
(part #1 of 2)

stitch inside Hind Leg here

tummy seam

C
●

♥ ♥ ♥ ♥ ♥

Endangered Species Appliques

♥ ♥ ♥ ♥ ♥

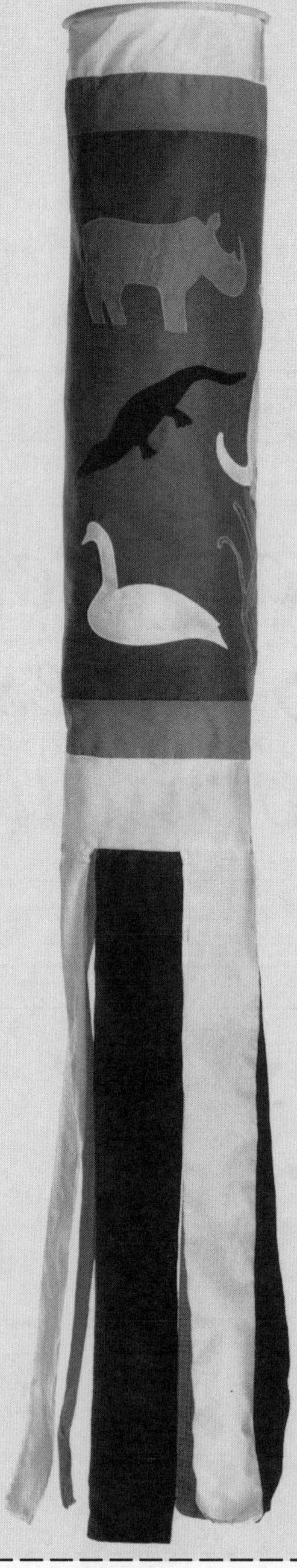

WINDSOCK

Windsocks are easy to construct and inexpensive to make. Purchase the nylon taffeta or ripstop nylon fabric at your local fabric store. Swivels, plastic tubing, and fishing line are hardware store finds. All can be ordered through the mail (see Sources).

A nifty invention, Wonder-Under™ by Pellon, is a fusible web backed with a peel-off paper. It makes applique a breeze! Find it at your local fabric store.

These easy instructions will guide you through the applique process, even if this is your first time. To maintain the beauty of your creation, hang away from direct sunlight.

Instructions are given below for satin stitching the appliques to the windsock. An easier method is to apply fabric paint over the unfinished raw edges in place of the stitching. This is a quicker and easier method, though perhaps not as strong or long lasting as stitching. If you choose to use the fabric paint, purchase it in the easy applicator bottles at your local crafts store or from the source listed at the end of the book. Apply the paint at the point in the instructions when you are directed to satin stitch.

MATERIALS

⅝ yard kelly green windsock fabric

⅓ yard yellow windsock fabric

¼ yard red windsock fabric

¼ yard each of four other colors for streamers. I used pink, purple, blue, and magenta.

½ yard Wonder-Under™

Thread or fabric paint to match each of the applique fabric colors

⅝ yard windsock tubing
(If you use hardware store tubing, also get a dowel to fit inside.
All you need is a ½" long piece of it.)

One swivel

Fishing line

INSTRUCTIONS

Note: All seam allowances are ¼".

1. Cut the fabrics as directed below. Refer to the illustrations below to see where the pieces fit.

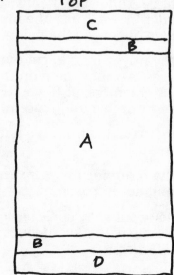

1 kelly green 19½" x 21½" for windsock body/applique background (piece a)
2 red 2½" x 21½" bands (piece b)
1 yellow 4½" x 21½" band for top of windsock (piece c)
1 yellow 3½" x 21½" band for bottom edge of windsock body (piece d)
7 streamers of 7 different colors, each 3" x 23"

2. Prevent the raw edges of the nylon from unraveling by searing them with a candle or oil lamp flame. Experiment on a scrap until you become adept at melting just the bare edge of the fabric. An alternative is to apply Fray Check™.

Note: In their finished form, appliques will be reversed.

3. Lay the kelly green 19½" x 21½" windsock body/applique background on your work surface, right side up, long measurement horizontal. Turn to the animal applique shapes following these instructions. Decide which animals you wish to use on your windsock. I used seven. You may certainly use fewer, or fit more by overlapping them a bit.

Paper side up, place the Wonder-Under™ over an animal applique design in the book. Trace the design. Cut around the design roughly, ¼" or more to the outside of the design lines. Decide which colors each of the animals will be. Following the instructions on the Wonder-Under™, fuse the rough side of the Wonder-Under™ to the nylon.

Cut along the traced lines to cut out the animal shapes. Arrange them on the background, cut some more, until you are satisfied with their number and placement.

Peel the paper backing from the back of the appliques.

Following the manufacturer's instructions, fuse the appliques in place.

Note: You may want to try appliqueing an animal on a scrap of windsock fabric to work out your satin stitch.

To applique the animal shapes, turn to the satin stitch instructions on page 12 in chapter 1. Use thread colors to match the appliques.

4. Stitch a red band to each 21½"-long edge of the kelly green windsock body. Stitch the wider (4" x 21½") yellow band to the top red band and the 3½" x 21½" yellow band to the bottom red band.

5. Pin the streamers to the bottom of the narrower yellow band, side by side but not overlapping. They should take up the full bottom edge with a ¼" seam allowance remaining on each end. Stitch.

6. Fold the windsock in half vertically, right side in. Stitch the vertical side seam. Press (permanent press, no steam) the seam allowances to one side.

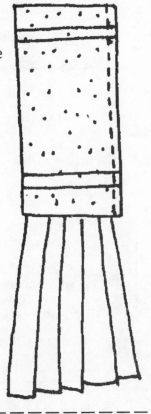

7. Press top edge ¼" to inside. Press another ¾" to inside. Topstitch close to bottom fold, leaving a ½" gap in the stitching, backstitching at each side of the gap.

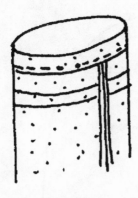

8. Turn windsock right side out. Measure around the circumference of the top of the windsock. Divide the measurement into three. Mark these thirds just below the bottom fold created in step 7. Make ¼"-long buttonholes at these markings. (The buttonholes are optional. You can just run fishing line through the markings in step 10 below. Buttonholes will be stronger though.)

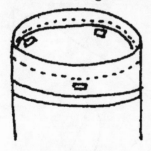

9. Cut a piece of the tubing ½" less than the circumference measured in step 8. Insert one end into the casing and run it through. Cut a piece of the tubing insert supplied with the tubing or dowel you bought (½" long). Insert into one end of the tubing and then the other to form a connection. Topstitch the gap in the casing stitching closed. If you can't get the tubing under the sewing machine foot, remove the foot, slide the tubing filled casing to the other side, and put the foot back on. Or, leave the gap unstitched.

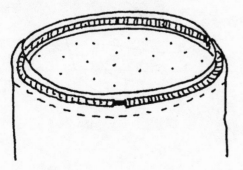

10. Cut three pieces of fishing line, each 20" long. Attach them as illustrated. If you didn't make buttonholes in step 8, thread the fishing line onto a large-eyed needle and run it through the markings. (Seal the holes with Fray Check™ when the windsock is complete). Either way, complete according to the illustrations below. Seal the knots carefully with a flame.

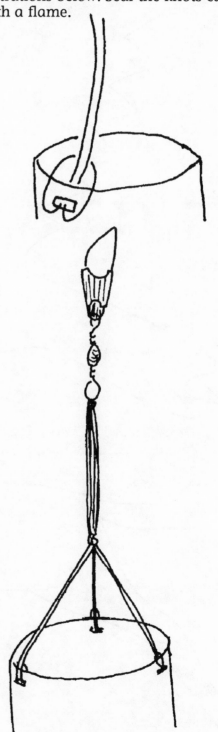

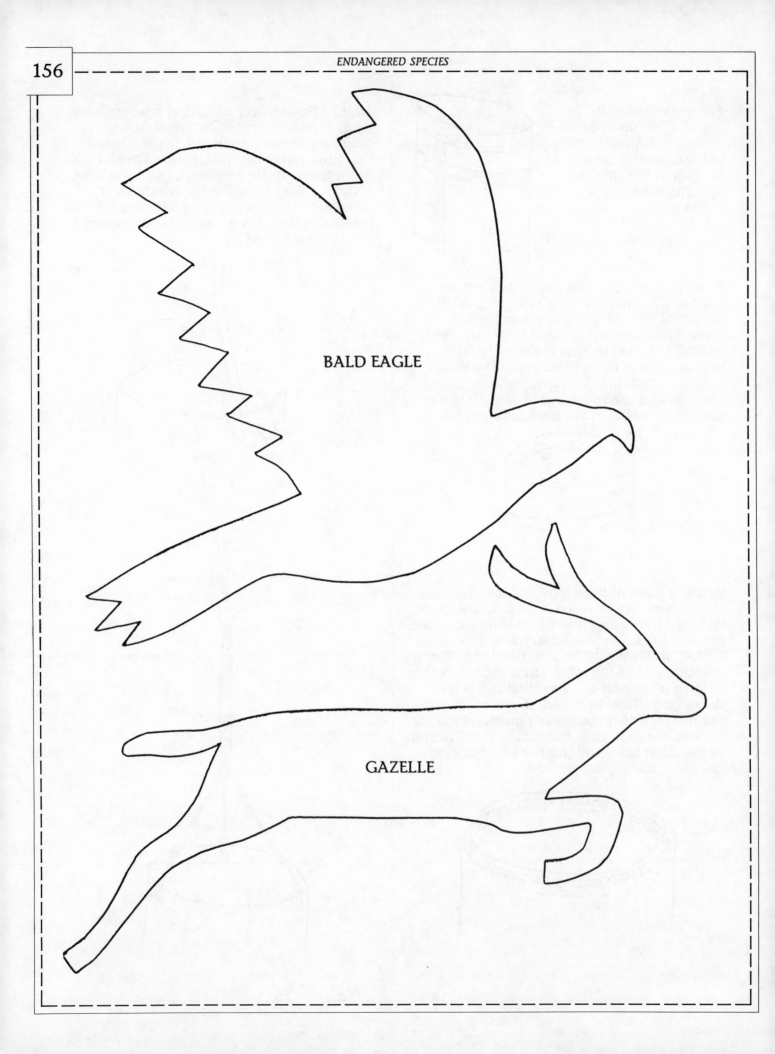

BALD EAGLE

GAZELLE

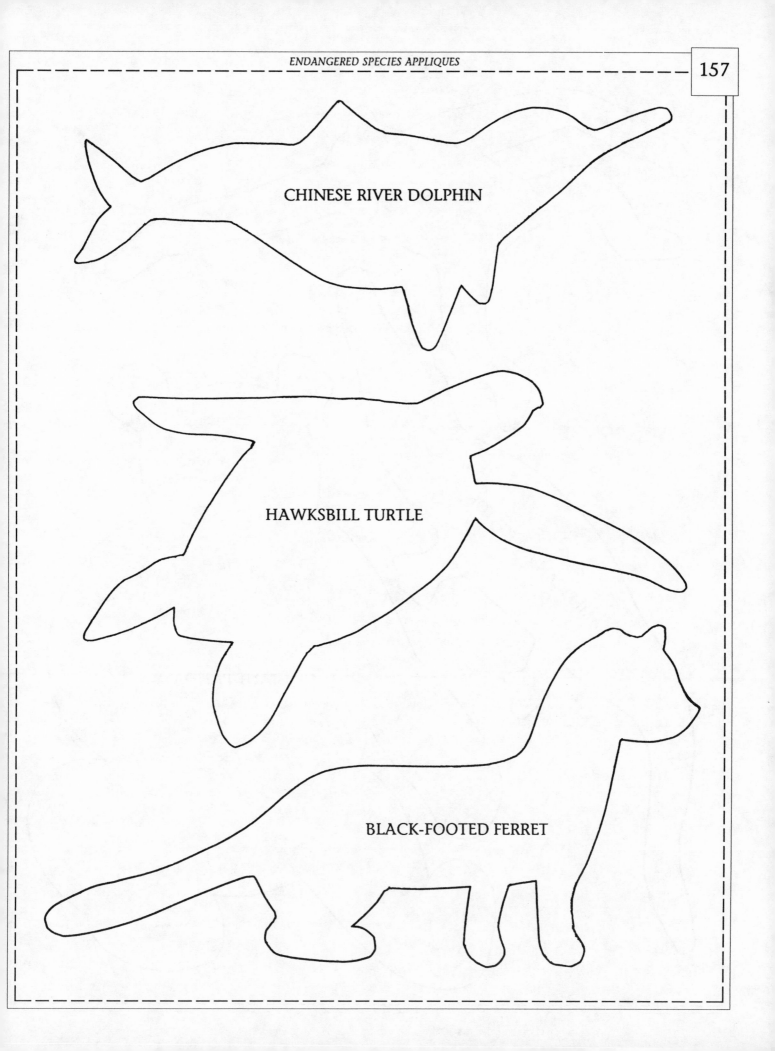

CHINESE RIVER DOLPHIN

HAWKSBILL TURTLE

BLACK-FOOTED FERRET

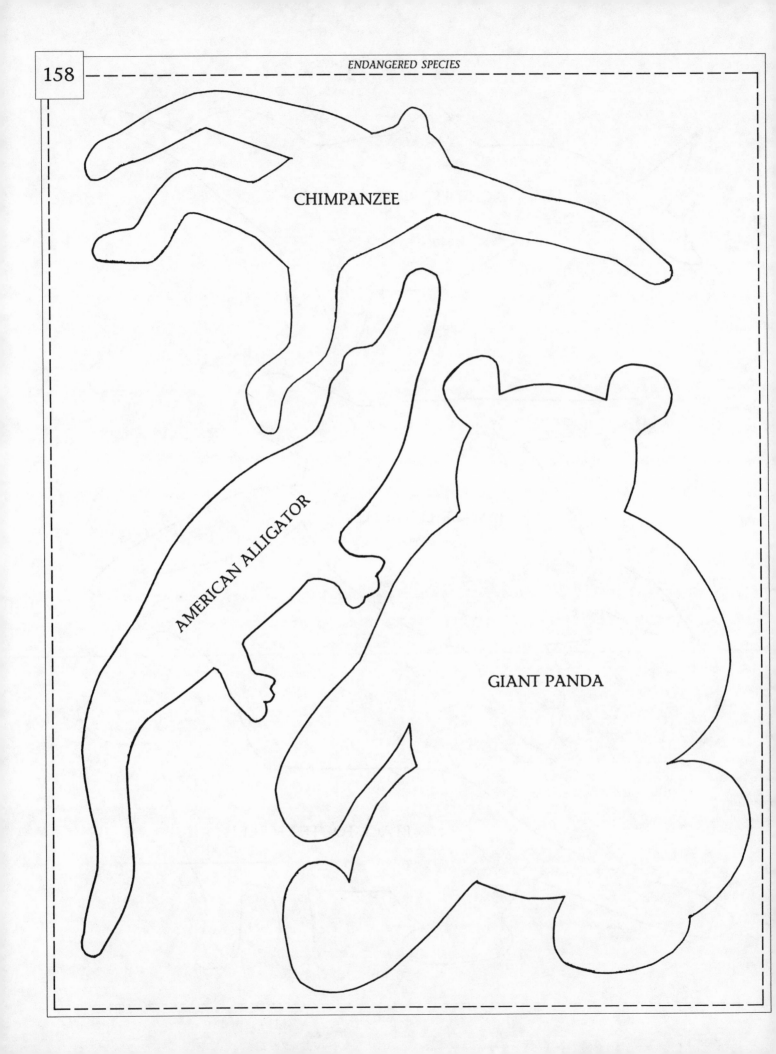

CHIMPANZEE

AMERICAN ALLIGATOR

GIANT PANDA

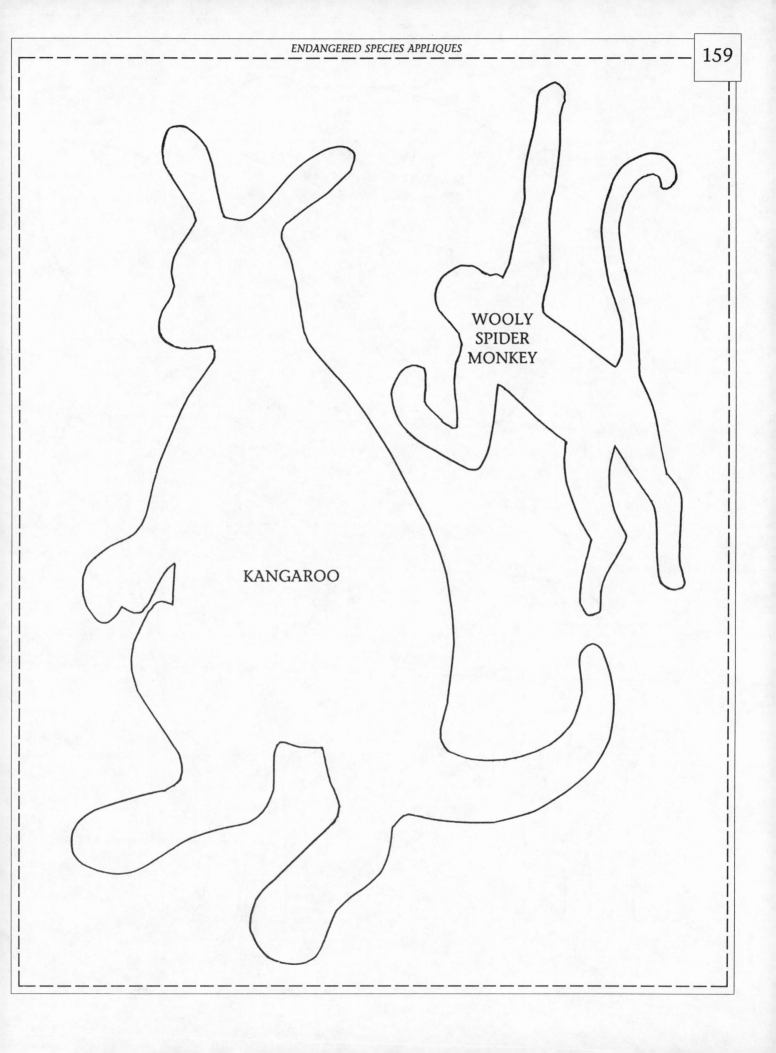

KANGAROO

WOOLY
SPIDER
MONKEY

SCARLET
MACAW

WHALE

WOLF

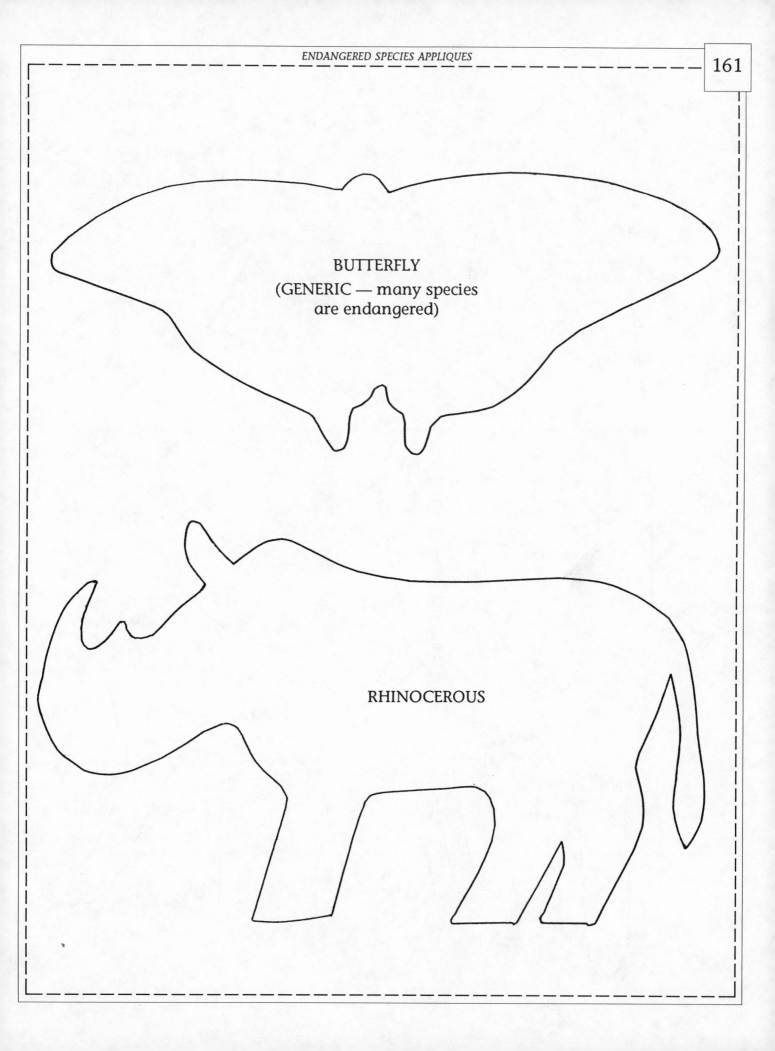

BUTTERFLY
(GENERIC — many species
are endangered)

RHINOCEROUS

MANATEE

TRUMPETER SWAN

CHEETAH

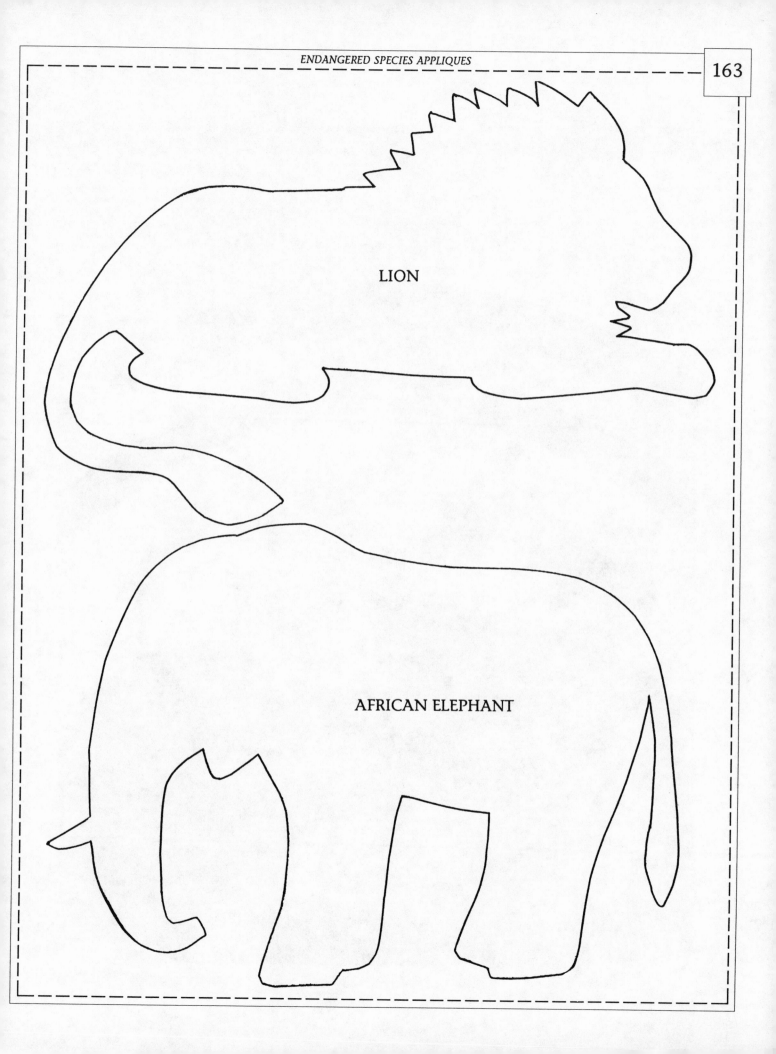

LION

AFRICAN ELEPHANT

HOUSE BANNER

Decorate your house, indoors or out, with a planet full of colorful animals. This quick and easy project hangs from a wooden dowel decorated with finials (see Sources).

Look for nylon taffeta or ripstop nylon at your local fabric store, or turn to the back of the book for mail order sources.

Instructions are given below for satin stitching the appliques to the banner. An easier method is to apply fabric paint over the unfinished raw edges in place of the stitching. This is a quicker and easier method, though not as strong or long lasting. If you choose to use the fabric paint, purchase it in the easy applicator bottles at your local crafts store or from the source listed at the end of the book. Apply the paint at the point in the instructions when you are directed to satin stitch.

MATERIALS

1 yard sky blue nylon taffeta
5/8 yard medium blue for the earth
1/2 yard medium green for the continents
1/2 yard each red, yellow, and kelly green for the rainbow
Scraps of other colorful nylon taffeta for animal appliques
Matching thread or fabric paint for all colors
3 yards Wonder-Under™
3 yards tear away stabilizer
One 1" dowel
2 finials (see Sources)
Stain and varnish for dowel and finials

INSTRUCTIONS

Note: All seam allowances are 1/4".

1. Cut a rectangle 42" x 30" from the sky blue fabric. This will be the background of the banner.

2. As instructed in chapter 1, make patterns for the earth, continents, rainbow, and eight or more animal appliques. Don't forget the eagle which will soar in the rainbow. Trace around the patterns onto the paper (smooth, not bumpy) side of the Wonder-Under™. Cut the shapes outside of the marked lines.

Fuse all of the Wonder-Under™ to the wrong sides of the colored fabrics. Cut out the shapes along the lines traced on the Wonder-Under™.

3. Lay the sky blue banner background on a flat surface with the short width horizontal. Remove the paper backing from the medium blue earth. Pin it to the sky blue banner background matching the bottom edges to those of the background. Place on an ironing board and fuse.

Remove the paper backing from the green continents. Fuse them to the blue earth.

Following the instructions on page 12 in chapter 1, satin stitch the raw edges of the earth and the planets to the background. There is no need to satin stitch any raw edges along the outside edges of the banner. These will be finished later.

4. Remove the paper backings from the three rainbow pieces. Pin the yellow bottom band to the sky blue banner background. The bottom side edges of the band should be 8" above the earth applique.

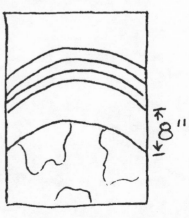

Fuse, removing the pins as you go so as not to iron over them.

Place the red band above the yellow band overlapping 1/8". Pin. Fuse.

Repeat for the green band.

Satin stitch over the raw edges with thread to match the darkest band being stitched.

5. Turn 3/8" of one short edge of banner to the back. Do the same for the other short edge. Topstitch. Repeat for the two long sides.

Turn 2" of the top of the banner to the back. Topstitch over the first topstitching to form a casing for the rod.

6. Remove the paper backings from the animal appliques. Arrange them on the banner. Pin. Fuse. Satin stitch in place with matching thread.

7. Cut the dowel to 32". Sand the dowel and finials. Stain. Allow to dry. Varnish. Set aside to dry.

Put one finial on one end of the dowel. Insert the other end of the dowel into the casing. Install the remaining finial.

To hang, put two screw eyes, 31" apart, into the wall at the desired height for the top of the banner. Tie cording to screw eyes and around the rod.

ASSEMBLING EARTH & CONTINENTS:

EARTH

1. Butt & tape to form half of patterns as shown

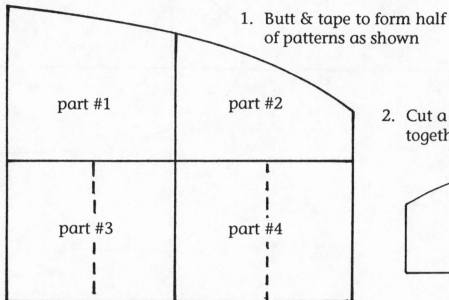

part #1

part #2

part #3

part #4

2. Cut a mirror image & tape together to form full pattern

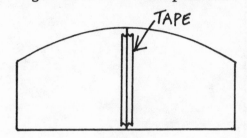

TAPE

CONTINENT OF EUROPE & AFRICA

CONTINENT OF NORTH AMERICA

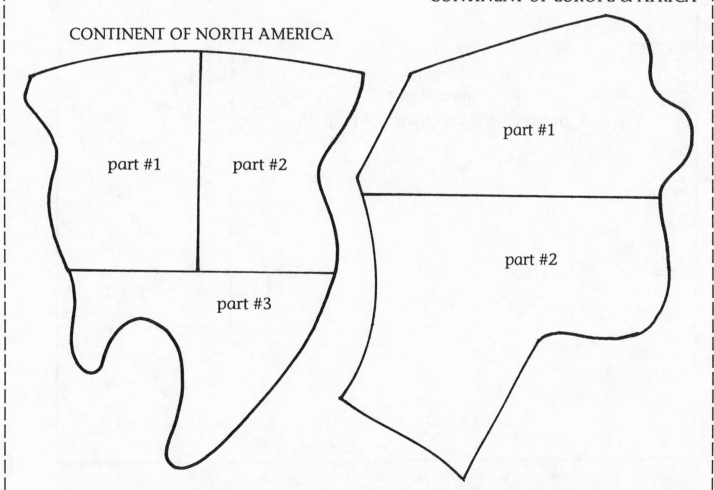

part #1

part #2

part #3

part #1

part #2

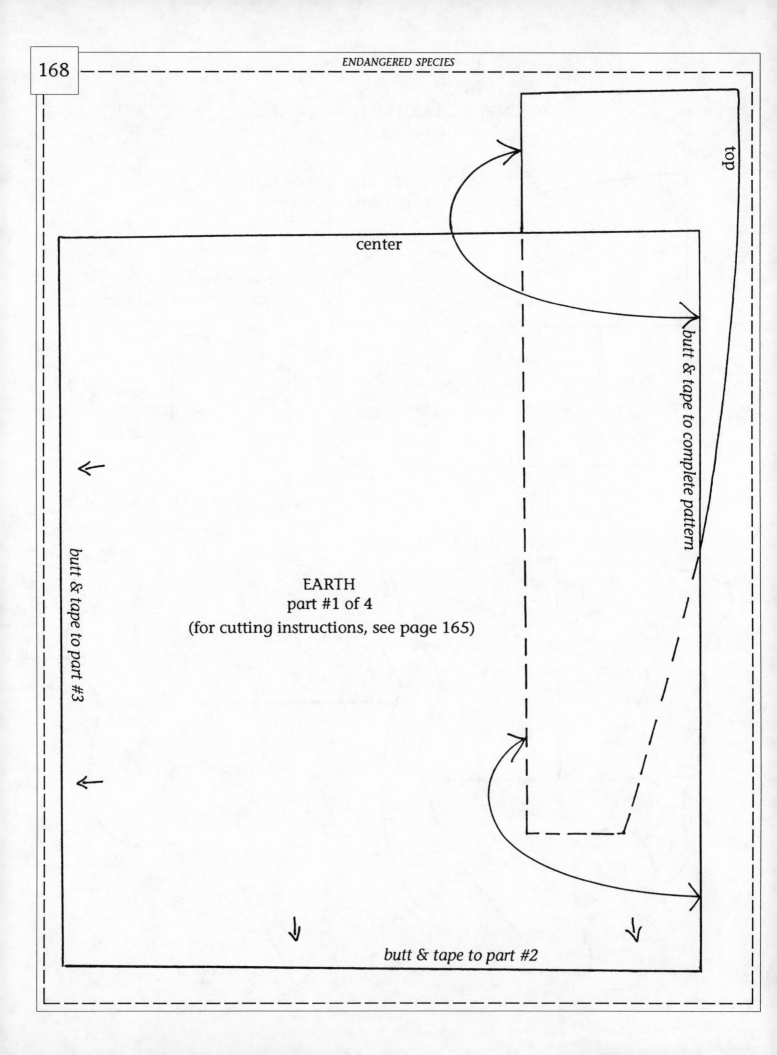

top

center

butt & tape to complete pattern

butt & tape to part #3

EARTH
part #1 of 4
(for cutting instructions, see page 165)

butt & tape to part #2

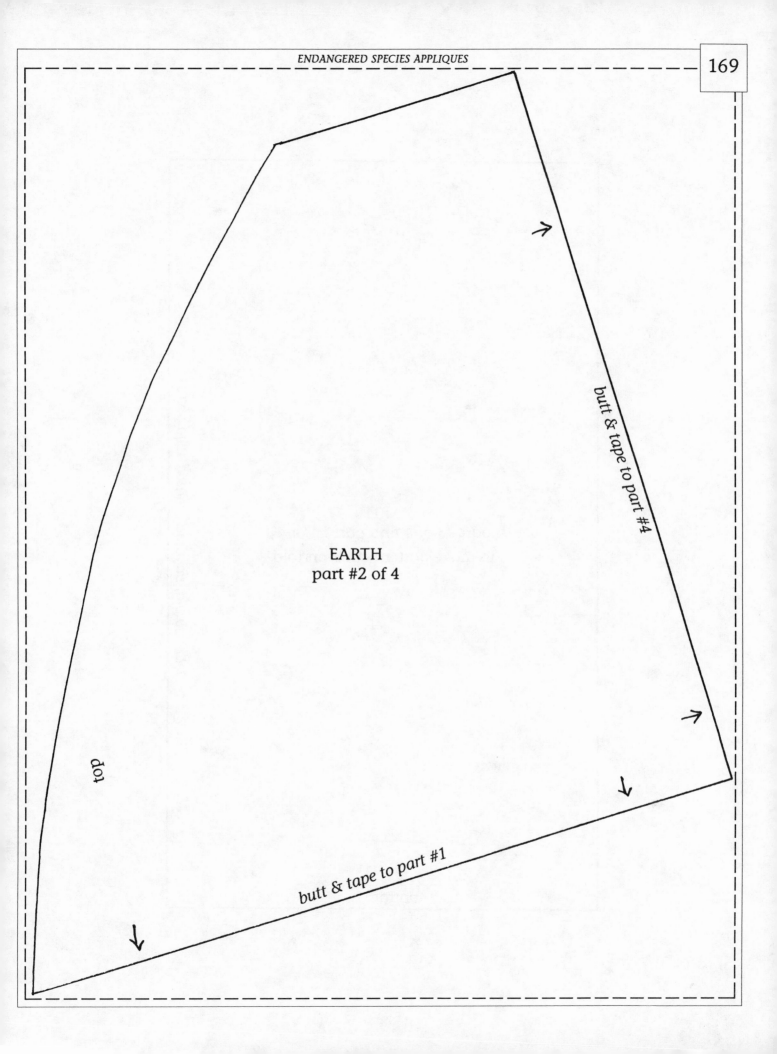

EARTH
part #2 of 4

butt & tape to part #4

top

butt & tape to part #1

EARTH
part #3 of 4 and part #4 of 4
to make pattern cut 2 on fold

bottom

to complete pattern: place on fold of paper

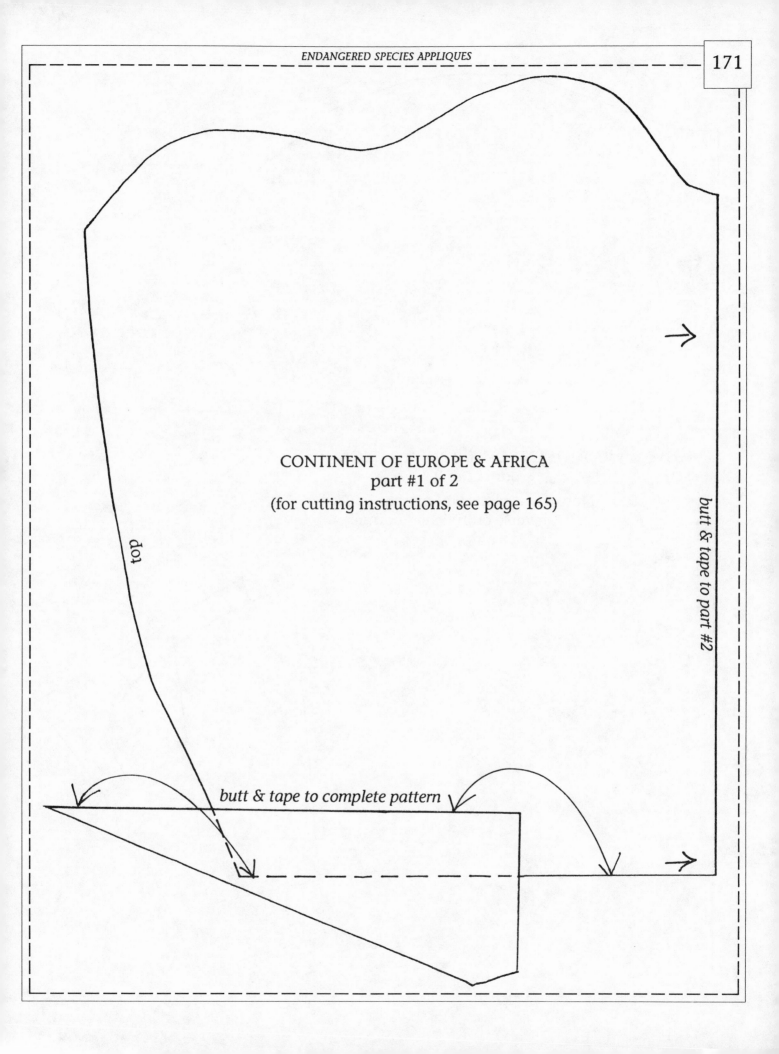

CONTINENT OF EUROPE & AFRICA
part #1 of 2
(for cutting instructions, see page 165)

top

butt & tape to part #2

butt & tape to complete pattern

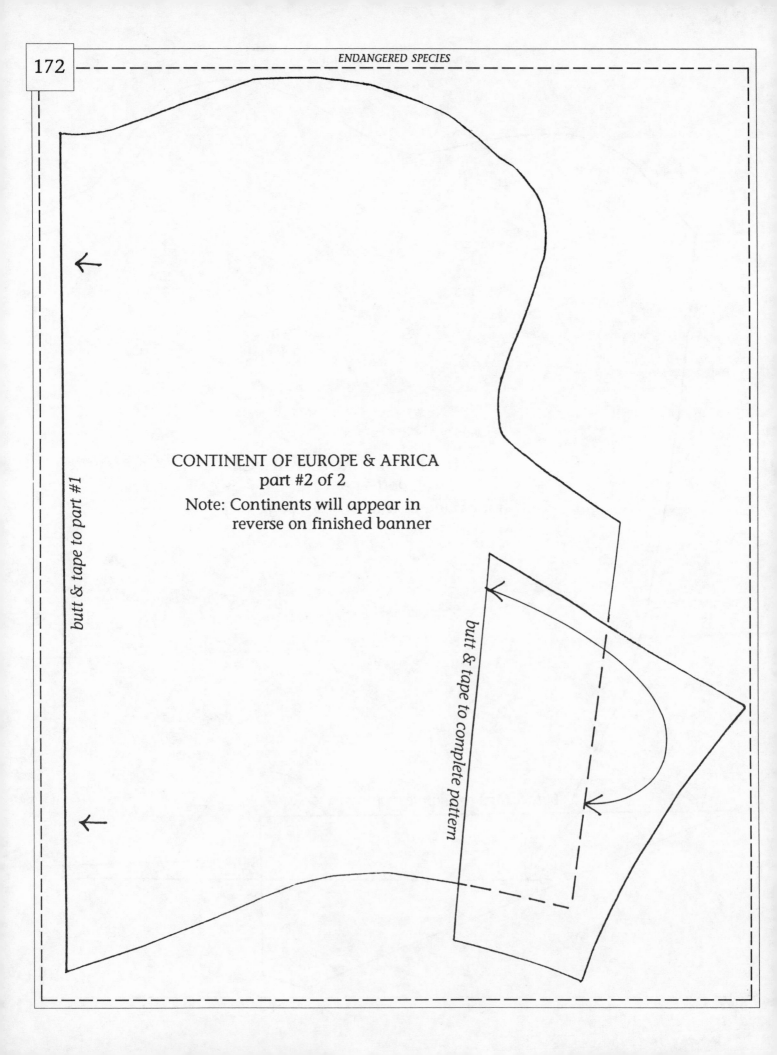

CONTINENT OF EUROPE & AFRICA
part #2 of 2

Note: Continents will appear in
reverse on finished banner

butt & tape to part #1

butt & tape to complete pattern

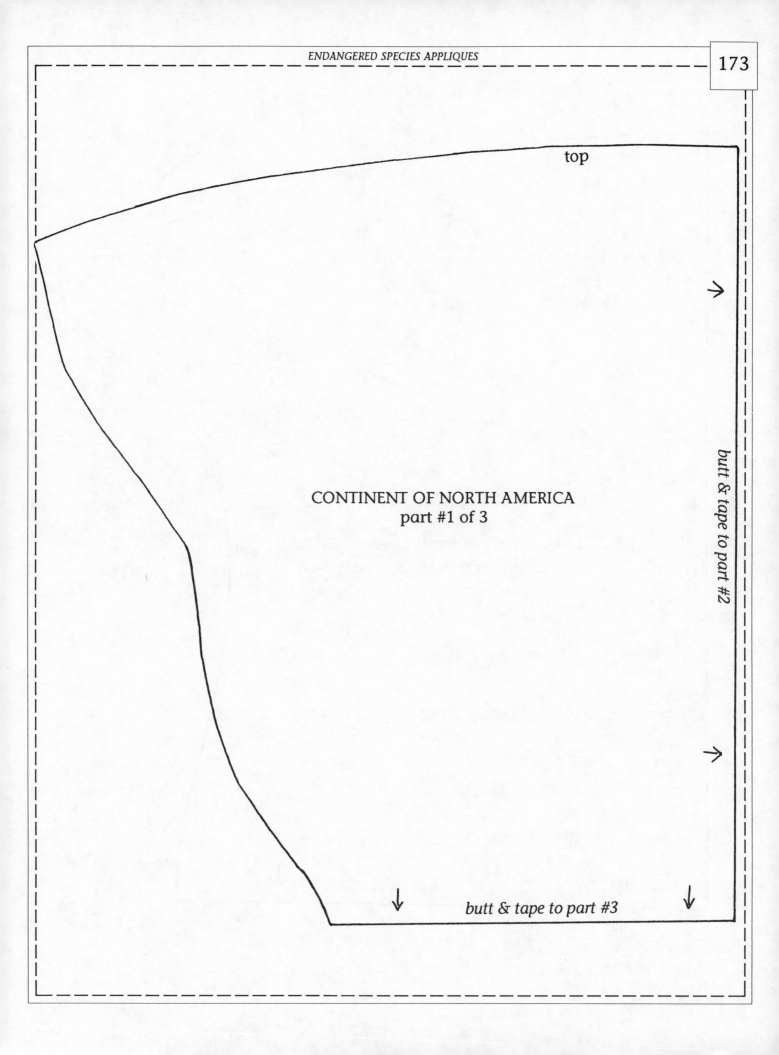

top

CONTINENT OF NORTH AMERICA
part #1 of 3

butt & tape to part #2

butt & tape to part #3

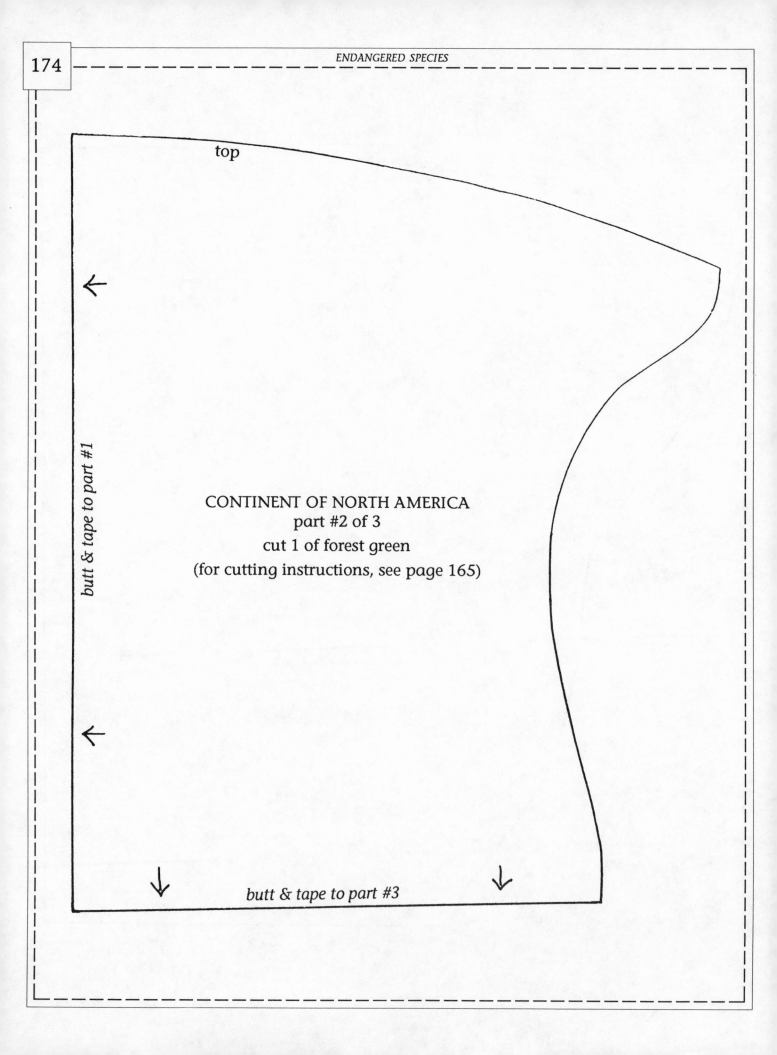

top

butt & tape to part #1

CONTINENT OF NORTH AMERICA
part #2 of 3
cut 1 of forest green
(for cutting instructions, see page 165)

butt & tape to part #3

CONTINENT OF NORTH AMERICA
part #3 of 3
Note: Continents will appear in
reverse on finished banner

butt & tape to part #1 & part #2

bottom

*butt & tape to
complete pattern*

top

CONTINENT OF SOUTH AMERICA
cut 1 of forest green
(for cutting instructions, see page 165)

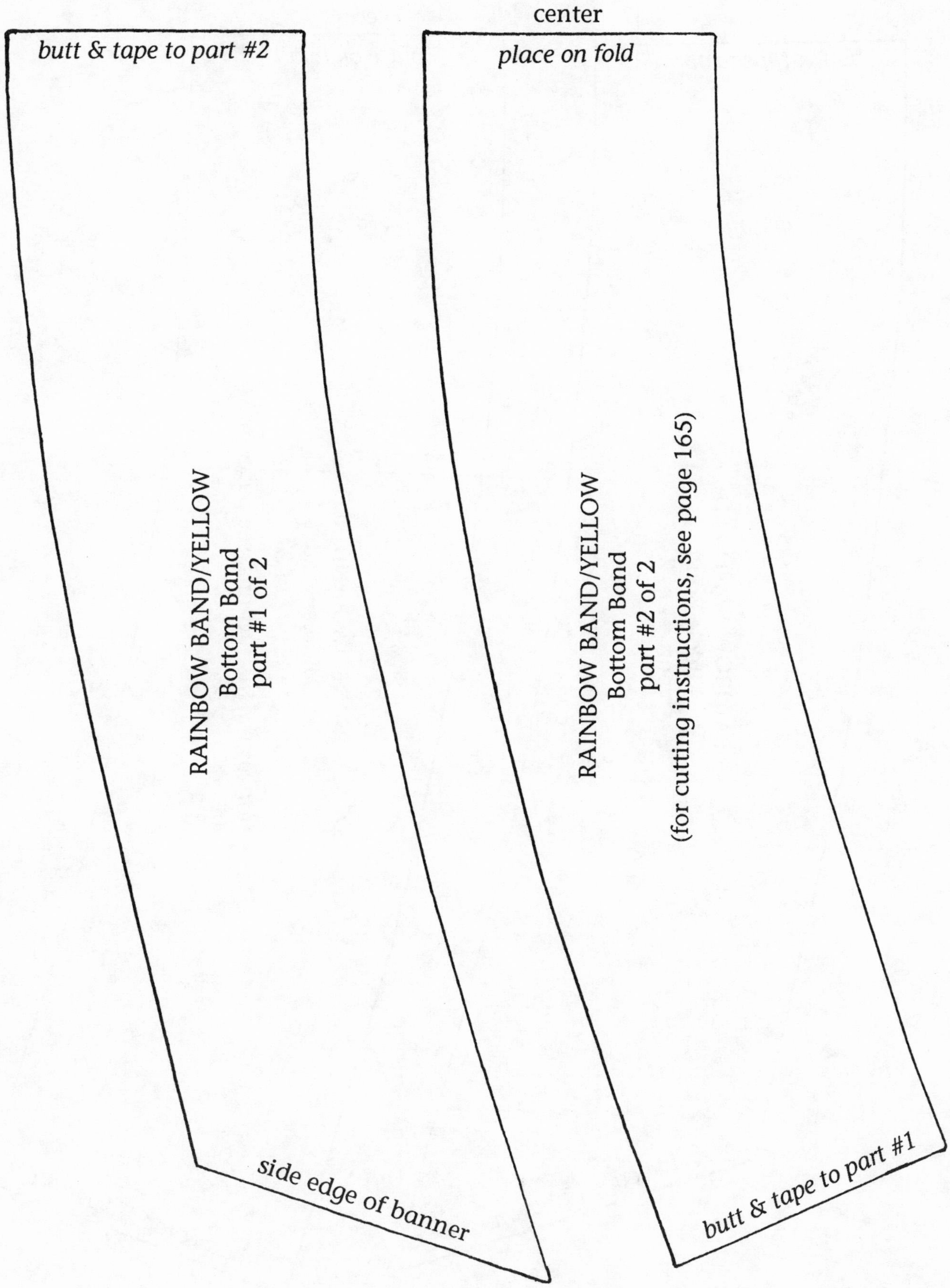

butt & tape to part #2

center

place on fold

RAINBOW BAND/YELLOW
Bottom Band
part #1 of 2

RAINBOW BAND/YELLOW
Bottom Band
part #2 of 2
(for cutting instructions, see page 165)

side edge of banner

butt & tape to part #1

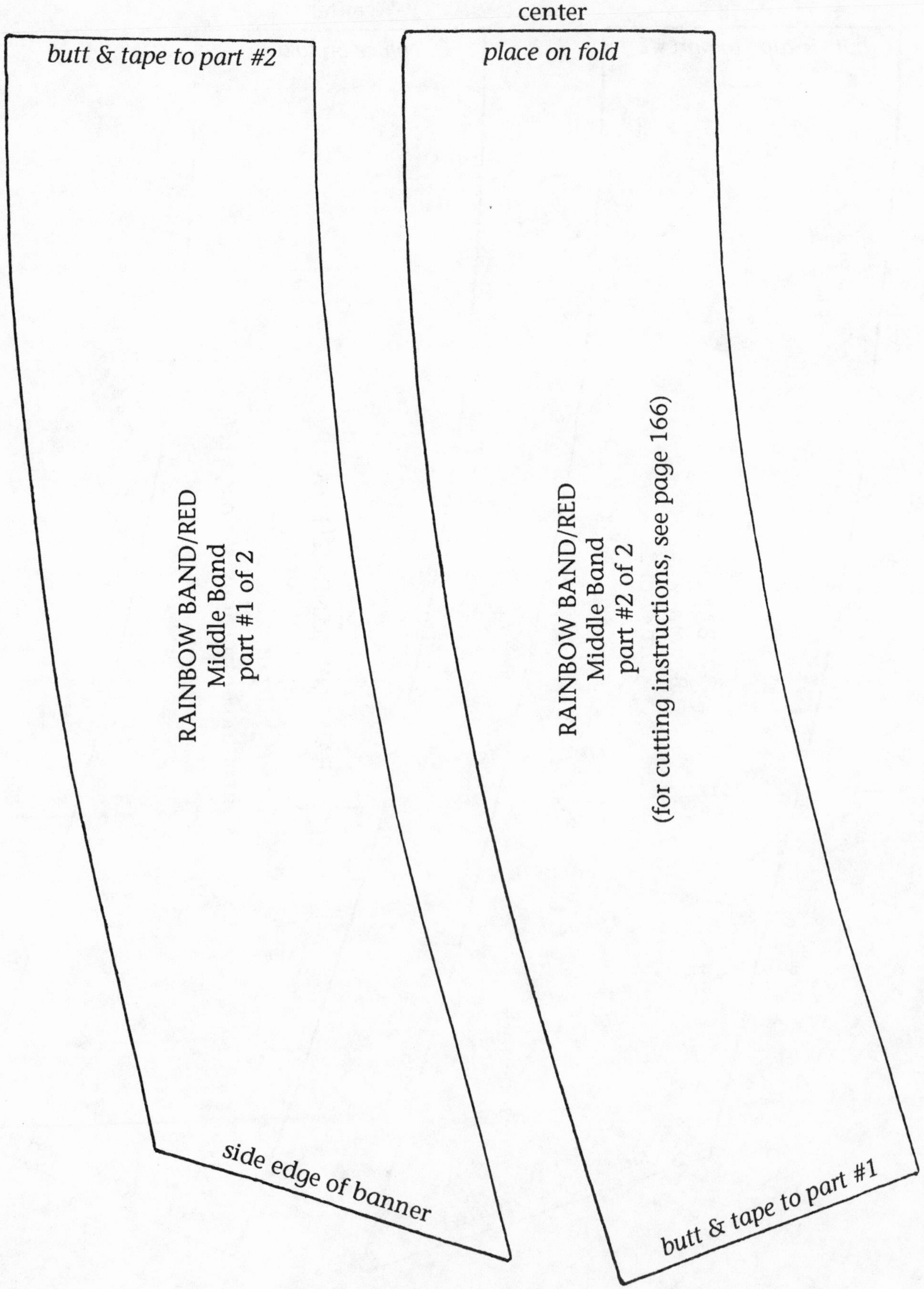

center

place on fold

butt & tape to part #2

RAINBOW BAND/RED
Middle Band
part #1 of 2

RAINBOW BAND/RED
Middle Band
part #2 of 2

(for cutting instructions, see page 166)

side edge of banner

butt & tape to part #1

butt & tape to part #2

center

place on fold

RAINBOW BAND/KELLY GREEN
Top Band
part #1 of 2

RAINBOW BAND/KELLY GREEN
Top Band
part #2 of 2
(for cutting instructions, see page 166)

side edge of banner

butt & tape to part #1

PILLOW & QUILT

Add endangered animals to your decor in the form of these soft furnishings. Quick strip machine piecing and machine quilting simplify and speed the construction process.

Choose pastel-colored prints and solids for a soft effect, or go Amish-style with bright, vibrant colors against a black background for a dramatic statement.

The quilt measures 34" x 50", and the pillow measures 18" x 18".

MATERIALS

Pillow

½ yard cotton fabric for pillow backing
Matching thread
18" square of muslin or plain fabric for quilting backing
⅓ yard each of 9 assorted coordinated print and/or solid fabrics
Matching thread for all colors
⅓ yard Wonder-Under™
⅓ yard tear away stabilizer
¾ yard batting (This is a great opportunity to use leftover scraps. You will need one 17" x 17" piece for quilting the pillow and strips 3" long.)
One 16" x 16" pillow form

Quilt

1½ yards cotton fabric for backing, cut to measure approximately 40" x 56"
Matching thread
1 yard each of 9 assorted coordinated print and/or solid fabrics
Approximately 40" x 50" polyester batting
2 yards Wonder-Under™
2 yards tear away stabilizer

INSTRUCTIONS

Note: All seam allowances are ¼".

To make borders/edging for pillow and/or quilt:

1. Cut strips from each color 1½" wide and the width of the fabric (44" or 45" wide). For each pillow, cut two sets, one of each color; for each quilt, 10 sets. Stitch each set together. Press seam allowances in one direction.

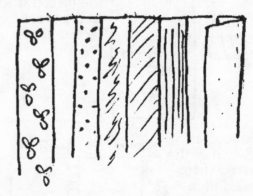

Cut these pieced sets into 4 strips 1½" wide and 10 strips 5" wide for each pillow. Cut into 32 strips 1½" wide each and 21 strips 2½" wide for the quilt. Set aside.

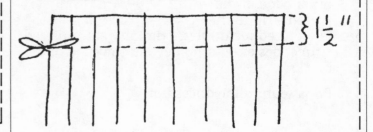

2. For each pillow top or quilt block, cut two 8" squares, one 8" x 10" rectangle, and one 6" x 8" rectangle. For the six quilt blocks, you will need a total of 12 8" x 8" squares, 6 8" x 10" rectangles, and 6 8" x 8" rectangles. If you are making an Amish-inspired quilt or pillow, cut them all from solid black. For the multi-fabric quilt or pillow, cut them from all nine different fabrics. Lay them out as you cut so they will result in a pleasing arrangement.

3. To assemble a pillow or quilt, block stitch one strip that was pieced in step 1 to one edge of an 8" square. Stitch the other edge of the pieced strip to the other 8" square.

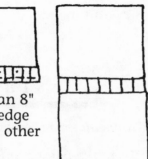

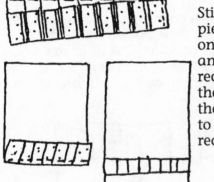

Stitch another pieced strip to one short edge of an 8" x 10" rectangle. Stitch the other side of the pieced strip to the 6" x 8" rectangle.

Stitch one short end of each of the two pieced strips together. Stitch them to one long side of the 8" x 8" block strip that was pieced above. Stitch the other edge of the pieced strip to the two pieced rectangles. Trim any extra pieced strip edges extending beyond the edge of the blocks.

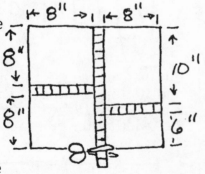

Press seam allowances flat.

For the pillow:

Skip to step 4.

For the quilt:

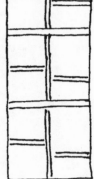

After constructing all the blocks, put together two strips of three blocks each, using pieced strips as was done to form the blocks.

Sew six pieced strips together. Stitch to the block strips as shown.

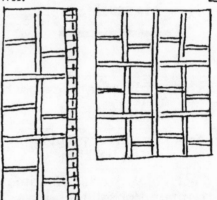

4. *Note: In their finished form, appliques will appear in the reverse of how they appear in the book.*

Choose the animals you want to make and the fabrics you wish to use. Paper side up, place the Wonder-Under™ over an animal applique design in the book. Trace the design. Cut around the design, leaving space around the shape. Be sure not to cut on the design lines. Following the instructions on the Wonder Under™, fuse the rough side to the fabric.

Cut along the design lines to cut out the animal shape. Repeat until you have 4 animals for each pillow or 24 animals for the quilt.

Arrange the animals on the pillow or quilt. Remove the paper backing from each animal and pin it in place. Keep in mind the 1/4" seam allowance on the raw edges of the quilt top or pillow. Fuse, removing the pins before doing so.

Turn to page 12 in chapter 1 for satin stitch instructions.

5. Quilt edging:

For pillows, skip to step 6.

Stitch the short ends of 7 2¹/₂"-wide pieced strips together for one long side of the quilt top. Repeat to make a strip for the other long edge.

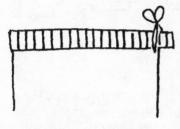

Stitch 4 2¹/₂"-wide strips together for one short edge of the quilt top. Repeat for the other short edge.

Stitch the shorter strips to the short edges. Trim any extra.

Stitch the longer strips to the long edges. Trim any extra strip edges extending beyond the edge.

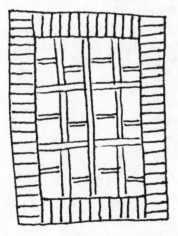

6. Quilting

Lay the muslin (for the pillow) or backing fabric (for the quilt) on a flat surface. Lay the batting on top. Place the pillow or quilt top right side up on top of both, centering it over the batting and backing which are larger than the quilt/pillow top.

Pin the three layers together with safety pins.

To quilt, "stitch in the ditch" (along the seam lines) of the pieced strips, joining the appliqued squares and rectangles. For best results, loosen the top thread tension of your machine slightly. A walking foot is ideal for straight quilting. If you don't have one, choose an open-toed satin stitch or applique foot so you can see your work as you sew.

Choose a bobbin color to match the backing and a neutral (black for Amish) color for the top thread. Use the satin stitch foot to quilt around the edges of the appliques. For the quilt top only: Stitch in the ditch along the seam line where the edging is sewn to the quilt top.

7. To finish quilt:

Press ¹/₂" on pieced edging to wrong side all the way around. Press under another ¹/₂". Lay quilt right side down on a flat surface.

Trim the backing and batting even with the second pressed fold line — 1" from the raw edge of the edging.

Fold the edging along the fold lines to the back of the quilt, encasing the raw edges of the batting and backing. Pin. Hand stitch in place.

To finish the pillow:

Stitch the short ends of 10 5"-wide pieced strips together. Join the two remaining short raw edges to form a circle.

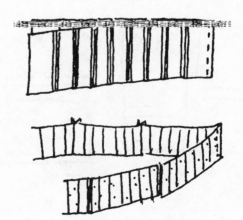

Cut strips of batting 3" wide. Lay them on the wrong side of the circle strip. Fold the strip around the batting and match and baste the raw edges of the strip together with a long machine stitch.

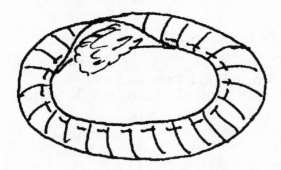

Cut two pieces for the pillow back, each 12" x 16½". Press under ¼" and another ¼" on one long side of each piece. Topstitch.

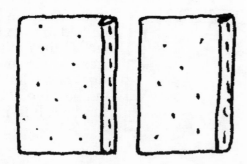

To round the corners of the pillows, use the template to mark the corners of the pillow backs and fronts. Cut along the marked lines.

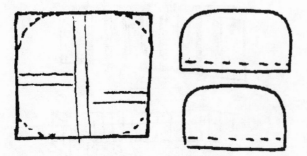

Fold as shown to divide the circle edging into quarters. Mark fold with pins.

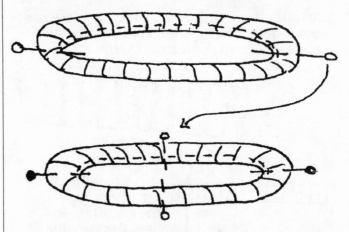

Lay pillow top down right side up. Find the centers of each side of the pillow edges. Mark with pins. Match and pin the pins on circle edging to pins on pillow top as shown. Pin raw edges of circle to raw edge of pillow. When you come to the corners, pull up on the basting stitches to gather the circle edging to fit. Baste.

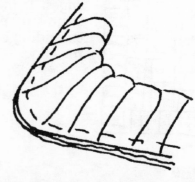

Pin the pillow backings over the pillow and pin to edges, overlapping the two pillow backs over one another 3". Stitch through all layers. Trim extra batting and muslin. Turn pillow right side out. Slip pillow form in through backs.

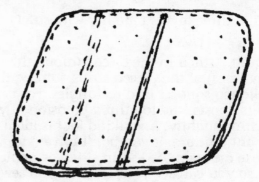

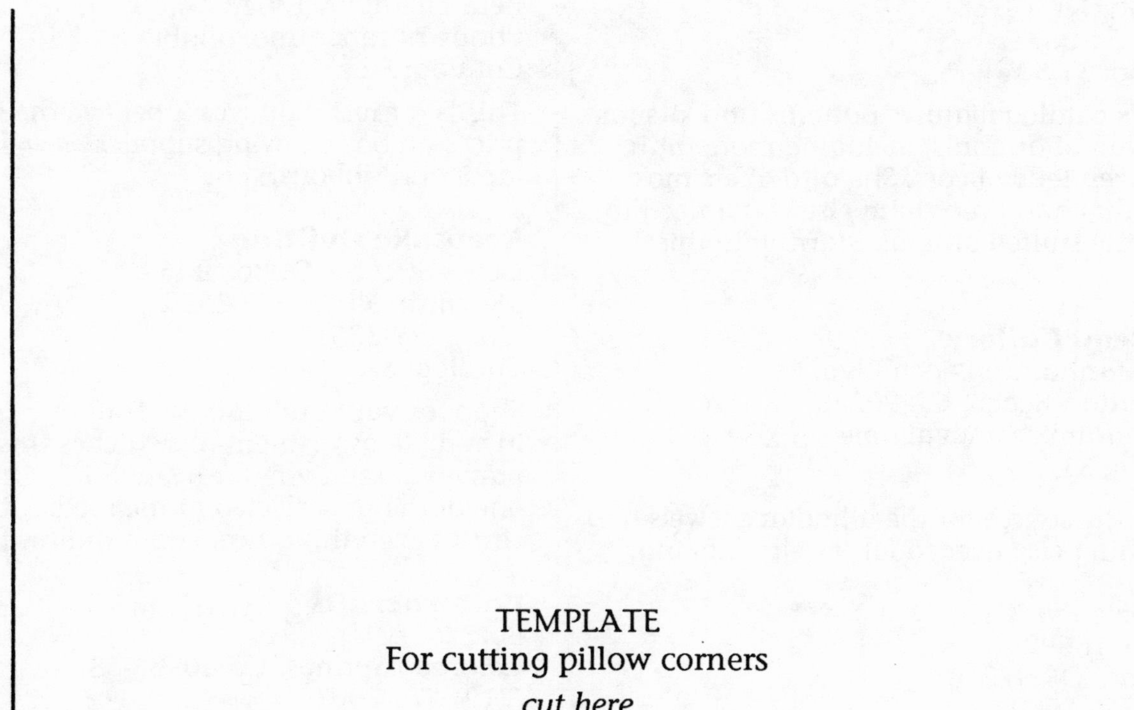

TEMPLATE
For cutting pillow corners
cut here

♥ ♥ ♥ ♥ ♥   *Sources*   ♥ ♥ ♥ ♥ ♥

by Diane
1126 Ivon Avenue
Endicott, NY 13760
(607) 754-0391
Catalog: $1.50

Diane's catalog features patterns and kits for a zoo-full of animals, including more than two dozen teddy bears. She also offers most of the furs and everything else you'll need to make the stuffed animals starring in this book.

The Bead Gallery
1809 Manhattan Beach Blvd.
Manhattan Beach, CA 90266
Phone number unavailable
Catalog: $1

This is the source for the alligator's jewels and everything else needed for jewelry making.

Carver's Eye Co.
PO Box 16692
Portland, OR 97216
(503) 666-5680
Catalog: $1

You'll find the eagle's eyes as well as safety eyes and bear noses in this catalog. They offer plastic joints and great prices on bulk orders.

Craft King
PO Box 90637
Lakeland, FL 33084
(813) 686-9600
Catalog: $2

Order Scribbles Fashion Writers for an easy applique method for your windsock or banner. They offer many other great craft supplies at discount prices.

CR's Crafts
Box 8
Leland, IA 50453
(515) 567-3652
Catalog: $2

In this wonderful source for general crafts supplies, you'll find the joints, eyes, seam brush, Pretty Hair™, and fur mentioned throughout this book.

Home Sew
Dept. JD
Bethlehem, PA 18018
Phone number unavailable
Catalog: Free

This is a must. You won't believe the low prices on basic sewing supplies as well as laces and ribbons.

Keepsake Quilting
Dover Street, P.O. Box 1459
Meredith, NH 03253-1459
(603) 279-3351
Catalog: $2

Shop for your quilt fabrics at home with the incredible assortment of swatches this company will send you for a small fee. Or choose one of the pre-selected fabric medleys. Also carries everything needed for quilting.

Patterncrafts
Box 25370
Colorado Springs, CC 80936-5370
(719) 574-2007
Catalog: $2

Color photos of more than 700 patterns, including dolls and stuffed animals, are featured in this extraordinary catalog of patterns collected from the best sources. Also carries the Stuff-It™ tool.

The Rain Shed
707 NW 11th Street
Corvallis, OR 97330
(503) 753-8900
Catalog: $1

The Rain Shed carries everything you'll need for the windsock: fabric, swivels, and tubing. To make your fabric color choices, include an extra dollar and request the nylon taffeta color swatch set.

Unfinished Business, Inc.
P.O. Box 246
Wingate, NC 28174
(704) 233-4295
Catalog: $3

Order the unfinished wooden finials and dowel for hanging the banner here. You'll also find many other fun, unfinished items.

Bibliography

The A to Z Soft Animals by Carolyn Hall, Prentice Hall Press, NY.

Unfortunately this book has gone out of print since publication in 1986. If you can find a copy, you will be pleased with the patterns.

The Cloth Dollmaker's Sourcebook by Diane Patterson Dee, Betterway Publications, Inc., White Hall, VA.

This is a topnotch book for doll and stuffed animal making. Contemporary designers are featured as well as suppliers of materials and accessories.

Let's Make Windsocks by Valerie J. Lund, Central Coast Creations, San Louis Obispo, CA, 1989

Lots of windsocks, all with complete instructions. Available from Patterncrafts (see Sources).

Reader's Digest Complete Guide To Sewing, Reader's Digest Books.

An excellent general sewing guide.

More good books from
♛ WILLIAMSON PUBLISHING

To order additional copies of **Easy-To-Make Endangered Species To Stitch & Stuff**, please enclose $13.95 per copy plus $2.50 shipping and handling. Follow "To Order" instructions on the last page. Thank you.

Easy-to-Make TEDDY BEARS & ALL THE TRIMMINGS
by Jodie Davis

Now you can make the most lovable, huggable, plain or fancy teddy bears imaginable, for a fraction of store-bought costs. Step-by-step instructions and easy patterns drawn to actual size for large, soft-bodied bears, quilted bears, and even jointed bears. Plus patterns for clothes, accessories — even teddy bear furniture!

208 pages, 8^1/2 x 11, illustrations and patterns
Quality paperback, $13.95

Easy-To-Make CLOTH DOLLS & ALL THE TRIMMINGS
by Jodie Davis

Jodie Davis turns her many talents to making the most adorable and personable cloth dolls imaginable. With her expert directions and clear full-sized patterns, anyone can create these instant friends for a special child or friend. Includes seven 18-inch dolls like Santa, Raggedy Ann, and a clown; a 20-inch baby doll plus complete wardrobe; a 25-inch boy and girl doll plus a wardrobe including sailor suits; and 10 dolls from around the world, including a Japanese kimono doll and Amish dolls. Absolutely beautiful and you can do it!

224 pages, 8^1/2 x 11, illustrations and patterns
Quality paperback, $13.95

Easy-To-Make STUFFED ANIMALS & ALL THE TRIMMINGS
by Jodie Davis

With Jodie Davis's complete and easy instructions, creating adorable stuffed animals has never been easier. Whether you are making gifts for children or additions for a special doll collection, these fuzzy animals are sure to delight anyone. Includes 14-inch unicorn, Rudolph doll, and a large assortment of farm animals — complete with clothing patterns!

208 pages, 8^1/2 x 11, illustrations and patterns
Quality paperback, $13.95

THE KIDS' NATURE BOOK
365 Indoor/Outdoor Activities and Experiences
by Susan Milord

Winner of the Parents' Choice Gold Award for learning and doing books, *The Kids' Nature Book* is loved by children, grandparents, and friends alike. Simple projects and activities emphasize fun while quietly reinforcing the wonder of the world we all share. Packed with facts and fun!

160 pages, 11 x 8¹/₂, 425 illustrations
Quality paperback, $12.95

KIDS CREATE!
Art & Craft Experiences for 3– to 9–year–olds
by Laurie Carlson

What's the most important experience for children ages 3 to 9? Why, to create something by themselves. Carlson provides over 150 creative experiences ranging from making dinosaur sculptures to clay cactus gardens, from butterfly puppets to windsocks. Plenty of help for the parents working with the kids, too! A delightfully innovative book.

160 pages, 11 x 8¹/₂, over 400 illustrations
Quality paperback, $12.95

KIDS & WEEKENDS!
Creative Ways to Make Special Days
by Avery Hart and Paul Mantell

Packed with truly creative ways to play, have fun, learn, grow, and build self-esteem and positive relationships, this book is a must for every parent, grandparent, baby-sitter, and teacher. Hart and Mantell will inspire us all to transform some part of every weekend — even if it is only 30 minutes — into a special experience. Everything from backyard nature to putting on a magic show to creating a bird sanctuary to writing a book about yourself to environmentally sound activities indoors and out. Whatever your interests, no matter how busy you are, kids and their families will savor special weekend moments.

176 pages, 11 x 8¹/₂, over 400 illustrations
Quality paperback, $12.95

ADVENTURES IN ART
Art & Craft Experiences for 7- to 14-year-olds
by Susan Milord

Imagine an art book that encourages children to explore, to experience, to touch and to see, to learn and to create . . . imagine a true adventure in art. Here's a book that teaches artisans' skills without stifling creativity. Covers making handmade papers, puppets, masks, paper seascapes, seed art, tin can lantern, berry ink, still life, silk screen, batiking, carving, and so much more. Perfect for the older child. Let the adventure begin!

160 pages, 11 x 8¹/₂, 500 illustrations
Quality paperback, $12.95

KIDS COOK!
Fabulous Food For The Whole Family
by Sarah Williamson and Zachary Williamson

Kids Cook! is filled with over 150 recipes for great tasting foods that kids ages 8 and up can cook for themselves and for their families and friends, too. Recipes from sections like "Breakfast Bonanzas," "Dynamite Dinners," and "Soda Fountain Treats" include real, healthy foods — not cutesy recipes that are no fun to eat. Plus Nutri Notes, Safety First, and plenty of special menus for Father's Day, Grandma's Teatime, picnics, and parties. One terrific book!

160 pages, 11 x 8¹/2, over 150 recipes, illustrations
Quality paperback, $12.95

DOING CHILDREN'S MUSEUMS
A Guide to 265 Hands-On Museums, Expanded and Updated
by Joanne Cleaver

Turn an ordinary day into a spontaneous "vacation" by taking a child to some of the 265 participatory children's museums, discovery rooms, and nature centers covered in this highly acclaimed, one-of-a-kind book. Filled with museum specifics to help you pick and plan the perfect place for the perfect day, Cleaver has created a most valuable resource for anyone who loves kids!

224 pages, 6 x 9
Quality paperback, $13.95

PARENTS ARE TEACHERS, TOO
Enriching Your Child's First Six Years
by Claudia Jones

Winner of the Parents' Choice Seal of Approval! Be the best teacher your child ever has. Jones shares hundreds of ways to help any child learn in playful home situations. Lots on developing reading, writing, math skills. Plenty on creative and critical thinking, too. A book you'll love using!

192 pages, 6 x 9, illustrations
Quality paperback, $9.95

<u>MORE</u> PARENTS ARE TEACHERS, TOO
Encouraging Your 6- to 12-Year-Old
by Claudia Jones

Winner of the Parents' Choice Seal of Approval! Help your children be the best they can be! When parents are involved, kids do better. When kids do better, they feel better, too. Here's a wonderfully creative book of ideas, activities, teaching methods and more to help you help your children over the rough spots and share in their growing joy in achieving. Plenty on reading, writing, math, problem-solving, creative thinking. Everything for parents who wants to help but not push their children.

224 pages, 6 x 9, illustrations
Quality paperback, $10.95

THE HOMEWORK SOLUTION
by Linda Agler Sonna

Put homework responsibilities where they belong — in the student's lap! Here it is! The simple remedy for the millions of parents who are tired of waging the never-ending nightly battle over kids' homework. Dr. Sonna's "One Step Solution" will relieve parents, kids and their siblings of the ongoing problem within a single month.

192 pages, 6 x 9
Quality paperback, $10.95

THE BROWN BAG COOKBOOK
Nutritious Portable Lunches for Kids and Grown-Ups
by Sara Sloan

Now in its ninth printing, this popular book has more than 1,000 brown bag lunch ideas with 150 recipes for simple, quick, nutritious lunches that kids will love. Breakfast ideas, too! The more people care what they eat, the more popular this book becomes.

192 pages, 8$\frac{1}{4}$ x 7$\frac{1}{4}$, illustrations
Quality paperback, $9.95

SUGAR–FREE TODDLERS
Over 100 Recipes
by Susan Watson

Give your toddlers the gift of lifelong healthy eating habits and a great start on good health by getting the sugar out of their diets now. Susan Watson doesn't just pay lip service to the idea of "sugar-free" — she shows you how to take refined sugars out of your children's mouths. Over 100 recipes packed with good nutrition and great taste, not empty calories. Plus over 200 popular commercial products such as peanut butters and cereals are rated for sugar content.

176 pages, 8$\frac{1}{4}$ x 7$\frac{1}{4}$, illustrations
Quality paperback, $9.95

GOLDE'S HOMEMADE COOKIES
by Golde Soloway

Over 50,000 copies of this marvelous cookbook have been sold. Now it's in its second edition with 135 of the most delicious cookie recipes imaginable. *Publishers Weekly* says, "Cookies are her chosen realm and how sweet a world it is to visit." You're sure to agree!

162 pages, 8$\frac{1}{4}$ x 7$\frac{1}{4}$, illustrations
Quality paperback, $8.95

PRACTICAL POLE BUILDING CONSTRUCTION
by Leigh Seddon

Saves money, time, labor; no excavation. Complete how-to-build information with original architectural plans and specs for small barn, horse barn, shed, animal shelter, cabins, and more.

186 pages, 8½ x 11, over 100 architectural renderings, tables
Quality paperback, $10.95

BUILDING FENCES OF WOOD, STONE, METAL & PLANTS
by John Vivian

Complete how-to on wood fence, stone fence, block, brick and mud fence, living fence and hedgerows, primitive fence, wire livestock fence, electric barrier fence, and classic horse fence.

224 pages, 8½ x 11, hundreds of drawings, photos, tables, charts
Quality paperback, $13.95

To Order:

At your bookstore or order directly from Williamson Publishing. We accept Visa and MasterCard (please include number and expiration date), or send check to:

> Williamson Publishing Company
> Church Hill Road, P.O. Box 185
> Charlotte, Vermont 05445

> Toll-free phone orders with credit cards:
> 1-800-234-8791

Please add $2.50 for postage and handling. Satisfaction is guaranteed or full refund without questions or quibbles.